Hands-On Data Structures and Algorithms with Python
Second Edition

Write complex and powerful code using the latest features of Python 3.7

Dr. Basant Agarwal
Benjamin Baka

BIRMINGHAM - MUMBAI

Hands-On Data Structures and Algorithms with Python
Second Edition

Commissioning Editor: Richa Tripathi
Acquisition Editor: Denim Pinto
Content Development Editor: Tiksha Sarang
Technical Editor: Mehul Singh
Copy Editor: Safis Editing
Project Coordinator: Prajakta Naik
Proofreader: Safis Editing
Indexer: Rekha Nair
Graphics: Jisha Chirayil
Production Coordinator: Shraddha Falebhai

First published: May 2017
Second edition: October 2018

Production reference: 2221118

Published by Packt Publishing Ltd.
Livery Place
35 Livery Street
Birmingham
B3 2PB, UK.

ISBN 978-1-78899-557-3

www.packtpub.com

This book is dedicated to my parents, wife, and kids Charvi, Kaavy.

- Dr. Basant Agarwal

`mapt.io`

Mapt is an online digital library that gives you full access to over 5,000 books and videos, as well as industry leading tools to help you plan your personal development and advance your career. For more information, please visit our website.

Why subscribe?

- Spend less time learning and more time coding with practical eBooks and videos from over 4,000 industry professionals
- Improve your learning with skill plans designed especially for you
- Get a free eBook or video every month
- Mapt is fully searchable
- Copy and paste, print, and bookmark content

Packt.com

Did you know that Packt offers eBook versions of every book published, with PDF and ePub files available? You can upgrade to the eBook version at `www.packt.com` and, as a print book customer, you are entitled to a discount on the eBook copy. Get in touch with us at `customercare@packtpub.com` for more details.

At `www.packt.com`, you can also read a collection of free technical articles, sign up for a range of free newsletters, and receive exclusive discounts and offers on Packt books and eBooks.

Contributors

About the authors

Dr. Basant Agarwal works as an associate professor at Swami Keshvanand Institute of Technology, Management, and Gramothan, India. He has been awarded an M.Tech and Ph.D. from MNIT, Jaipur, India, and has more than 8 years' experience in academia and research. He has been awarded the prestigious PostDoc Fellowship by ERCIM (the European Research Consortium for Informatics and Mathematics) through the Alain Bensoussan Fellowship Programme. He has also worked at Temasek Laboratories, the National University of Singapore. He has authored a book on sentiment analysis in the Springer Book Series: Socio-Affective Computing series, and is published in more than 50 reputed conferences and journals. His research interests are focused on NLP, machine learning, and deep learning.

Benjamin Baka works as a software developer who considers himself to be language agnostic and thus seeks out the elegant solutions to which his toolset can enable him to accomplish. Notable amongst ones are C, Java, Python, and Ruby. With a huge interest in algorithms, he seeks to always write code that borrows from Dr. Knuth's words, both simple and elegant. He also enjoys playing the bass guitar and listening to silence. He currently works with mPedigree Network.

About the reviewers

David Julian has written two books *Designing Machine Learning Systems with Python*, and *Deep Learning with Pytorch Quickstart Guide* both published by Packt. He has worked for Urban Ecological Systems Pty Ltd on a project to detect insect outbreaks in greenhouse environments using machine learning. He currently works as a technical consultant and information technology trainer for several private and non-government organizations.

Yogendra Sharma is a developer with experience in architecture, design, and the development of scalable and distributed applications, with a core interest in microservices and Spring. He is currently working as an IoT and cloud architect at Intelizign Engineering Services, Pune. He also has hands-on experience with technologies such as AWS Cloud, IoT, Python, J2SE, J2EE, NodeJS, Angular, MongoDB, and Docker. He is constantly exploring technical novelties, and is open-minded and eager to learn about new technologies and frameworks.

Packt is searching for authors like you

If you're interested in becoming an author for Packt, please visit `authors.packtpub.com` and apply today. We have worked with thousands of developers and tech professionals, just like you, to help them share their insight with the global tech community. You can make a general application, apply for a specific hot topic that we are recruiting an author for, or submit your own idea.

Acknowledgments

This book would not have been possible without the contribution of many individuals, to whom I would like to express my sincere appreciation and gratitude. First of all, I would like to acknowledge the great support of the Packt Publishing team. I am very grateful to the editor of the book, Tiksha Sarang, whose support throughout its development was marvelous. I would like to express my sincere gratitude to the acquisition editor of the book, Denim Pinto, who has given me the chance to contribute to this book. I would also like to thank Benjamin Baka for great work in the first edition of the book.

I would especially like to thank the editors and technical reviewers of the book for performing the extensive review process. I would like to express my thanks to all the reviewers for their constructive comments and suggestions. I am also grateful to Mehul Singh for his fantastic efforts as a technical reviewer. I would also like to express my gratitude to all those who were involved in the copy editing, proofreading, and production of this book.

I am grateful to the Swami Keshvanand Institute of Technology for providing me with a fantastic work environment and their kind cooperation. I would also like to express my sincere gratitude and thanks to Prof. S. L. Surana, Director (Academics), SKIT, for being a constant source of support and motivation. I am especially thankful to Prof. C. M. Choudhary, head of the Department of Computer Science and Engineering, for his help, advice, support, and encouragement. Special thanks also to all my wonderful friends and colleagues for helping me in eradicating the minor errors and for proofreading the book. I would also like to thank Dr. Mukesh Gupta, Dr. S.R. Dogiwal, and Gaurav Arora for their help.

And last, but by no means least, my sincere thanks go to my family and friends, for their endless encouragement and support throughout the production of this book. They always motivated me to work harder on the book. For any inadequacies that may remain in this book, the responsibility is entirely my own.

Table of Contents

Preface

Data structures and algorithms are two of the most important core subjects in the study of information technology and computer science engineering. This book aims to provide in-depth knowledge, along with programming implementation experience, of data structures and algorithms. It is designed for graduates and undergraduates who are studying data structures with Python programming at beginner and intermediate level, and explains the complex algorithms through the use of examples.

In this book, you will learn the essential Python data structures and the most common algorithms. This book will provide a basic knowledge of Python and give the reader an insight into data algorithms. In it, we provide Python implementations and explain them in relation to almost every important and popular data structure algorithm. We will look at algorithms that provide solutions to the most common problems in data analysis, including searching and sorting data, as well as being able to extract important statistics from data. With this easy-to-read book, you will learn how to create complex data structures, such as linked lists, stacks, heaps, and queues, as well as sort algorithms, including bubble sort, insertion sort, heapsort, and quicksort. We also describe a variety of selection algorithms, including randomized and deterministic selection. We provide a detailed discussion of various data structure algorithms and design paradigms, such as greedy algorithms, divide-conquer algorithms, and dynamic programming, along with how they can be used in real-time applications. In addition, complex data structures, such as trees and graphs, are explained using straightforward pictorial examples to explore the concepts of these useful data structures. You will also learn various important string processing and pattern matching algorithms, such as KMP, and Boyer-Moore algorithms, along with their easy implementation in Python. You will learn the common techniques and structures used in tasks, including preprocessing, modeling, and transforming data.

The importance of having a good understanding of data structures and algorithms cannot be overemphasized. It is an important arsenal to have at your disposal in order to understand new problems and find elegant solutions to them. By gaining a deeper understanding of algorithms and data structures, you may find uses for them in many more ways than originally intended. You will develop a consideration for the code you write and how it affects the amount of memory. Python has further opened the door to many professionals and students to come to appreciate programming. The language is fun to work with and concise in its description of problems. We leverage the language's mass appeal to examine a number of widely studied and standardized data structures and algorithms. The book begins with a concise tour of the Python programming language. As such, it is not required that you know Python before picking up this book.

Who this book is for

This book is intended for Python developers who are studying courses concerned with data structures and algorithms at a beginner or intermediate level. The book is also designed for all those undergraduate and graduate engineering students who attend, or have attended, courses on data structures and algorithms, as it covers almost all the algorithms, concepts, and designs that are studied in this course. Thus, this book can also be adapted as a textbook for data structure and algorithm courses. This book is also a useful tool for generic software developers who want to deploy various applications using a specific data structure as it provides efficient ways of storing the relevant data. It also provides a practical and straightforward approach to learning complex algorithms.

It is assumed that the reader has some basic knowledge of Python. However, it is not mandatory as we provide a quick overview of Python and its object-oriented concepts in this book. There is no requirement to have any prior knowledge of computer-related concepts in order to understand this book, since all the concepts and algorithms are explained in sufficient detail, with a good number of examples and pictorial representations. Most of the concepts are explained with the help of everyday scenarios to make the concepts and algorithms easy to understand.

What this book covers

Chapter 1, *Python Objects, Types, and Expressions*, introduces you to the basic types and objects of Python. We will give an overview of the language features, execution environment, and programming styles. We will also review the common programming techniques and language functionality.

Chapter 2, *Python Data Types and Structures*, explains Python's various built-in data types. It also describes each of the five numeric and five sequence data types, as well as one mapping and two set data types, and examines the operations and expressions applicable to each type. We will also provide many examples of typical use cases.

Chapter 3, *Principles of Algorithm Design,* covers various important data structure design paradigms, such as greedy algorithms, dynamic programming, divide and conquer, recursion, and backtracking. In general, the data structures we create need to conform to a number of principles. These principles include robustness, adaptability, reusability, and separating the structure from a function. We look at the role iteration plays and introduce recursive data structures. We also discuss various Big O notations and complexity classes.

Chapter 4, *Lists and Pointer Structures*, covers linked lists, which are one of the most common data structures, and are often used to implement other structures, such as stacks and queues. In this chapter, we describe their operation and implementation. We compare their behavior to arrays and discuss the relative advantages and disadvantages of each.

Chapter 5, *Stacks and Queues*, discusses the behavior of these linear data structures and demonstrates a number of implementations. We give examples of typical real-life example applications.

Chapter 6, *Trees*, looks at how to implement a binary tree. Trees form the basis of many of the most important advanced data structures. We will examine how to traverse trees and retrieve and insert values. We discuss binary and ternary search trees. We will also look at how to create structures such as heaps.

Chapter 7, *Hashing and Symbol Tables*, describes symbol tables, gives some typical implementations, and discusses various applications. We will look at the process of hashing, provide an implementation of a hash table, and discuss the various design considerations.

Chapter 8, *Graphs and Other Algorithms*, looks at some of the more specialized structures, including graphs and spatial structures. Representing data as a set of nodes and vertices is convenient in a number of applications and, from this, we can create structures including directed and undirected graphs. We will also introduce a number of other structures and concepts, such as priority queues, heaps, and selection algorithms.

Chapter 9, *Searching*, discusses the most common searching algorithms, for example, binary search and interpolation searching algorithms. We also give examples of their uses in relation to various data structures. Searching for a data structure is a key task and there are a number of different approaches.

Chapter 10, *Sorting*, looks at the most common approaches to sorting. These approaches include bubble sort, insertion sort, selection sort, quick sort, and heap sort algorithms. This chapter provides a detailed explanation of each, along with their Python implementation.

Chapter 11, *Selection Algorithms*, covers algorithms that involve finding statistics, such as the minimum, maximum, or median elements in a list. The chapter also discusses various selection algorithms for locating a specific element in a list by sorting, as well as randomized and deterministic selection algorithms.

Chapter 12, *String Algorithms and Techniques*, covers basic concepts and definitions related to strings. Various string and pattern matching algorithms are discussed in detailed, such as the naïve approach, Knuth-Morris-Pratt (KMP), and Boyer-Moore pattern matching algorithms.

Chapter 13, *Design Techniques and Strategies*, relates to how we look for solutions for similar problems when we are trying to solve a new problem. Understanding how we can classify algorithms and the types of problem that they most naturally solve is a key aspect of algorithm design. There are many ways in which we can classify algorithms, but the most useful classifications tend to revolve around either the implementation method or the design method. This chapter explains various algorithm design paradigms using many important applications, such as mergesort, Dijkstra's shortest path algorithm, and the coin-counting problem.

Chapter 14, *Implementations, Applications, and Tools*, discusses a variety of real-world applications. These include data analysis, machine learning, prediction, and visualization. In addition, there are libraries and tools that make our work with algorithms more productive and enjoyable.

To get the most out of this book

1. The code in the book will require you to run on Python 3.7 or higher.
2. The Python interactive environment can also be used to run the code snippets.
3. Readers are advised to learn the algorithms and concepts by executing the codes provided in the book that are designed to facilitate understanding of the algorithms.
4. The book aims to give readers practical exposure, so it is recommended that you carry out programming for all the algorithms in order to get the maximum out of this book.

Download the example code files

You can download the example code files for this book from your account at www.packt.com. If you purchased this book elsewhere, you can visit www.packt.com/support and register to have the files emailed directly to you.

You can download the code files by following these steps:

1. Log in or register at www.packt.com.
2. Select the **SUPPORT** tab.
3. Click on **Code Downloads & Errata**.
4. Enter the name of the book in the **Search** box and follow the onscreen instructions.

Once the file is downloaded, please make sure that you unzip or extract the folder using the latest version of:

- WinRAR/7-Zip for Windows
- Zipeg/iZip/UnRarX for Mac
- 7-Zip/PeaZip for Linux

The code bundle for the book is also hosted on GitHub at `https://github.com/PacktPublishing/Hands-On-Data-Structures-and-Algorithms-with-Python-Second-Edition`. In case there's an update to the code, it will be updated on the existing GitHub repository.

We also have other code bundles from our rich catalog of books and videos available at `https://github.com/PacktPublishing/`. Check them out!

Download the color images

We also provide a PDF file that has color images of the screenshots/diagrams used in this book. You can download it here: `https://www.packtpub.com/sites/default/files/downloads/9781788995573_ColorImages.pdf`

Conventions used

There are a number of text conventions used throughout this book.

`CodeInText`: Indicates code words in text, database table names, folder names, filenames, file extensions, pathnames, dummy URLs, user input, and Twitter handles. Here is an example: "We instantiate the `CountVectorizer` class and pass `training_data.data` to the `fit_transform` method of the `count_vect` object."

A block of code is set as follows:

```
class Node:
    def __init__(self, data=None):
        self.data = data
        self.next = None
```

When we wish to draw your attention to a particular part of a code block, the relevant lines or items are set in bold:

```
def dequeue(self):
    if not self.outbound_stack:
        while self.inbound_stack:
            self.outbound_stack.append(self.inbound_stack.pop())
    return self.outbound_stack.pop()
```

Any command-line input or output is written as follows:

```
   0     1      2
0   4.0   45.0   984.0
1   0.1    0.1     5.0
2  94.0   23.0    55.0
```

Bold: Indicates a new term, an important word, or words that you see on screen.

Warnings or important notes appear like this.

Tips and tricks appear like this.

Get in touch

Feedback from our readers is always welcome.

General feedback: If you have questions about any aspect of this book, mention the book title in the subject of your message and email us at customercare@packtpub.com.

Errata: Although we have taken every care to ensure the accuracy of our content, mistakes do happen. If you have found a mistake in this book, we would be grateful if you would report this to us. Please visit www.packt.com/submit-errata, selecting your book, clicking on the Errata Submission Form link, and entering the details.

Piracy: If you come across any illegal copies of our works in any form on the internet, we would be grateful if you would provide us with the location address or website name. Please contact us at copyright@packtpub.com with a link to the material.

If you are interested in becoming an author: If there is a topic that you have expertise in and you are interested in either writing or contributing to a book, please visit authors.packtpub.com.

Reviews

Please leave a review. Once you have read and used this book, why not leave a review on the site that you purchased it from? Potential readers can then see and use your unbiased opinion to make purchase decisions, we at Packt can understand what you think about our products, and our authors can see your feedback on their book. Thank you!

For more information about Packt, please visit packt.com.

Python Objects, Types, and Expressions

1

Data structures and algorithms are two of the core elements of a large and complex software project. They are a systematic way of storing and organizing data in software so that it can be used efficiently. Python has efficient high-level data structures and an effective object-oriented programming language. Python is the language of choice for many advanced data tasks, for a very good reason. It is one of the easiest advanced programming languages to learn. Intuitive structures and semantics mean that for people who are not computer scientists, but maybe biologists, statisticians, or the directors of a start-up, Python is a straightforward way to perform a wide variety of data tasks. It is not just a scripting language, but a full-featured, object-oriented programming language.

In Python, there are many useful data structures and algorithms built into the language. Also, because Python is an object-based language, it is relatively easy to create custom data objects. In this book, we will examine Python's internal libraries and some of the external libraries, and we'll learn how to build your own data objects from first principles.

In this chapter, we will look at the following topics:

- Obtaining a general working knowledge of data structures and algorithms
- Understanding core data types and their functions
- Exploring the object-oriented aspects of the Python programming language

Technical requirements

The data structures and algorithms are presented using the Python programming language (version 3.7) in this book. This book does assume that you know Python. However, if you are a bit rusty, coming from another language, or do not know Python at all, don't worry—this first chapter should get you quickly up to speed.

The following is the GitHub link: `https://github.com/PacktPublishing/Hands-On-Data-Structures-and-Algorithms-with-Python-Second-Edition/tree/master/Chapter01`.

 If you are not familiar with Python, then visit `https://docs.python.org/3/tutorial/index.html`, and you can also find the documentation at `https://www.python.org/doc/`. These are all excellent resources for easily learning this programming language.

Installing Python

To install Python, we use the following method.

Python is an interpreted language, and statements are executed line by line. A programmer can typically write down the series of commands in a source code file. For Python, the source code is stored in a file with a `.py` file extension.

Python is fully integrated and usually already installed on most of the Linux and Mac operating systems. Generally, the pre-installed Python version is 2.7. You can check the version installed on the system using the following commands:

```
>>> import sys
>>> print(sys.version)
3.7.0 (v3.7.0:1bf9cc5093, Jun 27 2018, 04:06:47) [MSC v.1914 32 bit
(Intel)]
```

You can also install a different version of Python using the following commands on Linux:

1. Open the Terminal
2. `sudo apt-get update`
3. `sudo apt-get install -y python3-pip`
4. `pip3 install <package_name>`

Python has to be installed on systems with Windows operating systems, as it is not pre-installed, unlike Linux/macOS. Any version of Python can be downloaded from this link: `https://www.python.org/downloads/`. You can download the software installer and run it—select **Install for all users** and then click on **Next**. You need to specify the location where you want to install the package, then click **Next**. After that, select the option **Add Python to environment variables** in the Customize Python dialog box, then just click **Next** again for final installation. When the installation is finished, you can confirm the installation by opening up Command Prompt and typing the following command:

```
python -V
```

The latest stable Python version is Python 3.7.0. The Python program can be executed by typing the following in the command line:

```
python <sourcecode_filename>.py
```

Understanding data structures and algorithms

Algorithms and data structures are the most fundamental concepts in computing. They are the main building blocks from which complex software is built. Having an understanding of these foundation concepts is extremely important in software design and this involves the following three characteristics:

- How algorithms manipulate information contained within data structures
- How data is arranged in memory
- What the performance characteristics of particular data structures are

In this book, we will examine the topic from several perspectives. Firstly, we will look at the fundamentals of the Python programming language from the perspective of data structures and algorithms. Secondly, it is important that we have the correct mathematical tools. We need to understand the fundamental concepts of computer science and for this we need mathematics. By taking a heuristic approach, developing some guiding principles means that, in general, we do not need any more than high school mathematics to understand the principles of these key ideas.

Another important aspect is an evaluation. Measuring the performance of algorithms requires an understanding of how the increase in data size affects operations on that data. When we are working on large datasets or real-time applications, it is essential that our algorithms and structures are as efficient as they can be.

Finally, we need a strong experimental design strategy. Being able to conceptually translate a real-world problem into the algorithms and data structures of a programming language involves being able to understand the important elements of a problem and a methodology for mapping these elements to programming structures.

To better understand the importance of algorithmic thinking, let's consider a real-world example. Imagine we are at an unfamiliar market and we are given the task of purchasing a list of items. We assume that the market is laid out randomly, each vendor sells a random subset of items, and some of these items may be on our list. Our aim is to minimize the price for each item we buy, as well as minimize the time spent at the market. One way to approach this problem is to write an algorithm like the following:

1. Does the vendor have items that are on our list and the cost is less than a predicted cost for that item?

2. If yes, buy and remove from list; if no, move on to the next vendor.

3. If no more vendors, end.

This is a simple iterator, with a decision and an action. If we have to implement this using programming language, we would need data structures to define and store in memory both the list of items we want to buy and the list of items the vendor is selling. We would need to determine the best way of matching items in each list and we need some sort of logic to decide whether to purchase or not.

There are several observations that we can make regarding this algorithm. Firstly, since the cost calculation is based on a prediction, we don't know what the real cost is. As such, we do not purchase an item because we underpredicted the cost of the item, and we reach the end of the market with items remaining on our list. To handle this situation, we need an effective way of storing the data so that we can efficiently backtrack to the vendor with the lowest cost.

Also, we need to understand the time taken to compare items on our shopping list with the items being sold by each vendor. It is important because as the number of items on our shopping list, or the number of items sold by each vendor, increases, searching for an item takes a lot more time. The order in which we search through items and the shape of the data structures can make a big difference to the time it takes to do a search. Clearly, we would like to arrange our list as well as the order we visit each vendor in such a way that we minimize the search time.

Also, consider what happens when we change the buy condition to purchase at the *cheapest* price, not just the below-average predicted price. This changes the problem entirely. Instead of sequentially going from one vendor to the next, we need to traverse the market once and, with this knowledge, we can order our shopping list with regards to the vendors we want to visit.

Obviously, there are many more subtleties involved in translating a real-world problem into an abstract construct such as a programming language. For example, as we progress through the market, our knowledge of the cost of a product improves, so our predicted average-price variable becomes more accurate until, by the last stall, our knowledge of the market is perfect. Assuming any kind of backtracking algorithm incurs a cost, we can see cause to review our entire strategy. Conditions such as high price variability, the size and shape of our data structures, and the cost of backtracking all determine the most appropriate solution. The whole discussion clearly demonstrates the importance of data structures and algorithms in building a complex solution.

Python for data

Python has several built-in data structures, including lists, dictionaries, and sets, which we use to build customized objects. In addition, there are a number of internal libraries, such as collections and math object, which allow us to create more advanced structures as well as perform calculations on those structures. Finally, there are the external libraries such as those found in the SciPy packages. These allow us to perform a range of advanced data tasks such as logistic and linear regression, visualization, and mathematical calculations, such as operations on matrices and vectors. External libraries can be very useful for an out-of-the-box solution. However, we must also be aware that there is often a performance penalty compared to building customized objects from the ground up. By learning how to code these objects ourselves, we can target them to specific tasks, making them more efficient. This is not to exclude the role of external libraries and we will look at this in Chapter 12, *Design Techniques and Strategies*.

To begin, we will take an overview of some of the key language features that make Python such a great choice for data programming.

The Python environment

Python is one of the most popular and extensively used programming languages all over the world due to its **readability and flexibility**. A feature of the Python environment is its interactive console, allowing you to both use Python as a desktop-programmable calculator and also as an environment to write and test snippets of code.

The `read...evaluate...print` loop of the console is a very convenient way to interact with a larger code base, such as to run functions and methods or to create instances of classes. This is one of the major advantages of Python over compiled languages such as C/C++ or Java, where the `write...compile...test...recompile` cycle can increase development time considerably compared to Python's `read...evaluate...print` loop. Being able to type in expressions and get an immediate response can greatly speed up data science tasks.

There are some excellent distributions of Python apart from the official CPython version. Two of the most popular are available at: Anaconda (`https://www.continuum.io/downloads`) and Canopy (`https://www.enthought.com/products/canopy/`). Most distributions come with their own developer environments. Both Canopy and Anaconda include libraries for scientific, machine learning, and other data applications. Most distributions come with an editor.

There are also a number of implementations of the Python console, apart from the CPython version. Most notable among these is the IPython/Jupyter platform which is based on a web-based computational environment.

Variables and expressions

To solve a real-world problem through algorithm implementation, we first have to select the variables and then apply the operations on these variables. Variables are labels that are attached to the objects. Variables are not objects nor containers for objects; they only act as a pointer or a reference to the object. For example, consider the following code:

```
In [1]: a=[2,4,6]

In [2]: b=a

In [3]: a.append(8)

In [4]: b
Out[4]: [2, 4, 6, 8]
```

Here, we have created a variable, a, that points to a list object. We create another variable, b, that points to this same list object. When we append an element to this list object, this change is reflected in both a and b.

In Python, variable names are attached to different data types during the program execution; it is not required to first declare the datatype for the variables. Each value is of a type (for example, a string or integer); however, the variable name that points to this value does not have a specific type. More specifically, variables point to an object that can change their type depending on the kind of values assigned to them. Consider the following example:

```
In [1]: a=1

In [2]: type(a)
Out[2]: int

In [3]: a=a+0.1

In [4]: type(a)
Out[4]: float
```

In the preceding code example, the type of a is changed from int to float, depending upon the value stored in the variable.

Variable scope

Scoping rules of variables inside functions are important. Whenever a function executes, a local environment (namespace) is created. This local namespace contains all the variables and parameter names that are assigned by the functions. Whenever a function is called, Python Interpreter first looks into the local namespace that is the function itself—if no match is found, then it looks at the global namespace. If the name is still not found, then it searches in the built-in namespace. If it is not found, then the interpreter would raise a NameError exception. Consider the following code:

```
a=15;b=25
def my_function():
  global a
  a=11;b=21

my_function()
print(a)   #prints 11
print(b)   #prints 25
```

In the preceding code, we define two global variables. We need to tell the interpreter, using the keyword global, that inside the function we are referring to a global variable. When we change this variable to 11, these changes are reflected in the global scope. However, the b variable we set to 21 is local to the function, and any changes made to it inside the function are not reflected in the global scope. When we run the function and print b, we see that it retains its global value.

In addition, let's consider another interesting example:

```
>>> a = 10
>>> def my_function():
...       print(a)
>>> my_function ()
10
```

The code works, and gives an output of 10, but see the following code:

```
>>> a = 10
>>> def my_function():
...       print(a)
...       a= a+1
>>> my_function()

UnboundLocalError: local variable 'a' referenced before assignment
```

The preceding code gives an error because assignment to a variable in a scope makes that variable a local variable to that scope. In the preceding example, in the my_function() assignment to the a variable, the compiler assumes a as a local variable, and that is why the earlier print() function tries to print a local variable a, which is not initialized as a local variable; thus, it gives an error. It can be resolved by accessing the outer scope variable by declaring it as global:

```
>>> a = 10
>>> def my_function():
...       global a
...       print(a)
...       a = a+1
>>> my_function()
10
```

So, in Python, the variables that are referenced inside a function are global implicitly, and if the a variable is assigned a value anywhere inside the function's body, it is assumed to be a local variable unless explicitly declared as global.

Flow control and iteration

Python programs consist of a sequence of statements. The interpreter executes each statement in order until there are no more statements. This is true if files run as the main program, as well as if they are loaded via `import`. All statements, including variable assignment, function definitions, class definitions, and module imports, have equal status. There are no special statements that have higher priority than any other, and every statement can be placed anywhere in a program. All the instructions/statements in the program are executed in sequence in general. However, there are two main ways of controlling the flow of program execution—conditional statements and loops.

The `if...else` and `elif` statements control the conditional execution of statements. The general format is a series of `if` and `elif` statements followed by a final `else` statement:

```
x='one'
if x==0:
    print('False')
elif  x==1:
    print('True')
else:  print('Something else')

#prints'Something else'
```

Note the use of the `==` operator to compare the two values. This returns `True` if both the values are equal; it returns `False` otherwise. Note also that setting `x` to a string will return `Something else` rather than generate a type error as may happen in languages that are not dynamically typed. Dynamically typed languages, such as Python, allow flexible assignment of objects with different types.

The other way of controlling program flow is with loops. Python offers two ways of constructing looping, such as the `while` and `for` loop statements. A `while` loop repeats executing statements until a Boolean condition is true. A `for` loop provides a way of repeating the execution into the loop through a series of elements. Here is an example:

```
In [5]: x=0

In [6]: while x < 3 : print(x); x +=1
0
1
2
```

In this example, the `while` loop executes the statements until the condition `x < 3` is true. Let's consider another example that uses a *for* loop:

```
>>>words = ['cat', 'dog', 'elephant']
>>> for w in words:
...      print(w)
...

cat
dog
elephant
```

In this example, the *for* loop executes iterating for all the items over the list.

Overview of data types and objects

Python contains various built-in data types. These include four numeric types (`int`, `float`, `complex`, `bool`), four sequence types (`str`, `list`, `tuple`, `range`), one mapping type (`dict`), and two set types. It is also possible to create user-defined objects, such as functions or classes. We will look at the string and the list data types in this chapter and the remaining built-in types in the next chapter.

All data types in Python are **objects**. In fact, pretty much everything is an object in Python, including modules, classes, and functions, as well as literals such as strings and integers. Each object in Python has a **type**, a **value,** and an **identity**. When we write `greet=` `"helloworld"`, we are creating an instance of a string object with the value "hello world" and the identity of `greet`. The identity of an object acts as a pointer to the object's location in memory. The type of an object, also known as the object's class, describes the object's internal representation, as well as the methods and operations it supports. Once an instance of an object is created, its identity and type cannot be changed.

We can get the identity of an object by using the built-in function `id()`. This returns an identifying integer and on most systems, this refers to its memory location, although you should not rely on this in any of your code.

Also, there are a number of ways to compare objects; for example, see the following:

```
if a==b:    # a and b have the same value

if a is b:    # if a and b are the same object

if type(a) is type(b):   #a and b are the same type
```

An important distinction needs to be made between **mutable** and **immutable** objects. Mutable objects such as lists can have their values changed. They have methods, such as `insert()` or `append()`, that change an object's value. Immutable objects such as strings cannot have their values changed, so when we run their methods, they simply return a value rather than change the value of an underlying object. We can, of course, use this value by assigning it to a variable or using it as an argument in a function. For example, the `int` class is immutable—once an instance of it is created, its value cannot be changed, however, an identifier referencing this object can be reassigned another value.

Strings

Strings are immutable sequence objects, with each character representing an element in the sequence. As with all objects, we use methods to perform operations. Strings, being immutable, do not change the instance; each method simply returns a value. This value can be stored as another variable or given as an argument to a function or method.

The following table is a list of some of the most commonly used string methods and their descriptions:

Method	Description
`s.capitalize`	Returns a string with only the first character capitalized, the rest remaining lowercase.
`s.count(substring, [start,end])`	Counts occurrences of a substring.
`s.expandtabs([tabsize])`	Replaces tabs with spaces.
`s.endswith(substring, [start, end]`	Returns `True` if a string ends with a specified substring.
`s.find(substring, [start,end])`	Returns index of first presence of a substring.
`s.isalnum()`	Returns `True` if all chars are alphanumeric of string `s`.
`s.isalpha()`	Returns `True` if all chars are alphabetic of string `s`.
`s.isdigit()`	Returns `True` if all chars are digits in the string.
`s.split([separator], [maxsplit])`	Splits a string separated by whitespace or an optional separator. Returns a list.
`s.join(t)`	Joins the strings in sequence `t`.
`s.lower()`	Converts the string to all lowercase.
`s.replace(old, new[maxreplace])`	Replaces old substring with a new substring.

`s.startswith(substring, [start, end]])`	Returns `True` if the string starts with a specified substring.
`s.swapcase()`	Returns a copy of the string with swapped case in the string.
`s.strip([characters])`	Removes whitespace or optional characters.
`s.lstrip([characters])`	Returns a copy of the string with leading characters removed.

Strings, like all sequence types, support indexing and slicing. We can retrieve any character from a string by using its index `s[i]`. We can retrieve a slice of a string by using `s[i:j]`, where `i` and `j` are the start and end points of the slice. We can return an extended slice by using a stride, as in the following—`s[i:j:stride]`. The following code should make this clear:

```
In [19]: greet = 'hello world'

In [20]: greet[1]
Out[20]: 'e'

In [21]: greet[0:8]
Out[21]: 'hello wo'

In [22]: greet[0:8:2]
Out[22]: 'hlow'

In [23]: greet[0::2]
Out[23]: 'hlowrd'
```

The first two examples are pretty straightforward, returning the character located at index `1` and the first seven characters of the string, respectively. Notice that indexing begins at `0`. In the third example, we are using a stride of `2`. This results in every second character being returned. In the final example, we omit the end index and the slice returns every second character in the entire string.

You can use any expression, variable, or operator as an index as long as the value is an integer:

```
In [9]: greet[1+2]
Out[9]: 'l'

In [10]: greet[len(greet)-1]
Out[10]: 'd'
```

Another common operation is traversing through a string with a loop:

```
In [24]: for i in enumerate(greet[0:5]): print(i)
(0, 'h')
(1, 'e')
(2, 'l')
(3, 'l')
(4, 'o')
```

Given that strings are immutable, a common question that arises is how we perform operations such as inserting values. Rather than changing a string, we need to think of ways to build new string objects for the results we need. For example, if we wanted to insert a word into our greeting, we could assign a variable to the following:

```
In [19]: greet[:5] + ' wonderful' + greet[5:]
Out[19]: 'hello wonderful world'
```

As this code shows, we use the slice operator to split the string at index position 5 and use + to concatenate. Python never interprets the contents of a string as a number. If we need to perform mathematical operations on a string, we need to first convert them to a numeric type:

```
In [15]: x='3'; y='2'

In [16]: x + y #concatenation
Out[16]: '32'

In [17]: int(x) + int(y) #addition
Out[17]: 5
```

Lists

List is one of the most commonly used built-in data structures, as they can store any number of different data types. They are simple representations of objects and are indexed by integers starting from zero, as we saw in the case of *strings.*

The following table contains the most commonly used list methods and their descriptions:

Method	Description
`list(s)`	Returns a list of sequence `s`.
`s.append(x)`	Appends element `x` at the end of list `s`.
`s.extend(x)`	Appends list `x` at the end of list `s`.
`s.count(x)`	Returns the count of the occurrence of `x` in list `s`.
`s.index(x, [start], [stop])`	Returns the smallest index `i`, where `s[i]==x`. We can include an optional start and stop index for the lookup.
`s.insert(i,e)`	Inserts `x` at index `i`.
`s.pop(i)`	Returns the element `i` and removes it from the list `s`.
`s.remove(x)`	Removes element `x` from the list `s`.
`s.reverse()`	Reverses the order of list `s`.
`s.sort(key, [reverse])`	Sorts list `s` with optional key and reverses it.

In Python, lists implementation is different when compared to other languages. Python does not create multiple copies of a variable. For example, when we assign a value of one variable in another variable, both variables point to the same memory address where the value is stored. A copy would only be allocated if the variables change their values. This feature makes Python memory efficient, in the sense that it only creates multiple copies when it is required.

This has important consequences for mutable compound objects such as lists. Consider the following code:

```
In [8]: x=1;y=2;z=3

In [9]: list1 =[x,y,z]

In [10]: list2 = list1

In [11]: list2[1] = 4

In [12]: list1
Out[12]: [1, 4, 3]
```

In the preceding code, both the `list1` and `list2` variables are pointing to the same memory location. However, when we change the `y` through `list2` to 4, we are actually changing the same `y` variable that `list1` is pointing to as well.

An important feature of `list` is that it can contain nested structures; that is, list can contain other lists. For example, in the following code, list `items` contains three other lists:

```
In [5]: items = [["rice",2.4, 8 ],["flour", 1.9, 5], ["Corn", 4.7, 6] ]

In [6]: for item in items:
   ...:     print("Product: %s Price: %.2f Quality: %i" % (item[0], item[1], item[2]))
   ...:
Product: rice Price: 2.40 Quality: 8
Product: flour Price: 1.90 Quality: 5
Product: Corn Price: 4.70 Quality: 6
```

We can access the values of the list using the bracket operators and, since lists are mutable, they are copied in place. The following example demonstrates how we can use this to update elements; for example, here we are raising the price of flour by 20 percent:

```
In [26]: items[1][1] = items[1][1] * 1.2

In [27]: items[1][1]
Out[27]: 2.28
```

We can create a list from expressions using a very common and intuitive method; that is, **list comprehensions.** It allows us to create a list through an expression directly into the list. Consider the following example, where a list `l` is created using this expression:

```
In [27]: l= [2,4,8,16]

In [28]: [i**3 for i in l]
Out[28]: [8, 64, 512, 4096]
```

List comprehensions can be quite flexible; for example, consider the following code. It essentially shows two different ways to performs a function composition, where we apply one function (x*4) to another (x*2). The following code prints out two lists representing the function composition of `f1` and `f2`, calculated first using a for loop and then using a list comprehension:

```
def f1(x): return x*2
def f2(x): return x*4

lst=[]
for i in range(16):
    lst.append(f1(f2(i)))

print(lst)
print([f1(x) for x in range(64) if x in [f2(j) for j in range(16)]])
```

The first line of output is from the for loop construct. The second is from the list comprehension expression:

```
[0, 8, 16, 24, 32, 40, 48, 56, 64, 72, 80, 88, 96, 104, 112, 120]
[0, 8, 16, 24, 32, 40, 48, 56, 64, 72, 80, 88, 96, 104, 112, 120]
```

List comprehensions can also be used to replicate the action of nested loops in a more compact form. For example, we multiply each of the elements contained within list1 with each other:

```
In [13]: list1= [[1,2,3], [4,5,6]]

In [14]: [i * j for i in list1[0] for j in list1[1]]
Out[14]: [4, 5, 6, 8, 10, 12, 12, 15, 18]
```

We can also use list comprehensions with other objects such as strings, to build more complex structures. For example, the following code creates a list of words and their letter count:

```
In [20]: words = 'here is a sentence'.split()

In [21]: [[word, len(word)] for word in words]
Out[21]: [['here', 4], ['is', 2], ['a', 1], ['sentence', 8]]
```

As we will see, lists form the foundation of many of the data structures we will look at. Their versatility, ease of creation, and use enable them to build more specialized and complex data structures.

Functions as first class objects

In Python, it is not only data types that are treated as objects. Both functions and classes are what are known as first class objects, allowing them to be manipulated in the same ways as built-in data types. By definition, first class objects are the following:

- Created at runtime
- Assigned as a variable or in a data structure
- Passed as an argument to a function
- Returned as the result of a function

In Python, the term **first class object** is a bit of a misnomer, since it implies some sort of hierarchy, whereas all Python objects are essentially first class.

To have a look at how this works, let's define a simple function:

```
def greeting(language):
    if language=='eng':
        return 'hello world'
    if language =='fr'
        return 'Bonjour le monde'
    else: return  'language not supported'
```

Since user-defined functions are objects, we can do things such as include them in other objects, such as lists:

```
In [9]: l=[greeting('eng'), greeting('fr'), greeting('ger')]

In [10]: l[1]
Out[10]: ' Bonjour le monde'
```

Functions can also be used as arguments for other functions. For example, we can define the following function:

```
In [14]: def callf(f):
    ...:       lang='eng'
    ...:       return (f(lang))
    ...:

In [15]: callf(greeting)
Out[15]: 'hello world'
```

Here, `callf()` takes a function as an argument, sets a language variable to `'eng'`, and then calls the function with the language variable as its argument. We could see how this would be useful if, for example, we wanted to produce a program that returns specific sentences in a variety of languages, perhaps for some sort of natural language application. Here, we have a central place to set the language. As well as our greeting function, we could create similar functions that return different sentences. By having one point where we set the language, the rest of the program logic does not have to worry about this. If we want to change the language, we simply change the language variable and we can keep everything else the same.

Higher order functions

Functions that take other functions as arguments, or that return functions, are called **higher order functions**. Python 3 contains two built-in higher order functions—filter() and map(). Note that in earlier versions of Python, these functions returned lists; in Python 3, they return an iterator, making them much more efficient. The map() function provides an easy way to transform each item into an iterable object. For example, here is an efficient, compact way to perform an operation on a sequence. Note the use of the lambda anonymous function:

```
In [40]: list = [1,2,3,4]
In [41]: for item in map(lambda n: n*2, list): print(item)
Out [41]:
2
4
6
8
```

Similarly, we can use the filter built-in function to filter items in a list:

```
In [3]: list = [1,2,3,4]
In [4]: for item in filter(lambda n: n<4, list): print(item)
Out [4]:
1
2
3
```

Note that both map and filter perform the same function similar to what can be achieved by list comprehensions. There does not seem to be a great deal of difference in the performance characteristics, apart from a slight performance advantage when using the in-built functions map and filter without the lambda operator, compared to list comprehensions. Despite this, most style guides recommend the use of list comprehensions over built-in functions, possibly because they tend to be easier to read.

Creating our own higher order functions is one of the hallmarks of functional programming style. A practical example of how higher order functions can be useful is demonstrated by the following. Here, we are passing the `len` function as the key to the sort function. This way, we can sort a list of words by length:

```
In [19]: words=str.split('The longest word in this sentence')

In [20]: sorted(words, key=len)
Out[20]: ['in', 'The', 'word', 'this', 'longest', 'sentence']
```

Here is another example for case-insensitive sorting:

```
In [84]: sl=['A','b','a', 'C', 'c']

In [85]: sl.sort(key=str.lower)

In [86]: sl
Out[86]: ['A', 'a', 'b', 'C', 'c']

In [87]: sl.sort()

In [88]: sl
Out[88]: ['A', 'C', 'a', 'b', 'c']
```

Note the difference between the `list.sort()` method and the sorted built-in function. The `list.sort()` method, a method of the list object, sorts the existing instance of a list without copying it. This method changes the target object and returns `None`. It is an important convention in Python that functions or methods that change the object return `None`, to make it clear that no new object was created and that the object itself was changed.

On the other hand, the sorted built-in function returns a new list. It actually accepts any iterable object as an argument, but it will always return a list. Both *list sort* and *sorted* take two optional keyword arguments as key.

A simple way to sort more complex structures is to use the index of the element to sort, using the lambda operator, for example:

```
In [3]: items= [['rice',2.4,8],["flour",1.9,5],["Corn", 4.7,6]]

In [4]: items.sort(key=lambda item: item[1])

In [5]: print(items)

Out [5]: [['flour', 1.9, 5], ['rice', 2.4, 8], ['Corn', 4.7, 6]]
```

Here we have sorted the items by price.

Recursive functions

Recursion is one of the most fundamental concepts of computer science. It is called *recursion* when a function takes one or more calls to itself during execution. Loop iterations and recursion are different in the sense that *loops* execute statements repeatedly through a Boolean condition or through a series of elements, whereas recursion repeatedly calls a function. In Python, we can implement a recursive function simply by calling it within its own function body. To stop a recursive function turning into an infinite loop, we need at least one argument that tests for a terminating case to end the recursion. This is sometimes called the base case. It should be pointed out that recursion is different from iteration. Although both involve repetition, iteration loops through a sequence of operations, whereas recursion repeatedly calls a function. Technically, recursion is a special case of iteration known as tail iteration, and it is usually always possible to convert an iterative function to a recursive function and vice versa. The interesting thing about recursive functions is that they are able to describe an infinite object within a finite statement.

The following code should demonstrate the difference between recursion and iteration. Both these functions simply print out numbers between low and high, the first one using iteration and the second using recursion:

```
def iterTest(low,high):
    while low <= high:
        print(low)
        low=low+1

def recurTest(low,high):
    if low <= high:
        print(low)
        recurTest(low+1, high)
```

Notice that for `iterTest`, the iteration example, we use a while statement to test for the condition, then call the print method, and finally increment the low value. The recursive example tests for the condition, prints, then calls itself, incrementing the low variable in its argument. In general, iteration is more efficient; however, recursive functions are often easier to understand and write. Recursive functions are also useful for manipulating recursive data structures such as linked lists and trees, as we will see.

Generators and co-routines

We can create functions that do not just return one result but rather an entire sequence of results, by using the yield statement. These functions are called **generators.** Python contains generator functions, which are an easy way to create iterators and are especially useful as a replacement for unworkably long lists. A generator yields items rather than builds lists. For example, the following code shows why we might choose to use a generator, as opposed to creating a list:

```python
#compares the running time of a list compared to a generator
import time
#generator function creates an iterator of odd numbers between n and m
def oddGen(n,m):
    while n<m:
      yield n
      n+=2


#builds a list of odd numbers between n and m
def oddLst(n,m):
    lst=[]
    while n<m:
        lst.append(n)
        n+=2
    return lst

#the time it takes to perform sum on an iterator
t1=time.time()
sum(oddGen(1,1000000))
print("Time to sum an iterator: %f" % (time.time() - t1))
#the time it takes to build and sum a list
t1=time.time()
sum(oddLst(1,1000000))
print("Time to build and sum a list: %f" % (time.time() - t1))
```

This prints out the following:

```
Time to sum an iterator: 0.133119
Time to build and sum a list: 0.191172
```

As we can see, building a list to do this calculation takes significantly longer. The performance improvement as a result of using generators is because the values are generated on demand, rather than saved as a list in memory. A calculation can begin before all the elements have been generated and elements are generated only when they are needed.

In the preceding example, the sum method loads each number into memory when it is needed for the calculation. This is achieved by the generator object repeatedly calling the __next__ () special method. Generators never return a value other than None.

Typically, generator objects are used in for loops. For example, we can make use of the oddLst generator function created in the preceding code to print out odd integers between 1 and 10:

```
for i in oddLst (1,10):print(i)
```

We can also create a **generator expression**, which, apart from replacing square brackets with parentheses, uses the same syntax and carries out the same operation as list comprehensions. Generator expressions, however, do not create a list; they create a **generator object**. This object does not create the data, but rather creates that data on demand. This means that generator objects do not support sequence methods such as append() and insert().

You can, however, change a generator into a list using the list() function:

```
In [5]: lst1= [1,2,3,4]

In [6]: gen1 = (10**i for i in lst1)

In [7]: gen1
Out[7]: <generator object <genexpr> at 0x000001B981504C50>

In [8]: for x in gen1: print(x)
10
100
1000
10000
```

Classes and object programming

Classes are a way to create new kinds of objects and they are central to object-oriented programming. A class defines a set of attributes that are shared across instances of that class. Typically, classes are sets of functions, variables, and properties.

The object-oriented paradigm is compelling because it gives us a concrete way to think about and represent the core functionality of our programs. By organizing our programs around objects and data rather than actions and logic, we have a robust and flexible way to build complex applications. The actions and logic are still present, of course, but by embodying them in objects, we have a way to encapsulate functionality, allowing objects to change in very specific ways. This makes our code less error-prone, easier to extend and maintain, and able to model real-world objects.

Classes are created in Python using the class statement. This defines a set of shared attributes associated with a collection of class instances. A class usually consists of a number of methods, class variables, and computed properties. It is important to understand that defining a class does not, by itself, create any instances of that class. To create an instance, a variable must be assigned to a class. The class body consists of a series of statements that execute during the class definition. The functions defined inside a class are called **instance methods.** They apply some operations to the class instance by passing an instance of that class as the first argument. This argument is called self by convention, but it can be any legal identifier. Here is a simple example:

```python
class Employee(object):
    numEmployee=0
    def init (self,name,rate):
        self.owed=0
        self.name=name
        self.rate=rate
      Employee.numEmployee += 1

    def del (self):
        Employee.numEmployee-=1

    def hours(self,numHours):
        self.owed += numHours*self.rate
        return ("%.2f hours worked" % numHours)

    def pay(self):
        self.owed=0
        return("payed %s " % self.name)
```

Class variables, such as numEmployee, share values among all the instances of the class. In this example, numEmployee is used to count the number of employee instances. Note that the Employee class implements the __init__ and __del__ special methods, which we will discuss in the next section.

We can create instances of the `Employee` objects, run methods, and return class and instance variables by doing the following:

```
In [3]: emp1=Employee("Jill", 18.50)

In [4]: emp2=Employee("Jack", 15.50)

In [5]: Employee.numEmployee
Out[5]: 2

In [6]: emp1.hours(20)
Out[6]: '20.00 hours worked'

In [7]: emp1.owed
Out[7]: 370.0

In [8]: emp1.pay()
Out[8]: 'payed Jill '
```

Special methods

We can use the `dir(object)` function to get a list of attributes of a particular object. The methods that begin and end with two underscores are called **special methods.** Apart from the following exception, special methods are generally called by the Python interpreter rather than the programmer; for example, when we use the + operator, we are actually invoking a to `_add_ ()` call. For example, rather than using `my_object._len_ ()`, we can use `len(my_object)`; using `len()` on a string object is actually much faster, because it returns the value representing the object's size in memory, rather than making a call to the object's `_len_` method.

The only special method we actually call in our programs, as common practice, is the `_init_` method, to invoke the initializer of the superclass in our own class definitions. It is strongly advised not to use the double underscore syntax for your own objects because of potential current or future conflicts with Python's own special methods.

We may, however, want to implement special methods in custom objects, to give them some of the behavior of built-in types. In the following code, we create a class that implements the `_repr_` method. This method creates a string representation of our object that is useful for inspection purposes:

```python
class my_class():
    def __init__(self,greet):
        self.greet=greet
    def __repr__(self):
        return 'a custom object (%r) ' % (self.greet)
```

When we create an instance of this object and inspect it, we can see we get our customized string representation. Notice the use of the `%r` format placeholder to return the standard representation of the object. This is useful and best practice because, in this case, it shows us that the `greet` object is a string indicated by the quotation marks:

```
In [13]: a=my_class('giday')

In [14]: a
Out[14]: a custom object ('giday')
```

Inheritance

Inheritance is one of the most powerful features of object-oriented programming languages. It allows us to inherit the functionality from other classes. It is possible to create a new class that modifies the behavior of an existing class through inheritance. Inheritance means that if an object of one class is created by inheriting another class, then the object would have all the functionality, methods, and variables of both the classes; that is, the parent class and new class. The existing class from which we inherit the functionalities is called the parent/base class, and the new class is called the derived/child class.

Inheritance can be explained with a very simple example—we create an `employee` class with attributes such as name of employee and rate at which he is going to be paid hourly. We can now create a new `specialEmployee` class inheriting all the attributes from the `employee` class.

Inheritance in Python is done by passing the inherited class as an argument in the class definition. It is often used to modify the behavior of existing methods.

An instance of the `specialEmployee` class is identical to an `Employee` instance, except for the changed `hours()` method. For example, in the following code we create a new `specialEmployee` class that inherits all the functionalities of the `Employee` class, and also change the `hours()` method:

```
class specialEmployee(Employee):
    def hours(self,numHours):
        self.owed += numHours*self.rate*2
        return("%.2f hours worked" % numHours)
```

For a subclass to define new class variables, it needs to define an __init__() method, as follows:

```
class specialEmployee(Employee):
    def __init__(self,name,rate,bonus):
        Employee.__init__(self,name,rate)      #calls the base classes
        self.bonus=bonus

    def   hours(self,numHours):
        self.owed += numHours*self.rate+self.bonus
        return("%.2f hours worked" % numHours)
```

Notice that the methods of the base class are not automatically invoked and it is necessary for the derived class to call them. We can test for the class membership using the built-in isinstance(obj1,obj2) function. This returns True if obj1 belongs to the class of obj2 or any class derived from obj2. Let's consider the following example to understand this, where obj1 and obj2 are the objects of the Employee and specialEmployee classes respectively:

```
#Example issubclass() to check whether a class is a subclass of another
class
#Example isinstance() to check if an object belongs to a class or not

print(issubclass(specialEmployee, Employee))
print(issubclass(Employee, specialEmployee))

d = specialEmployee("packt", 20, 100)
b = Employee("packt", 20)
print(isinstance(b, specialEmployee))
print(isinstance(b, Employee))

# the output prints
True
False
False
True
```

Generally, all the methods operate on the instance of a class defined within a class. However, it is not a requirement. There are two types of methods—**static methods** and **class methods**. A static method is quite similar to a class method, which is mainly bound to the class, and not bound with the object of the class. It is defined within a class and does not require an instance of a class to execute. It does not perform any operations on the instance and it is defined using the @staticmethod class decorator. Static methods cannot access the attributes of an instance, so their most common usage is as a convenience to group utility functions together.

A class method operates on the class itself and does not work with the instances. A class method works in the same way that class variables are associated with the classes rather than instances of that class. Class methods are defined using the `@classmethod` decorator and are distinguished from instance methods in the class. It is passed as the first argument, and this is named `cls` by convention. The `exponentialB` class inherits from the `exponentialA` class and changes the base class variable to 4. We can also run the parent class's `exp()` method as follows:

```python
class exponentialA(object):
    base=3
    @classmethod
    def exp(cls,x):
        return(cls.base**x)

    @staticmethod
    def addition(x, y):
        return (x+y)

class exponentialB(exponentialA):
        base=4

a = exponentialA()
b= a.exp(3)
print("the value: 3 to the power 3 is", b)
print('The sum is:', exponentialA.addition(15, 10))
print(exponentialB.exp(3))

#prints the following output
the value: 3 to the power 3 is 27
The sum is: 25
64
```

The difference between a static method and a class method is that a static method doesn't know anything about the class, it only deals with the parameters, whereas the class method works only with the class, and its parameter is always the class itself.

There are several reasons why class methods may be useful. For example, because a subclass inherits all the same features of its parent, there is the potential for it to break inherited methods. Using class methods is a way to define exactly what methods are run.

Data encapsulation and properties

Unless otherwise specified, all attributes and methods are accessible without restriction. This also means that everything defined in a base class is accessible from a derived class. This may cause problems when we are building object-oriented applications where we may want to hide the internal implementation of an object. This can lead to namespace conflicts between objects defined in derived classes with the base class. To prevent this, the methods we define private attributes with have a double underscore, such as `__privateMethod()`. These method names are automatically changed to `__Classname_privateMethod()` to prevent name conflicts with methods defined in base classes. Be aware that this does not strictly hide private attributes, rather it just provides a mechanism for preventing name conflicts.

It is recommended to use private attributes when using a class **property** to define mutable attributes. A property is a kind of attribute that rather than returning a stored value computes its value when called. For example, we could redefine the `exp()` property with the following:

```
class Bexp(Aexp):
    base=3
    def exp(self):
        return(x**cls.base)
```

Summary

This chapter has given us a basic fundamental and an introduction to the Python programming. We described various data structures and algorithms provided by the python. We covered the use of variables, lists, a couple of control structures, and learned how to use the conditional statement. We also discussed how functions are used in python. The various kinds of objects were discussed, together with some materials on the object-oriented aspects of the Python language. We created our own objects and inherited from them.

There is still more that Python offers. As we prepare to examine the later chapters on some implementations of algorithms, the next chapter will focus on numbers, sequences, maps, and sets. These are also data types in Python that prove useful when organizing data for a series of operations.

Further reading

- *Learning Python* by Fabrizio Romano: `https://www.packtpub.com/application-development/learning-python`.

2

Python Data Types and Structures

In this chapter, we are going to examine Python data types in more detail. We have already introduced two data types, the string and list, `str()` and `list()`. However, these data types are not sufficient, and we often need more specialized data objects to represent/store our data. Python has various other standard data types that are used to store and manage data, which we will be discussing in this chapter. In addition to the built-in types, there are several internal modules that allow us to address common issues when working with data structures. First, we are going to review some operations and expressions that are common to all data types, and we will discuss more related to data types in Python.

This chapter's objectives are as follows:

- Understanding various important built-in data types supported in Python 3.7
- Exploring various additional collections of high-performance alternatives to built-in data types

Technical requirements

All of the code used in this chapter is given at the following GitHub link: `https://github.com/PacktPublishing/Hands-On-Data-Structures-and-Algorithms-with-Python-Second-Edition/tree/master/Chapter02`.

Built-in data types

Python data types can be divided into three categories: numeric, sequence, and mapping. There is also the None object that represents Null, or the absence of a value. It should not be forgotten that other objects such as classes, files, and exceptions can also properly be considered *types*; however, they will not be considered here.

Every value in Python has a data type. Unlike many programming languages, in Python you do not need to explicitly declare the type of a variable. Python keeps track of object types internally.

Python built-in data types are outlined in the following table:

Category	Name	Description
None	None	It is a null object.
Numeric	int	This is an integer data type.
	float	This data type can store a floating-point number.
	complex	It stores a complex number.
	bool	It is Boolean type and returns True or False.
Sequences	str	It is used to store a string of characters.
	liXst	It can store a list of arbitrary objects.
	Tuple	It can store a group of arbitrary items.
	range	It is used to create a range of integers.
Mapping	dict	It is a dictionary data type that stores data in *key/value* pairs.
	set	It is a mutable and unordered collection of unique items.
	frozenset	It is an immutable set.

None type

The None type is immutable. It is used as None to show the absence of a value; it is similar to null in many programming languages, such as C and C++. Objects return None when there is actually nothing to return. It is also returned by False Boolean expressions. None is often used as a default value in function arguments to detect whether a function call has passed a value or not.

Numeric types

Number types include integers (int), that is, whole numbers of unlimited range, floating-point numbers (float), complex numbers (complex), which are represented by two float numbers, and Boolean (bool) in Python. Python provides the int data type that allows standard arithmetic operators (+, −, * and /) to work on them, similar to other programming languages. A Boolean data type has two possible values, True and False. These values are mapped to 1 and 0, respectively. Let's consider an example:

```
>>> a=4; b=5    # Operator (=) assigns the value to variable
>>>print(a, "is of type", type(a))
4 is of type
<class 'int'>
>>> 9/5
1.8
>>>c= b/a   # division returns a floating point number
>>> print(c, "is of type", type(c))
1.25 is of type <class 'float'>
>>> c    # No need to explicitly declare the datatype
1.25
```

The a and b variables are of the int type and c is a floating-point type. The division operator (/) always returns a float type; however, if you wish to get the int type after division, you can use the floor division operator (//), which discards any fractional part and will return the largest integer value that is less than or equal to x. Consider the following example:

```
>>> a=4; b=5
>>>d= b//a
>>> print(d, "is of type", type(d))
1 is of type <class 'int'>
>>>7/5  # true division
1.4
>>> -7//5  # floor division operator
-2
```

It is advised that readers use the division operator carefully, as its function differs according to the Python version. In Python 2, the division operator returns only integer, not float.

The exponent operator (**) can be used to get the power of a number (for example, x ** y), and the modulus operator (%) returns the remainder of the division (for example, a% b returns the remainder of a/b):

```
>>> a=7; b=5
>>> e= b**a   # The operator (**)calculates power
>>>e
78125
>>>a%b
2
```

Complex numbers are represented by two floating-point numbers. They are assigned using the j operator to signify the imaginary part of the complex number. We can access the real and imaginary parts with f.real and f.imag, respectively, as shown in the following code snippet. Complex numbers are generally used for scientific computations. Python supports addition, subtraction, multiplication, power, conjugates, and so forth on complex numbers, as shown in the following:

```
>>> f=3+5j
>>>print(f, "is of type", type(f))
(3+5j) is of type <class 'complex'>
>>> f.real
3.0
>>> f.imag
5.0
>>> f*2    # multiplication
(6+10j)
>>> f+3   # addition
(6+5j)
>>> f -1   # subtraction
(2+5j)
```

In Python, Boolean types are represented using truth values, that is, True and False; it's similar to 0 and 1. There is a bool class in Python, which returns True or False. Boolean values can be combined with logical operators such as and, or, and not:

```
>>>bool(2)
True
>>>bool(-2)
True
>>>bool(0)
False
```

A Boolean operation returns either `True` or `False`. Boolean operations are ordered in priority, so if more than one Boolean operation occurs in an expression, the operation with the highest priority will occur first. The following table outlines the three Boolean operators in descending order of priority:

Operator	Example
not x	It returns `False` if x is `True`, and returns `True` if x is `False`.
x and y	It returns `True` if x and y are both `True`; otherwise, it returns `False`.
x or y	It returns `True` if either x or y is `True`; otherwise, it returns `False`.

Python is very efficient when evaluating Boolean expressions as it will only evaluate an operator if it needs to. For example, if x is `True` in an expression x or y, then there is no need to evaluate y since the expression is `True` anyway—that is why in Python the y is not evaluated. Similarly, in an expression x and y, if x is `False`, the interpreter will simply evaluate x and return `False`, without evaluating y.

The comparison operators (<, <=, >, >=, ==, and !=) work with numbers, lists, and other collection objects and return `True` if the condition holds. For collection objects, comparison operators compare the number of elements and the equivalence operator (==) returns `True` if each collection object is structurally equivalent, and the value of each element is identical. Let's see an example:

```
>>>See_boolean = (4 * 3 > 10) and (6 + 5 >= 11)
>>>print(See_boolean)
True
>>>if (See_boolean):
...    print("Boolean expression returned True")
   else:
...   print("Boolean expression returned False")
...

Boolean expression returned True
```

Representation error

It should be noted that the native double precision representation of floating-point numbers leads to some unexpected results. For example, consider the following:

```
>>> 1-0.9
0.09999999999999998
>>> 1-0.9==.1
False
```

This is a result of the fact that most decimal fractions are not exactly representable as a binary fraction, which is how most underlying hardware represents floating-point numbers. For algorithms or applications where this may be an issue, Python provides a decimal module. This module allows for the exact representation of decimal numbers and facilitates greater control of properties, such as rounding behavior, number of significant digits, and precision. It defines two objects, a `Decimal` type, representing decimal numbers, and a `Context` type, representing various computational parameters such as precision, rounding, and error handling. An example of its usage can be seen in the following snippet:

```
>>> import decimal
>>> x=decimal.Decimal(3.14)
>>> y=decimal.Decimal(2.74)
>>> x*y
Decimal('8.603600000000001010036498883')
>>> decimal.getcontext().prec=4
>>> x*y
Decimal('8.604')
```

Here we have created a global context and set the precision to `4`. The `Decimal` object can be treated pretty much as you would treat `int` or `float`. They are subject to all of the same mathematical operations and can be used as dictionary keys, placed in sets, and so on. In addition, `Decimal` objects also have several methods for mathematical operations, such as natural exponents, `x.exp()`; natural logarithms, `x.ln()`; and base 10 logarithms, `x.log10()`.

Python also has a `fractions` module that implements a rational number type. The following example shows several ways to create fractions:

```
>>> import fractions
>>> fractions.Fraction(3,4)
Fraction(3, 4)
>>> fractions.Fraction(0.5)
Fraction(1, 2)
>>> fractions.Fraction("0.25")
Fraction(1, 4)
```

It is also worth mentioning here the NumPy extension. This has types for mathematical objects, such as arrays, vectors, and matrices, and capabilities for linear algebra, calculation of Fourier transforms, eigenvectors, logical operations, and much more.

Membership, identity, and logical operations

Membership operators (`in` and `not in`) test for variables in sequences, such as lists or strings, and do what you would expect; `x in y` returns `True` if an `x` variable is found in `y`. The `is` operator compares object identity. For example, the following snippet shows contrast equivalence with object identity:

```
>>> x=[1,2,3]
>>> y=[1,2,3]
>>> x==y   # test equivalence
True
>>> x is y    # test object identity
False
>>> x=y    # assignment
>>> x is y
True
```

Sequences

Sequences are ordered sets of objects indexed by non-negative integers. Sequences include `string`, `list`, `tuple`, and `range` objects. Lists and tuples are sequences of arbitrary objects, whereas strings are sequences of characters. However, `string`, `tuple`, and `range` objects are immutable, whereas, the `list` object is mutable. All sequence types have a number of operations in common. Note that, for the immutable types, any operation will only return a value rather than actually change the value.

For all sequences, the indexing and slicing operators apply as described in the previous chapter. The `string` and `list` data types were discussed in detail in Chapter 1, *Python Objects, Types, and Expressions*. Here, we present some of the important methods and operations that are common to all of the sequence types (`string`, `list`, `tuple`, and `range` objects).

All sequences have the following methods:

Method	Description
`len(s)`	Returns the number of elements in s.
`min(s, [,default=obj, key=func])`	Returns the minimum value in s (alphabetically for strings).
`max(s, [,default=obj, key=func])`	Returns the maximum value in s (alphabetically for strings).

	Returns the sum of the elements (returns `TypeError` if `s` is not numeric).
`sum(s, [, start=0])`	
`all(s)`	Returns `True` if all elements in `s` are `True` (that is, not `0`, `False`, or `Null`).
`any(s)`	Checks whether any item in `s` is `True`.

In addition, all sequences support the following operations:

Operation	Description
`s+r`	Concatenates two sequences of the same type.
`s*n`	Makes n copies of `s`, where `n` is an integer.
`v1,v2...,vn=s`	Unpacks n variables from `s` to `v1`, `v2`, and so on.
`s[i]`	Indexing returns the `i` element of `s`.
`s[i:j:stride]`	Slicing returns elements between `i` and `j` with optional stride.
`x in s`	Returns `True` if the `x` element is in `s`.
`x not in s`	Returns `True` if the `x` element is not in `s`.

Let's consider an example code snippet implementing some of the preceding operations on the `list` data type :

```
>>>list() # an empty list
>>>list1 = [1,2,3, 4]
>>>list1.append(1)  # append value 1 at the end of the list
>>>list1
[1, 2, 3, 4, 1]
>>>list2 = list1 *2
[1, 2, 3, 4, 1, 1, 2, 3, 4, 1]
>>> min(list1)
1
>>> max(list1)
4
>>>list1.insert(0,2)  # insert an value 2 at index 0
>>> list1
[2, 1, 2, 3, 4, 1]
>>>list1.reverse()
>>> list1
[1, 4, 3, 2, 1, 2]
>>>list2=[11,12]
>>>list1.extend(list2)
>>> list1
[1, 4, 3, 2, 1, 2, 11, 12]
```

```
>>>sum(list1)
36
>>> len(list1)
8
>>> list1.sort()
>>> list1
[1, 1, 2, 2, 3, 4, 11, 12]
>>>list1.remove(12)    #remove value 12 form the list
>>> list1
[1, 1, 2, 2, 3, 4, 11]
```

Learning about tuples

Tuples are immutable sequences of arbitrary objects. A tuple is a comma-separated sequence of values; however, it is common practice to enclose them in parentheses. Tuples are very useful when we want to set up multiple variables in one line, or to allow a function to return multiple values of different objects. Tuple is an ordered sequence of items similar to the list data type. The only difference is that tuples are immutable; hence, once created they cannot be modified, unlike list. Tuples are indexed by integers greater than zero. Tuples are **hashable**, which means we can sort lists of them and they can be used as keys to dictionaries.

We can also create a tuple using the built-in function: tuple(). With no argument, this creates an empty tuple. If the argument to tuple() is a sequence then this creates a tuple of elements of that sequence. It is important to remember to use a trailing comma when creating a tuple with one element—without the trailing comma, this will be interpreted as a string. An important use of tuples is to allow us to assign more than one variable at a time by placing a tuple on the left-hand side of an assignment.

Consider an example:

```
>>> t= tuple()    # create an empty tuple
>>> type(t)
<class 'tuple'>
>>> t=('a',)  # create a tuple with 1 element
>>> t
('a',)
>>> print('type is ',type(t))
type is  <class 'tuple'>
>>> tpl=('a','b','c')
>>> tpl('a', 'b', 'c')
>>> tuple('sequence')
('s', 'e', 'q', 'u', 'e', 'n', 'c', 'e')
>>> x,y,z= tpl    #multiple assignment
```

```
>>> x
'a'
>>> y
'b'
>>> z
'c'
>>> 'a' in tpl   # Membership can be tested
True
>>> 'z' in tpl
False
```

Most operators, such as those for slicing and indexing, work as they do on lists. However, because tuples are immutable, trying to modify an element of a tuple will give you TypeError. We can compare tuples in the same way that we compare other sequences, using the ==, > and < operators. Consider an example code snippet:

```
>>> tupl = 1, 2,3,4,5  # braces are optional
>>>print("tuple value at index 1 is ", tupl[1])
tuple value at index 1 is  2
>>> print("tuple[1:3] is ", tupl[1:3])
tuple[1:3] is (2, 3)
>>>tupl2 = (11, 12,13)
>>>tupl3= tupl + tupl2   # tuple concatenation
>>> tupl3
(1, 2, 3, 4, 5, 11, 12, 13)
>>> tupl*2      # repetition for tuples
(1, 2, 3, 4, 5, 1, 2, 3, 4, 5)
>>> 5 in tupl    # membership test
True
>>> tupl[-1]     # negative indexing
5
>>> len(tupl)   # length function for tuple
5
>>> max(tupl)
5
>>> min(tupl)
1
>>> tupl[1] = 5 # modification in tuple is not allowed.
Traceback (most recent call last):
  File "<stdin>", line 1, in <module>
TypeError: 'tuple' object does not support item assignment
>>>print (tupl== tupl2)
False
>>>print (tupl>tupl2)
False
```

Let's consider another example to better understand tuples. For example, we can use multiple assignments to swap values in a tuple:

```
>>> l = ['one','two']
>>> x,y = l
('one', 'two')
>>> x,y = y,x
>>> x,y
('two', 'one')
```

Beginning with dictionaries

In Python, the `Dictionary` data type is one of the most popular and useful data types. A dictionary stores the data in a mapping of key and value pair. Dictionaries are mainly a collection of objects; they are indexed by numbers, strings, or any other immutable objects. Keys should be unique in the dictionaries; however, the values in the dictionary can be changed. Python dictionaries are the only built-in mapping type; they can be thought of as a mapping from a set of keys to a set of values. They are created using the `{key:value}` syntax. For example, the following code can be used to create a dictionary that maps words to numerals using different methods:

```
>>>a= {'Monday':1,'Tuesday':2,'Wednesday':3} #creates a dictionary
>>>b =dict({'Monday':1 , 'Tuesday': 2, 'Wednesday': 3})
>>> b
{'Monday': 1, 'Tuesday': 2, 'Wednesday': 3}
>>> c= dict(zip(['Monday','Tuesday','Wednesday'], [1,2,3]))
>>> c={'Monday': 1, 'Tuesday': 2, 'Wednesday': 3}
>>> d= dict([('Monday',1), ('Tuesday',2), ('Wednesday',3)])
>>>d
{'Monday': 1, 'Tuesday': 2, 'Wednesday': 3}
```

We can add keys and values. We can also update multiple values, and test for the membership or occurrence of a value using the `in` operator, as shown in the following code example:

```
>>>d['Thursday']=4      #add an item
>>>d.update({'Friday':5,'Saturday':6})  #add multiple items
>>>d
{'Monday': 1, 'Tuesday': 2, 'Wednesday': 3, 'Thursday': 4, 'Friday': 5,
'Saturday': 6}
>>>'Wednesday' in d  # membership test (only in keys)
True
>>>5 in d       # membership do not check in values
False
```

The `in` operator to find an element in a list takes too much time if the list is long. The running time required to look up an element in a list increases linearly with an increase in the size of the list. Whereas, the `in` operator in dictionaries uses a hashing function, which enables dictionaries to be very efficient, as the time taken in looking up an element is independent of the size of the dictionary.

Notice when we print out the `{key: value}` pairs of the dictionary it does so in no particular order. This is not a problem since we use specified keys to look up each dictionary value rather than an ordered sequence of integers, as is the case for strings and lists:

```
>>> dict(zip('packt', range(5)))
{'p': 0, 'a': 1, 'c': 2, 'k': 3, 't': 4}
>>> a = dict(zip('packt', range(5)))
>>> len(a)    # length of dictionary a
5
>>> a['c']   # to check the value of a key
2
>>> a.pop('a')
1
>>> a{'p': 0, 'c': 2, 'k': 3, 't': 4}
>>> b= a.copy()    # make a copy of the dictionary
>>> b
{'p': 0, 'c': 2, 'k': 3, 't': 4}
>>> a.keys()
dict_keys(['p', 'c', 'k', 't'])
>>> a.values()
dict_values([0, 2, 3, 4])
>>> a.items()
dict_items([('p', 0), ('c', 2), ('k', 3), ('t', 4)])
>>> a.update({'a':1})    # add an item in the dictionary
>>> a{'p': 0, 'c': 2, 'k': 3, 't': 4, 'a': 1}
>>> a.update(a=22)   # update the value of key 'a'
>>> a{'p': 0, 'c': 2, 'k': 3, 't': 4, 'a': 22}
```

The following table contains all the dictionary methods and their descriptions:

Method	Description
len(d)	Returns total number of items in the dictionary, d.
d.clear()	Removes all of the items from the dictionary, d.
d.copy()	Returns a shallow copy of the dictionary, d.
d.fromkeys(s[,value])	Returns a new dictionary with keys from the s sequence and values set to value.

d.get(k[,v])	Returns d[k] if it is found; otherwise, it returns v (None if v is not given).
d.items()	Returns all of the key:value pairs of the dictionary, d.
d.keys()	Returns all of the keys defined in the dictionary, d.
d.pop(k[,default])	Returns d[k] and removes it from d.
d.popitem()	Removes a random key:value pair from the dictionary, d, and returns it as a tuple.
d.setdefault(k[,v])	Returns d[k]. If it is not found, it returns v and sets d[k] to v.
d.update(b)	Adds all of the objects from the b dictionary to the d dictionary .
d.values()	Returns all of the values in the dictionary, d.

Python

It should be noted that the in operator, when applied to dictionaries, works in a slightly different way to when it is applied to a list. When we use the in operator on a list, the relationship between the time it takes to find an element and the size of the list is considered linear. That is, as the size of the list gets bigger, the corresponding time it takes to find an element grows, at most, linearly. The relationship between the time an algorithm takes to run compared to the size of its input is often referred to as its time complexity. We will talk more about this important topic in the next (and subsequent) chapters.

In contrast to the list object, when the in operator is applied to dictionaries, it uses a hashing algorithm, and this has the effect of an increase in each lookup time that is almost independent of the size of the dictionary. This makes dictionaries extremely useful as a way to work with large amounts of indexed data. We will talk more about this important topic of rates of growth hashing in Chapter 4, *Lists and Pointer Structures*, and Chapter 14, *Implementations, Applications, and Tools*.

Sorting dictionaries

If we want to do a simple sort on either the keys or values of a dictionary, we can do the following:

```
>>> d = {'one': 1, 'two': 2, 'three': 3, 'four': 4, 'five': 5, 'six': 6}
>>> sorted(list(d))
['five', 'four', 'one', 'six', 'three', 'two']
>>> sorted(list(d.values()))
[1, 2, 3, 4, 5, 6]
```

Note that the first line in the preceding code sorts the keys alphabetically and the second line sorts the values in order of the integer value.

The `sorted()` method has two optional arguments that are of interest: `key` and `reverse`. The `key` argument has nothing to do with the dictionary keys, but rather is a way of passing a function to the sort algorithm to determine the sort order. For example, in the following code, we use the `__getitem__` special method to sort the dictionary keys according to the dictionary values:

```
sorted(list(d), key = d.__getitem__)
['one', 'two', 'three', 'four', 'five', 'six']
```

Essentially, what the preceding code is doing is, for every key in `d`, it uses the corresponding value to sort. We can also sort the values according to the sorted order of the dictionary keys. However, since dictionaries do not have a method to return a key by using its value, the equivalent of the `list.index` method for lists, using the optional key argument to do this is a little tricky. An alternative approach is to use a list comprehension, as the following example demonstrates:

```
In [7]: [value for (key, value) in sorted(d.items())]
Out[7]: [5, 4, 1, 6, 3, 2]
```

The `sorted()` method also has an optional `reverse` argument, and unsurprisingly this does exactly what it says—reverses the order of the sorted list, as in the following example:

```
In [11]: sorted(list(d), key = d.__getitem__ , reverse=True)
Out[11]: ['six', 'five', 'four', 'three', 'two', 'one']
```

Now, let's say we are given the following dictionary, with English words as keys and French words as values. Our task is to place the string values in the correct numerical order:

```
d2={'one':'uno','two':'deux','three':'trois','four':'quatre','five':'cinq',
'six':'six'}
```

Of course, when we print this dictionary out, it will be unlikely to print in the correct order. Because all keys and values are strings, we have no context for numerical ordering. To place these items in correct order, we need to use the first dictionary we created, mapping words to numerals as a way to order our English to French dictionary:

```
In [15]: sorted(d2, key=d.__getitem__)
Out[15]: ['one', 'two', 'three', 'four', 'five', 'six']
```

Notice we are using the values of the first dictionary, d, to sort the keys of the second dictionary, d2. Since our keys in both dictionaries are the same, we can use a list comprehension to sort the values of the French to English dictionary:

```
In [16]: [d2[i] for i in sorted(d2, key=d.__getitem__)]
Out[16]: ['uno', 'deux', 'trois', 'quatre', 'cinq', 'six']
```

We can, of course, define our own custom method that we can use as the key argument to the sorted method. For example, here we define a function that simply returns the last letter of a string:

```
def corder(string):
    return (string[len(string)-1])
```

We can then use this as the key to our sorted function to sort each element by its last letter:

```
sorted(d2.values(), key=corder)
['quatre', 'uno', 'cinq', 'trois', 'deux', 'six']
```

Dictionaries for text analysis

A common use of dictionaries is to count the occurrences of like items in a sequence; a typical example is counting the occurrences of words in a body of text. The following code creates a dictionary where each word in the text is used as a key and the number of occurrences as its value. This uses a very common idiom of nested loops. Here we are using it to traverse the lines in a file in an outer loop and the keys of a dictionary on the inner loop:

```
def wordcount(fname):
    try:
        fhand=open(fname)
    except:
        print('File can not be opened')
```

```
            exit()

    count=dict()
    for line in fhand:
        words=line.split()
        for word in words:
            if word not in count:
                count[word]=1
            else:
                count[word]+=1
    return(count)
```

This will return a dictionary with an element for each unique word in the text file. A common task is to filter items such as these into subsets we are interested in. You will need a text file saved in the same directory as you run the code. Here we have used `alice.txt`, a short excerpt from *Alice in Wonderland*. To obtain the same results, you can download `alice.txt` from `davejulian.net/bo5630` or use a text file of your own. In the following code, we create another dictionary, filtered, containing a subset of items from `count`:

```
count=wordcount('alice.txt')
filtered={key:value for key, value in count.items() if value <20 and
value>16 }
```

When we print the filtered dictionary, we get the following:

```
{'once': 18, 'eyes': 18, 'There': 19, 'this,': 17, 'before': 19, 'take':
18, 'tried': 18, 'even': 17, 'things': 19, 'sort': 17, 'her,': 18, '`And':
17, 'sat': 17, '`But': 19, "it,'": 18, 'cried': 18, '`Oh,': 19, 'and,': 19,
"`I'm": 19, 'voice': 17, 'being': 19, 'till': 19, 'Mouse': 17, '`but': 19,
'Queen,': 17}
```

Note the use of the **dictionary comprehension** used to construct the filtered dictionary. Dictionary comprehensions work in an identical way to the list comprehensions we looked at in `Chapter 1`, *Python Objects, Types, and Expressions*.

Sets

Sets are unordered collections of unique items. Sets are themselves mutable—we can add and remove items from them; however, the items themselves must be immutable. An important distinction with sets is that they cannot contain duplicate items. Sets are typically used to perform mathematical operations such as intersection, union, difference, and complement.

Unlike sequence types, set types do not provide any indexing or slicing operations. There are two types of set objects in Python, the mutable `set` object and the immutable `frozenset` object. Sets are created using comma-separated values within curly braces. By the way, we cannot create an empty set using `a={}`, because this will create a dictionary. To create an empty set, we write either `a=set()` or `a=frozenset()`.

Methods and operations of sets are described in the following table:

Method	Description	
`len(a)`	Provides the total number of elements in the a set.	
`a.copy()`	Provides another copy of the a set.	
`a.difference(t)`	Provides a set of elements that are in the a set but not in t.	
`a.intersection(t)`	Provides a set of elements that are in both sets, a and t.	
`a.isdisjoint(t)`	Returns True if no element is common in both the sets, a and t.	
`a.issubset(t)`	Returns True if all of the elements of the a set are also in the t set.	
`a.issuperset(t)`	Returns True if all of the elements of the t set are also in the a set.	
`a.symmetric_difference(t)`	Returns a set of elements that are in either the a or t sets, but not in both.	
`a.union(t)`	Returns a set of elements that are in either the a or t sets.	

In the preceding table, the `t` parameter can be any Python object that supports iteration and all methods are available to both `set` and `frozenset` objects. It is important to be aware that the operator versions of these methods require their arguments to be sets, whereas the methods themselves can accept any iterable type. For example, `s-[1,2,3]`, for any set, `s`, will generate an unsupported operand type. Using the equivalent, `s.difference([1,2,3])` will return a result.

Mutable `set` objects have additional methods, described in the following table:

Method	Description
`s.add(item)`	Adds an item to s; nothing happens if the item is already added.
`s.clear()`	Removes all elements from the set, s.
`s.difference_update(t)`	Removes those elements from the s set that are also in the other set, t.
`s.discard(item)`	Removes the item from the set, s.

`s.intersection_update(t)`	Remove the items from the set, `s`, which are not in the intersection of the sets, `s` and `t`.
`s.pop()`	Returns an arbitrary item from the set, `s`, and it removes it from the `s` set.
`s.remove(item)`	Deletes the item from the `s` set.
`s.symetric_difference_update(t)`	Deletes all of the elements from the `s` set that are not in the symmetric difference of the sets, `s` and `t`.
`s.update(t)`	Appends all of the items in an iterable object, `t`, to the `s` set.

Here, consider a simple example showing addition, removal, discard, and clear operations:

```
>>> s1 = set()
>>> s1.add(1)
>>> s1.add(2)
>>> s1.add(3)
>>> s1.add(4)
>>> s1
{1, 2, 3, 4}
>>> s1.remove(4)
>>> s1
{1, 2, 3}
>>> s1.discard(3)
>>> s1
{1, 2}
>>>s1.clear()
>>>s1
set()
```

The following example demonstrates some simple set operations and their results:

```
In [1]: s1={'ab',3,4,(5,6)}

In [2]: s2={'ab',7,(7,6)}

In [3]: s1-s2 # same as s1.difference(s2)
Out[3]: {(5, 6), 3, 4}

In [4]: s1.intersection(s2)
Out[4]: {'ab'}

In [5]: s1.union(s2)
Out[5]: {3, 4, 'ab', 7, (5, 6), (7, 6)}
```

Notice that the `set` object does not care that its members are not all of the same type, as long as they are all immutable. If you try to use a mutable object such as a list or dictionary in a set, you will receive an unhashable type error. Hashable types all have a hash value that does not change throughout the lifetime of the instance. All built-in immutable types are hashable. All built-in mutable types are not hashable, so they cannot be used as elements of sets or keys to dictionaries.

Notice also in the preceding code that when we print out the union of `s1` and `s2`, there is only one element with the value `'ab'`. This is a natural property of sets in that they do not include duplicates.

In addition to these built-in methods, there are a number of other operations that we can perform on sets. For example, to test for membership of a set, use the following:

```
In [6]: 'ab' in s1
Out[6]: True

In [7]: 'ab' not in s1
Out[7]: False
```

We can loop through elements in a set using the following:

```
In [8]: for element in s1: print(element)
(5, 6)
ab
3
4
```

Immutable sets

Python has an immutable set type called `frozenset`. It works pretty much exactly like `set`, apart from not allowing methods or operations that change values such as the `add()` or `clear()` methods. There are several ways that this immutability can be useful.

For example, since normal sets are mutable and therefore not hashable, they cannot be used as members of other sets. On the other hand `frozenset` is immutable and therefore able to be used as a member of a set:

```
In [26]: s1.add(s2)
Traceback (most recent call last):

  File "<ipython-input-26-05d7ba45d78a>", line 1, in <module>
    s1.add(s2)

TypeError: unhashable type: 'set'

In [27]: s1.add(frozenset(s2))

In [28]: s1
Out[28]: {(5, 6), 'ab', 3, 4, frozenset({(7, 6), 'ab', 7})}
```

Also, the immutable property of `frozenset` means we can use it for a key to a dictionary, as in the following example:

```
In [38]: fs1 = frozenset(s1)

In [39]: fs2 = frozenset(s2)

In [40]: {fs1: 'fs1' , fs2: 'fs2'}
Out[40]: {frozenset({(7, 6), 'ab', 7}): 'fs2', frozenset({(5, 6), 'ab', 3, 4}): 'fs1'}
```

Modules for data structures and algorithms

In addition to the built-in types, there are several Python modules that we can use to extend the built-in types and functions. In many cases, these Python modules may offer efficiency and programming advantages that allow us to simplify our code.

So far, we have looked at the built-in datatypes of strings, lists, sets, and dictionaries as well as the decimal and fraction modules. They are often described by the term **Abstract Data Types** (**ADTs**). ADTs can be considered mathematical specifications for the set of operations that can be performed on data. They are defined by their behavior rather than their implementation. In addition to the ADTs that we have looked at, there are several Python libraries that provide extensions to the built-in datatypes. These will be discussed in the following section.

Collections

The `collections` module provides more specialized, high-performance alternatives for the built-in data types as well as a utility function to create named tuples. The following table lists the datatypes and operations of the collections module and their descriptions:

Datatype or operation	Description
`namedtuple()`	Creates tuple subclasses with named fields.
`deque`	Lists with fast appends and pops either end.
`ChainMap`	Dictionary-like class to create a single view of multiple mappings.
`Counter`	Dictionary subclass for counting hashable objects.
`OrderedDict`	Dictionary subclass that remembers the entry order.
`defaultdict`	Dictionary subclass that calls a function to supply missing values.
`UserDict UserList UserString`	These three data types are simply wrappers for their underlying base classes. Their use has largely been supplanted by the ability to subclass their respective base classes directly. Can be used to access the underlying object as an attribute.

Deques

Double-ended queues, or deques (usually pronounced *decks*), are list-like objects that support thread-safe, memory-efficient appends. Deques are mutable and support some of the operations of lists, such as indexing. Deques can be assigned by index, for example, `dq[1] = z`; however, we cannot directly slice deques. For example, `dq[1:2]` results in `TypeError` (we will look at a way to return a slice from a deque as a list shortly).

The major advantage of deques over lists is that inserting items at the beginning of a deque is much faster than inserting items at the beginning of a list, although inserting items at the end of a deque is very slightly slower than the equivalent operation on a list. Deques are thread-safe and can be serialized using the `pickle` module.

A useful way of thinking about deques is in terms of populating and consuming items. Items in deques are usually populated and consumed sequentially from either end:

```
In [18]: from collections import deque

In [19]: dq = deque('abc') #creates deque(['a','b','c'])

In [20]: dq.append('d') #adds the value 'd' to the right

In [21]: dq.appendleft('z') #adds the value 'z' to the left

In [22]: dq.extend('efg') #adds multiple items to the right

In [23]: dq.extendleft('yxw') #adds multiple items to the left

In [24]: dq
Out[24]: deque(['w', 'x', 'y', 'z', 'a', 'b', 'c', 'd', 'e', 'f', 'g'])
```

We can use the `pop()` and `popleft()` methods for consuming items in the deque, as in the following example:

```
In [25]: dq.pop() #returns and removes an item from the right
Out[25]: 'g'

In [26]: dq.popleft() #returns and removes an item from the left
Out[26]: 'w'

In [27]: dq
Out[27]: deque(['x', 'y', 'z', 'a', 'b', 'c', 'd', 'e', 'f'])
```

We can also use the `rotate(n)` method to move and rotate all items of n steps to the right for positive values of the n integer or negative values of n steps to the left, using positive integers as the argument, as in the following example:

```
In [45]: dq.rotate(2) #rotates all items 2 steps to the right

In [46]: dq
Out[46]: deque(['e', 'f', 'x', 'y', 'z', 'a', 'b', 'c', 'd'])

In [47]: dq.rotate(-2) #rotates all items 2 steps to the left

In [48]: dq
Out[48]: deque(['x', 'y', 'z', 'a', 'b', 'c', 'd', 'e', 'f'])
```

Note that we can use the `rotate` and `pop` methods to delete selected elements. Also worth knowing is a simple way to return a slice of a deque, as a list, which can be done as follows:

```
In [14]: dq
Out[14]: deque(['x', 'y', 'z', 'a', 'b', 'c', 'd', 'e', 'f'])

In [15]: list(itertools.islice(dq,3,9))
Out[15]: ['a', 'b', 'c', 'd', 'e', 'f']
```

The `itertools.islice()` method works in the same way that slice works on a list, except rather than taking a list for an argument, it takes an iterable and returns selected values, by start and stop indices, as a list.

A useful feature of deques is that they support a `maxlen` optional parameter that restricts the size of the deque. This makes it ideally suited to a data structure known as a **circular buffer**. This is a fixed-size structure that is effectively connected end to end and they are typically used for buffering data streams. The following is a basic example:

```
dq2=deque([],maxlen=3)
for i in range(6):
    dq2.append(i)
    print(dq2)
```

This prints out the following:

```
deque([0], maxlen=3)
deque([0, 1], maxlen=3)
deque([0, 1, 2], maxlen=3)
deque([1, 2, 3], maxlen=3)
deque([2, 3, 4], maxlen=3)
deque([3, 4, 5], maxlen=3)
```

In this example, we are populating from the right and consuming from the left. Notice that once the buffer is full the oldest values are consumed first and values are replaced from the right. We will look at circular buffers again in `Chapter 4`, *Lists and Pointer Structures*, when implementing circular lists.

ChainMap objects

The `collections.chainmap` class was added in Python 3.2, and it provides a way to link a number of dictionaries, or other mappings, so that they can be treated as one object. In addition, there is a `maps` attribute, a `new_child()` method, and a `parents` property. The underlying mappings for `ChainMap` objects are stored in a list and are accessible using the `maps[i]` attribute to retrieve the `ith` dictionary. Note that, even though dictionaries themselves are unordered, `ChainMap` objects are ordered lists of dictionaries.

`ChainMap` is useful in applications where we are using a number of dictionaries containing related data. The consuming application expects data in terms of a priority, where the same key in two dictionaries is given priority if it occurs at the beginning of the underlying list. `ChainMap` is typically used to simulate nested contexts such as when we have multiple overriding configuration settings. The following example demonstrates a possible use case for `ChainMap`:

```
>>> import collections
>>> dict1= {'a':1, 'b':2, 'c':3}
>>> dict2 = {'d':4, 'e':5}
>>> chainmap = collections.ChainMap(dict1, dict2)  # linking two
dictionaries
>>> chainmap
ChainMap({'a': 1, 'b': 2, 'c': 3}, {'d': 4, 'e': 5})
>>> chainmap.maps
[{'a': 1, 'b': 2, 'c': 3}, {'d': 4, 'e': 5}]
>>> chainmap.values
<bound method Mapping.values of ChainMap({'a': 1, 'b': 2, 'c': 3}, {'d': 4,
'e': 5})
>>>> chainmap['b']    #accessing values
2
>>> chainmap['e']
5
```

The advantage of using `ChainMap` objects, rather than just a dictionary, is that we retain previously set values. Adding a child context overrides values for the same key, but it does not remove it from the data structure. This can be useful when we may need to keep a record of changes so that we can easily roll back to a previous setting.

We can retrieve and change any value in any of the dictionaries by providing the `map()` method with an appropriate index. This index represents a dictionary in `ChainMap`. Also, we can retrieve the parent setting, that is, the default settings, by using the `parents()` method:

```
>>> from collections import ChainMap
>>> defaults= {'theme':'Default','language':'eng','showIndex':True,
```

```
'showFooter':True}
>>> cm= ChainMap(defaults)    #creates a chainMap with defaults
configuration
>>> cm.maps[{'theme': 'Default', 'language': 'eng', 'showIndex': True,
'showFooter': True}]
>>> cm.values()
ValuesView(ChainMap({'theme': 'Default', 'language': 'eng', 'showIndex':
True, 'showFooter': True}))
>>> cm2= cm.new_child({'theme':'bluesky'}) # create a new chainMap with a
child that overrides the parent.
>>> cm2['theme']   #returns the overridden theme'bluesky'
>>> cm2.pop('theme')   # removes the child theme value
'bluesky'
>>> cm2['theme']
'Default'
>>> cm2.maps[{}, {'theme': 'Default', 'language': 'eng', 'showIndex': True,
'showFooter': True}]
>>> cm2.parents
ChainMap({'theme': 'Default', 'language': 'eng', 'showIndex': True,
'showFooter': True})
```

Counter objects

Counter is a subclass of a dictionary where each dictionary key is a hashable object and the associated value is an integer count of that object. There are three ways to initialize a counter. We can pass it any sequence object, a dictionary of key:value pairs, or a tuple of the format (object=value,...), as in the following example:

```
>>> from collections import Counter
>>> Counter('anysequence')
Counter({'e': 3, 'n': 2, 'a': 1, 'y': 1, 's': 1, 'q': 1, 'u': 1, 'c': 1})
>>> c1 = Counter('anysequence')
>>> c2= Counter({'a':1, 'c': 1, 'e':3})
>>> c3= Counter(a=1, c= 1, e=3)
>>> c1
Counter({'e': 3, 'n': 2, 'a': 1, 'y': 1, 's': 1, 'q': 1, 'u': 1, 'c': 1})
>>> c2
Counter({'e': 3, 'a': 1, 'c': 1})
>>> c3
Counter({'e': 3, 'a': 1, 'c': 1})
```

We can also create an empty counter object and populate it by passing its `update` method an iterable or a dictionary. Notice how the `update` method adds the counts rather than replacing them with new values. Once the counter is populated, we can access stored values in the same way we would do for dictionaries, as in the following example:

```
>>> from collections import Counter
>>> ct = Counter()  # creates an empty counter object
>>> ct
Counter()
>>> ct.update('abca') # populates the object
>>> ct
Counter({'a': 2, 'b': 1, 'c': 1})
>>> ct.update({'a':3}) # update the count of 'a'
>>> ct
Counter({'a': 5, 'b': 1, 'c': 1})
>>> for item in ct:
...     print('%s: %d' % (item, ct[item]))
...
a: 5
b: 1
c: 1
```

The most notable difference between counter objects and dictionaries is that counter objects return a zero count for missing items rather than raising a key error. We can create an iterator out of a `Counter` object by using its `elements()` method. This returns an iterator where counts below one are not included and the order is not guaranteed. In the following code, we perform some updates, create an iterator from `Counter` elements, and use `sorted()` to sort the keys alphabetically:

```
>>> ct
Counter({'a': 5, 'b': 1, 'c': 1})
>>> ct['x']
0
>>> ct.update({'a':-3, 'b':-2, 'e':2})
>>> ct
Counter({'a': 2, 'e': 2, 'c': 1, 'b': -1})
>>>sorted(ct.elements())
['a', 'a', 'c', 'e', 'e']
```

Two other `Counter` methods worth mentioning are `most_common()` and `subtract()`. The most common method takes a positive integer argument that determines the number of most common elements to return. Elements are returned as a list of (key,value) tuples.

The subtract method works exactly like update except, instead of adding values, it subtracts them, as in the following example:

```
>>> ct.most_common()
[('a', 2), ('e', 2), ('c', 1), ('b', -1)]
>>> ct.subtract({'e':2})
>>> ct
Counter({'a': 2, 'c': 1, 'e': 0, 'b': -1})
```

Ordered dictionaries

The important thing about ordered dictionaries is that they remember the insertion order, so when we iterate over them, they return values in the order they were inserted. This is in contrast to a normal dictionary, where the order is arbitrary. When we test to see whether two dictionaries are equal, this equality is only based on their keys and values; however, with `OrderedDict`, the insertion order is also considered an equality test between two `OrderedDict` objects with the same keys and values, but a different insertion order will return `False`:

```
>>> import collections
>>> od1= collections.OrderedDict()
>>> od1['one'] = 1
>>> od1['two'] = 2
>>> od2 = collections.OrderedDict()
>>> od2['two'] = 2
>>> od2['one'] = 1
>>> od1==od2
False
```

Similarly, when we add values from a list using `update`, `OrderedDict` will retain the same order as the list. This is the order that is returned when we iterate the values, as in the following example:

```
>>> kvs = [('three',3), ('four',4), ('five',5)]
>>> od1.update(kvs)
>>> od1
OrderedDict([('one', 1), ('two', 2), ('three', 3), ('four', 4), ('five', 5)])
>>> for k, v in od1.items(): print(k, v)
```

```
...
one 1
two 2
three 3
four 4
five 5
```

`OrderedDict` is often used in conjunction with the sorted method to create a sorted dictionary. In the following example, we use a Lambda function to sort the values, and here we use a numerical expression to sort the integer values:

```
>>> od3 = collections.OrderedDict(sorted(od1.items(), key= lambda t :
(4*t[1])- t[1]**2))
>>>od3
OrderedDict([('five', 5), ('four', 4), ('one', 1), ('three', 3), ('two',
2)])
>>> od3.values()
odict_values([5, 4, 1, 3, 2])
```

defaultdict

The `defaultdict` object is a subclass of `dict`, and therefore they share methods and operations. It acts as a convenient way to initialize dictionaries. With `dict`, Python will throw `KeyError` when attempting to access a key that is not already in the dictionary. The `defaultdict` overrides one method, `missing (key)`, and creates a new instance variable, `default_factory`. With `defaultdict`, rather than throw an error, it will run the function supplied as the `default_factory` argument, which will generate a value. A simple use of `defaultdict` is to set `default_factory` to `int` and use it to quickly tally the counts of items in the dictionary, as in the following example:

```
>>> from collections import defaultdict
>>> dd = defaultdict(int)
>>> words = str.split('red blue green red yellow blue red green green red')
>>> for word in words: dd[word] +=1
...
>>> dd
defaultdict(<class 'int'>, {'red': 4, 'blue': 2, 'green': 3, 'yellow': 1})
```

You will notice that if we tried to do this with an ordinary dictionary, we would get a key error when we tried to add the first key. The `int` we supplied as an argument to the `defaultdict` is really the `int ()` function that simply returns a zero.

We can, of course, create a function that will determine the dictionary's values. For example, the following function returns `True` if the supplied argument is a primary color, that is `red`, `green`, or `blue`, or returns `False` otherwise:

```
def isprimary(c):
    if (c=='red') or (c=='blue') or (c=='green'):
        return True
    else:
        return False
```

Learning about named tuples

The `namedtuple` method returns a tuple-like object that has fields accessible with named indexes as well as the integer indexes of normal tuples. This allows for code that is, to a certain extent, self-documenting and more readable. It can be especially useful in an application where there are a large number of tuples and we need to easily keep track of what each tuple represents. Furthermore, `namedtuple` inherits methods from tuple and it is backward-compatible with tuple.

The field names are passed to the `namedtuple` method as comma and/or whitespace-separated values. They can also be passed as a sequence of strings. Field names are single strings, and they can be any legal Python identifier that does not begin with a digit or an underscore. A typical example is shown here:

```
>>> from collections import namedtuple
>>> space = namedtuple('space', 'x y z')
>>> s1= space(x=2.0, y=4.0, z=10) # we can also use space(2.0,4.0, 10)
>>> s1
space(x=2.0, y=4.0, z=10)
>>> s1.x * s1.y * s1.z    # calculate the volume
80.0
```

In addition to the inherited tuple methods, the named tuple also defines three methods of its own, `_make()`, `asdict()`, and `_replace`. These methods begin with an underscore to prevent potential conflicts with field names. The `_make()` method takes an iterable as an argument and turns it into a named tuple object, as in the following example:

```
>>> sl = [4,5,6]
>>> space._make(sl)
space(x=4, y=5, z=6)
>>> s1._1
4
```

The _asdict method returns an OrderedDict object with the field names mapped to index keys and the values mapped to the dictionary values. The _replace method returns a new instance of the tuple, replacing the specified values. In addition, _fields returns the tuple of string listing the fields names. The _fields_defaults method provides dictionary mapping field names to the default values. Consider the example code snippet:

```
>>> s1._asdict()
OrderedDict([('x', 3), ('_1', 4), ('z', 5)])
>>> s1._replace(x=7, z=9)
space2(x=7, _1=4, z=9)
>>> space._fields
('x', 'y', 'z')
>>> space._fields_defaults
{}
```

Arrays

The array module defines a data type array that is similar to the list data type except for the constraint that their contents must be of a single type of the underlying representation, as is determined by the machine architecture or underlying C implementation.

The type of an array is determined at creation time and it is indicated by one of the following type codes:

Code	C type	Python type	Minimum bytes
'b'	signedchar	int	1
'B'	unsignedchar	int	1
'u'	Py_UNICODE	Unicodecharacter	2
'h'	signedshort	int	2
'H'	unsignedshort	int	2
'i'	signedint	int	2
'I'	unsignedint	int	2
'l'	signedlong	int	4
'L'	unsignedlong	int	8
'q'	signedlonglong	int	8
'Q'	unsignedlonlong	int	8
'f'	float	float	4
'd'	double	float	8

The array objects support the attributes and methods:

Attribute or method	Description
a.itemsize	The size of one array item in bytes.
a.append(x)	Appends an x element at the end of the a array.
a.buffer_info()	Returns a tuple containing the current memory location and length of the buffer used to store the array.
a.byteswap()	Swaps the byte order of each item in the a array.
a.count(x)	Returns the occurrences of x in the a array.
a.extend(b)	Appends all the elements from iterable b at the end of the a array.
a.frombytes(s)	Appends elements from an s string, where the string is an array of machine values.
a.fromfile(f,n)	Reads n machine values from the file and appends them at the end of the array.
a.fromlist(l)	Appends all of the elements from the l list to the array.
a.fromunicode(s)	Extends an array of the u type with the Unicode string, s.
index(x)	Returns the first (smallest) index of the x element.
a.insert(i,x)	Inserts an item of which the value is x, in the array at i index position.
a.pop([i])	Returns the item at index, I, and removes it from the array.
a.remove(x)	Removes the first occurrence of the x item from the array.
a.reverse()	Reverses the order of items in the a array.
a.tofile(f)	Writes all the elements to the f file object.
a.tolist()	Converts the array into a list.
a.tounicode()	Converts an array of the u type into a Unicode string

Array objects support all of the normal sequence operations such as indexing, slicing, concatenation, and multiplication.

Using arrays, as opposed to lists, is a much more efficient way of storing data that is of the same type. In the following example, we have created an integer array of the digits from 0 to one million minus 1, and an identical list. Storing one million integers in an integer array requires around 90% of the memory of an equivalent list:

```
>>> import array
>>> ba = array.array('i', range(10**6))
>>> bl = list(range(10**6))
>>> import sys
>>> 100*sys.getsizeof(ba)/sys.getsizeof(bl)
90.92989871246161
```

Because we are interested in saving space, that is, we are dealing with large datasets and limited memory size, we usually perform in-place operations on arrays, and only create copies when we need to. Typically, enumerate is used to perform an operation on each element. In the following snippet, we perform the simple operation of adding one to each item in the array.

It should be noted that when performing operations on arrays that create lists, such as list comprehensions, the memory efficiency gains of using an array in the first place will be negated. When we need to create a new data object, a solution is to use a generator expression to perform the operation.

Arrays created with this module are unsuitable for work that requires a matrix of vector operations. In the next chapter, we will build our own abstract data type to deal with these operations. Also important for numerical work is the NumPy extension, available at www.numpy.org .

Summary

In the last two chapters, we presented the language features and data types of Python. We looked at the built-in data types and some internal Python modules, most notably the collections module. There are also several other Python modules that are relevant to the topic of this book, but rather than examining them separately, their use and functionality should become self-evident as we begin using them. There are also a number of external libraries, for example, SciPy.

In the next chapter, we will introduce the basic theory and techniques of algorithm design.

Principles of Algorithm Design 3

Why do we study algorithm design? There are, of course, many reasons, and our motivations for learning something is very much dependent on our own circumstances. There are, without a doubt, important professional reasons for being interested in algorithm design. Algorithms are the foundation of all computing. We can think of a computer as being a piece of hardware, with a hard drive, memory chips, processors, and so on. However, the essential component, the thing that, if missing, would render modern technology impossible, is algorithms. Let's learn more about it in the upcoming sections.

In this chapter, we will look at the following topics:

- An introduction to algorithms
- Recursion and backtracking
- Big O notation

Technical requirements

We will need to install the `matplotlib` library with Python to plot the diagram in this chapter.

It can be installed on Ubuntu/Linux by running the following commands on the terminal:

```
python3 -mpip install matplotlib
```

You can also use the following:

```
sudo apt-get install python3-matplotlib
```

To install `matplotlib` on Windows:

If Python is already installed on the Windows operating system, `matplotlib` can be obtained from the following link to install it on Windows: `https://github.com/matplotlib/matplotlib/downloads` or `https://matplotlib.org`.

Code files for this chapter can be found at: `https://github.com/PacktPublishing/Hands-On-Data-Structures-and-Algorithms-with-Python-Second-Edition/tree/master/Chapter03`.

An introduction to algorithms

The theoretical foundation of algorithms, in the form of the Turing machine, was established several decades before digital logic circuits could actually implement such a machine. The Turing machine is essentially a mathematical model that, using a predefined set of rules, translates a set of inputs into a set of outputs. The first implementations of Turing machines were mechanical and the next generation may likely see digital logic circuits replaced by quantum circuits or something similar. Regardless of the platform, algorithms play a central predominant role.

Another aspect is the effect algorithms have on technological innovation. As an obvious example, consider the page rank search algorithm, a variation of which the Google Search engine is based on. Using this and similar algorithms allows researchers, scientists, technicians, and others to quickly search through vast amounts of information extremely quickly. This has a massive effect on the rate at which new research can be carried out, new discoveries made, and new innovative technologies developed. An algorithm is a sequential set of instructions to execute a particular task. They are very important, as we can break a complex problem into a smaller one to prepare simple steps to execute a big problem—that is the most important part of algorithms. A good algorithm is key for an efficient program to solve a specific problem. The study of algorithms is also important because it trains us to think very specifically about certain problems. It can help to increase our problem-solving abilities by isolating the components of a problem and defining relationships between these components. In summary, there are some important reasons for studying algorithms:

- They are essential for computer science and *intelligent* systems
- They are important in many other domains (computational biology, economics, ecology, communications, ecology, physics, and so on)
- They play a role in technology innovation
- They improve problem-solving and analytical thinking

There are mainly two important aspects to solve a given problem. Firstly, we need an efficient mechanism to store, manage, and retrieve the data, which is important to solve a problem (this comes under data structures); secondly, we require an efficient algorithm which is a finite set of instructions to solve that problem. Thus, the study of data structures and algorithms is key to solving any problem using computer programs. An efficient algorithm should have the following characteristics:

- It should be as specific as possible
- It should have each instruction properly defined
- There should not be any ambiguous instruction
- All the instructions of the algorithm should be executable in a finite amount of time and in a finite number of steps
- It should have clear input and output to solve the problem
- Each instruction of the algorithm should be important in solving the given problem

Algorithms, in their simplest form, are just a sequence of actions—a list of instructions. It may just be a linear construct of the form do x, then do y, then do z, then finish. However, to make things more useful we add clauses to the effect of do x then do y; in Python, these are if-else statements. Here, the future course of action is dependent on some conditions; say the state of a data structure. To this, we also add the operation, iteration, the while, and the for statements. Expanding our algorithmic literacy further, we add recursion. Recursion can often achieve the same results as iteration, however, they are fundamentally different. A recursive function calls itself, applying the same function to progressively smaller inputs. The input of any recursive step is the output of the previous recursive step.

Algorithm design paradigms

In general, we can discern three broad approaches to algorithm design. They are:

- Divide and conquer
- Greedy algorithms
- Dynamic programming

As the name suggests, the divide and conquer paradigm involves breaking a problem into smaller simple sub-problems, and then solving these sub-problems, and finally, combining the results to obtain a global optimal solution. This is a very common and natural problem-solving technique, and is, arguably, the most commonly used approach to algorithm design. For example, merge sort is an algorithm to sort a list of n natural numbers increasingly.

In this algorithm, we divide the list iteratively in equal parts until each sub-list contains one element, and then we combine these sub-lists to create a new list in a sorted order. We will be discussing merge sort in more detail later in this section/chapter.

Some examples of divide and conquer algorithm paradigms are as follows:

- Binary search
- Merge sort
- Quick sort
- Karatsuba algorithm for fast multiplication
- Strassen's matrix multiplication
- Closest pair of points

Greedy algorithms often involve optimization and combinatorial problems. In greedy algorithms, the objective is to obtain the best optimum solution from many possible solutions in each step, and we try to get the local optimum solution which may eventually lead us to obtain the overall optimum solution. Generally, greedy algorithms are used for optimization problems. Here are many popular standard problems where we can use greedy algorithms to obtain the optimum solution:

- Kruskal's minimum spanning tree
- Dijkstra's shortest path
- Knapsack problem
- Prim's minimal spanning tree algorithm
- Travelling salesman problem

Greedy algorithms often involve optimization and combinatorial problems; the classic example is to apply the greedy algorithm to the traveling salesperson problem, where a greedy approach always chooses the closest destination first. This shortest-path strategy involves finding the best solution to a local problem in the hope that this will lead to a global solution.

Another classic example is to apply the greedy algorithm to the traveling salesperson problem; it is an NP-hard problem. In this problem, a greedy approach always chooses the closest unvisited city first from the current city; in this way, we are not sure that we get the best solution, but we surely get an optimal solution. This shortest-path strategy involves finding the best solution to a local problem in the hope that this will lead to a global solution.

The dynamic programming approach is useful when our sub-problems overlap. This is different from divide and conquer. Rather than breaking our problem into independent sub-problems, with dynamic programming, intermediate results are cached and can be used in subsequent operations. Like divide and conquer, it uses recursion; however, dynamic programming allows us to compare results at different stages. This can have a performance advantage over the divide and conquer for some problems because it is often quicker to retrieve a previously calculated result from memory rather than having to recalculate it. Dynamic programming also uses recursion to solve the problems. For example, the matrix chain multiplication problem can be solved using dynamic programming. The matrix chain multiplication problem determines the best effective way to multiply the matrices when a sequence of matrices is given, it finds the order of multiplication that requires the minimum number of operations.

For example, let's look at three matrices—*P*, *Q*, and *R*. To compute the multiplication of these three matrices, we have many possible choices (because the matrix multiplication is associative), such as *(PQ)R = P(QR)*. So, if the sizes of these matrices are—*P* is a 20 × 30, *Q* is 30 × 45, *R* is 45 x 50, then, the number of multiplications for *(PQ)R* and *P(QR)* will be:

- *(PQ)R* = 20 x 30 x 45 + 20 x 45 x 50 = 72,000
- *P(QR)* = 20 x 30 x 50 + 30 x 45 x 50 = 97,500

It can be observed from this example that if we multiply using the first option, then we would need 72,000 multiplications, which is less when compared to the second option/ This is shown in the following code:

```
def MatrixChain(mat, i, j):
    if i == j:
        return 0
    minimum_computations = sys.maxsize
    for k in range(i, j):
        count = (MatrixChain(mat, i, k) + MatrixChain(mat, k+1, j)+
mat[i-1] * mat[k] * mat[j])
        if count < minimum_computations:
            minimum_computations= count;
        return minimum_computations;

matrix_sizes = [20, 30, 45, 50];
print("Minimum multiplications are", MatrixChain(matrix_sizes , 1,
len(matrix_sizes)-1));

#prints 72000
```

Chapter 13, *Design Techniques and Strategies*, presents a more detailed discussion on the algorithm design strategy.

Recursion and backtracking

Recursion is particularly useful for divide and conquer problems; however, it can be difficult to understand exactly what is happening, since each recursive call is itself spinning off other recursive calls. A recursive function can be in an infinite loop, therefore, it is required that each recursive function adhere to some properties. At the core of a recursive function are two types of cases:

- **Base cases**: These tell the recursion when to terminate, meaning the recursion will be stopped once the base condition is met
- **Recursive cases**: The function calls itself and we progress towards achieving the base criteria

A simple problem that naturally lends itself to a recursive solution is calculating factorials. The recursive factorial algorithm defines two cases: the base case when n is zero (the terminating condition), and the recursive case when n is greater than zero (the call of the function itself). A typical implementation is the following:

```
def factorial(n):
    # test for a base case
    if  n==0:
        return 1
        #make a calculation and a recursive call
    else:
        f= n*factorial(n-1)
    print(f)
    return(f)

factorial(4)
```

To calculate the factorial of 4, we require four recursive calls plus the initial parent call. On each recursion, a copy of the method variables is stored in memory. Once the method returns it is removed from memory. The following is a way we can visualize this process:

It may not necessarily be clear if recursion or iteration is a better solution to a particular problem; after all, they both repeat a series of operations and both are very well-suited to divide and conquer approaches and to algorithm design. Iteration churns away until the problem is done with. Recursion breaks the problem down into smaller and smaller chunks and then combines the results. Iteration is often easier for programmers, because control stays local to a loop, whereas recursion can more closely represent mathematical concepts such as factorials. Recursive calls are stored in memory, whereas iterations are not. This creates a trade-off between processor cycles and memory usage, so choosing which one to use may depend on whether the task is processor or memory intensive. The following table outlines the key differences between recursion and iteration:

Recursion	Iteration
The function calls itself.	A set of instructions are executed repeatedly in the loop.
It stops when the termination condition is met.	It stops execution when the loop condition is met.
Infinite recursive calls may give an error related to stack overflow.	An infinite iteration will run indefinitely until the hardware is powered.
Each recursive call needs memory space.	Each iteration does not require memory storage.
The code size, in general, is comparatively smaller.	The code size, in general, is comparatively smaller.
Recursion is generally slower than iteration.	It is faster as it does not require a stack.

Backtracking

Backtracking is a form of recursion that is particularly useful for types of problems such as traversing tree structures, where we are presented with a number of options for each node, from which we must choose one. Subsequently, we are presented with a different set of options, and depending on the series of choices made, either a goal state or a dead end is reached. If it is the latter, we must backtrack to a previous node and traverse a different branch. Backtracking is a divide and conquer method for exhaustive searching. Importantly, backtracking **prunes** branches that cannot give a result.

An example of backtracking is given next. Here, we have used a recursive approach to generate all the possible arrangements of a given string, s, of a given length, n:

```
def bitStr(n,s):
  if n==1: return s
  return [digit + bits for digit in bitStr(1,s) for bits in bitStr(n-1,s)]

print(bitStr(3,'abc'))
```

This generates the following output:

```
['aaa', 'aab', 'aac', 'aba', 'abb', 'abc', 'aca', 'acb', 'acc', 'baa', 'bab', 'bac', 'bba',
'bbb', 'bbc', 'bca', 'bcb', 'bcc', 'caa', 'cab', 'cac', 'cba', 'cbb', 'cbc', 'cca', 'ccb', 'ccc']
```

Notice the double list compression and the two recursive calls within this comprehension. This recursively concatenates each element of the initial sequence, returned when $n = 1$, with each element of the string generated in the previous recursive call. In this sense, it is *backtracking* to uncover previously ungenerated combinations. The final string that is returned is all n letter combinations of the initial string.

Divide and conquer – long multiplication

For recursion to be more than just a clever trick, we need to understand how to compare it to other approaches, such as iteration, and to understand when its use will lead to a faster algorithm. An iterative algorithm that we are all familiar with is the procedure we learned in primary math classes, and is used to multiply two large numbers. That is long multiplication. If you remember, long multiplication involved iterative multiplying and carry operations followed by a shifting and addition operation.

Our aim here is to examine ways to measure how efficient this procedure is and attempt to answer the question—is this the most efficient procedure we can use for multiplying two large numbers together?

In the following diagram, we can see that multiplying two four-digit numbers together requires 16 multiplication operations, and we can generalize and say that an n digit number requires, approximately, n^2 multiplication operations:

$$
\begin{array}{ccccc}
 & & 1 & 2 & 3 & 4 \\
 & & 3 & 4 & 5 & 6 \quad \times \\
\hline
 & & 7 & 4 & 0 & 4 \\
 & 6 & 1 & 7 & 0 & 0 \\
4 & 9 & 3 & 6 & 0 & 0 \\
3 & 7 & 0 & 2 & 0 & 0 & 0 \\
4 & 2 & 6 & 4 & 7 & 0 & 4 \\
\end{array}
\quad \approx n^2 \, operations
$$

This method of analyzing algorithms, in terms of the number of computational primitives such as multiplication and addition, is important because it gives us a way to understand the relationship between the time it takes to complete a certain computation and the size of the input to that computation. In particular, we want to know what happens when the input, the number of digits, n, is very large. This topic, called **asymptotic analysis**, or **time complexity**, is essential to our study of algorithms and we will revisit it often during this chapter and the rest of this book.

The recursive approach

It turns out that in the case of long multiplication the answer is yes, there are in fact several algorithms for multiplying large numbers that require less operations. One of the most well-known alternatives to long multiplication is the **Karatsuba algorithm**, first published in 1962. This takes a fundamentally different approach: rather than iteratively multiplying single-digit numbers, it recursively carries out multiplication operations on progressively smaller inputs. Recursive programs call themselves on smaller subsets of the input. The first step in building a recursive algorithm is to decompose a large number into several smaller numbers. The most natural way to do this is to simply split the number into two halves, the first half of most-significant digits, and a second half of least-significant digits. For example, our four-digit number, 2345, becomes a pair of two-digit numbers, 23 and 45. We can write a more general decomposition of any two n digit numbers, x, and y using the following, where m is any positive integer less than n:

$$
x = 10^m a + b
$$

$$
y = 10^m c + d
$$

So now we can rewrite our multiplication problem x, y as follows:

$$
(10^m a + b)(10^m c + d)
$$

When we expand, we get the following:

$$10^{2m} ac + 10^m (ad + bc) + bd$$

More conveniently, we can write it like this (equation 3.1):

$$x \times y = 10^{2m} z_2 + 10^m z_1 + z_0 \qquad \ldots (3.1)$$

Where:

$$z_2 = ac; z_1 = ad + bc; z_0 = bd$$

It should be pointed out that this suggests a recursive approach to multiplying two numbers since this procedure does itself involve multiplication. Specifically, the products ac, ad, bc, and bd all involve numbers smaller than the input number and so it is conceivable that we could apply the same operation as a partial solution to the overall problem. This algorithm, so far, consists of four recursive multiplication steps and it is not immediately clear if it will be faster than the classic long multiplication approach.

What we have discussed so far in regards to the recursive approach to multiplication, has been well-known to mathematicians since the late nineteenth century. The Karatsuba algorithm improves on this by making the following observation. We really only need to know three quantities: $z_2 = ac$, $z_1 = ad + bc$, and $z_0 = bd$ to solve equation 3.1. We need to know the values of a, b, c, and d only in so far as they contribute to the overall sum and products involved in calculating the quantities z_2, z_1, and z_0. This suggests the possibility that perhaps we can reduce the number of recursive steps. It turns out that this is indeed the situation.

Since the products ac and bd are already in their simplest form, it seems unlikely that we can eliminate these calculations. We can, however, make the following observation:

$$(a + b)(c + d) = ac + bd + ad + bc$$

When we subtract the quantities ac and bd, which we have calculated in the previous recursive step, we get the quantity we need, namely $(ad + bc)$:

$$ac + bd + ad + bc - ac - bd = ad + bc$$

This shows that we can indeed compute the sum of *ad* + *bc* without separately computing each of the individual quantities. In summary, we can improve on equation 3.1 by reducing four recursive steps to three. These three steps are as follows:

1. Recursively calculate *ac*
2. Recursively calculate *bd*
3. Recursively calculate $(a + b)(c + d)$ and subtract *ac* and *bd*

The following example shows a Python implementation of the Karatsuba algorithm. In the following code, initially, we see if any one of the given numbers is less than 10, then there is no need to run recursive functions. Next, we identify the number of digits in the larger value, and add one if the number of digits is odd. Finally, we recursively call the function three times to calculate *ac*, *bd*, and $(a + d)(c + d)$. The following code prints the multiplication of any two digits; for example, it prints 4264704 for the multiplication of 1234 and 3456. The implementation of the Karatsuba algorithm is:

```python
from math import log10
def karatsuba(x,y):

    #The base case for recursion
    if x<10 or y<10:
        return x*y

    #sets n, the number of digits in the highest input number
    n=max(int(log10(x)+1), int(log10(y)+1))

    #rounds up n/2
    n_2 = int(math.ceil(n/2.0))
    #adds 1 if n is uneven
    n = n if n%2 == 0  else n+1
    #splits the input numbers
    a, b = divmod(x, 10**n_2)
    c, d = divmod(y,10**n_2)
    #applies the three recursive steps
    ac = karatsuba(a,c)
    bd = karatsuba(b,d)
    ad_bc = karatsuba((a+b),(c+d))-ac-bd

    #performs the multiplication
    return (((10**n)*ac)+bd+((10**n_2)*(ad_bc)))


t= karatsuba(1234,3456)
print(t)

# outputs - 4264704
```

Runtime analysis

The performance of an algorithm is generally measured by the size of its input data (**n**) and the time and the memory space used by the algorithm. **Time** required is measured by the key operations to be performed by the algorithm (such as comparison operations), whereas the space requirements of an algorithm is measured by the storage needed to store the variables, constants, and instructions during the execution of the program. The space requirements of an algorithm may also change dynamically during execution as it depends on variable size, which is to be decided at runtime, such as dynamic memory allocation, memory stacks, and so on.

The running time required by an algorithm depends on the input size; as the input size (**n**) increases, the runtime also increases. For example, a sorting algorithm will have more running time to sort the list of input size 5,000 as compared to the other list of input size 50. Therefore, it is clear that to compute the time complexity, the input size is important. Further, for a specific input, the running time depends on the key operations to be executed in the algorithm. For example, the key operation for a sorting algorithm is a **comparison operation** that will take most of the time as compared to assignment or any other operation. The more is the number of key operations to be executed, the longer it will take to run the algorithm.

It should be noted that an important aspect to algorithm design is gauging the efficiency both in terms of space (memory) and time (number of operations). It should be mentioned that an identical metric is used to measure an algorithm's memory performance. There are a number of ways we could, conceivably, measure runtime and probably the most obvious way is to simply measure the total time taken by the algorithm. The major problem with this approach is that the time taken for an algorithm to run is very much dependent on the hardware it is run on. A platform-independent way to gauge an algorithm's runtime is to count the number of operations involved. However, this is also problematic as there is no definitive way to quantify an operation. This is dependent on the programming language, the coding style, and how we decide to count operations. We can use this idea, though, of counting operations, if we combine it with the expectation that as the size of the input increases the runtime will increase in a specific way. That is, there is a mathematical relationship between *n*, the size of the input, and the time it takes for the algorithm to run. There are essentially three things that characterize an algorithm's runtime performance; these can be described as follows:

- Worst-case complexity is the upper-bound complexity; it is the maximum running time required for an algorithm to execute. In this case, the key operations would be executed the maximum number of times.

- Best-case complexity is the lower-bound complexity; it is the minimum running time required for an algorithm to execute. In this case, the key operations would be executed the minimum number of times.
- Average-case complexity is the average running time required for an algorithm to execute.

Worst-case analysis is useful because it gives us a tight upper bound that our algorithm is guaranteed not to exceed. Ignoring small constant factors, and lower-order terms, is really just about ignoring the things that, at large values of the input size, n, do not contribute, in a large degree, to the overall run time. Not only does this make our work mathematically easier, but it also allows us to focus on the things that are having the most impact on performance.

We saw with the Karatsuba algorithm that the number of multiplication operations increased to the square of the size, n, of the input. If we have a four-digit number the number of multiplication operations is 16; an eight-digit number requires 64 operations. Typically, though, we are not really interested in the behavior of an algorithm at small values of n, so we most often ignore factors that increase at slower rates, say linearly with n. This is because at high values of n, the operations that increase the fastest as we increase n will dominate.

We will explain this in more detail with an example: the merge sort algorithm. Sorting is the subject of `Chapter 10`, *Sorting*, however, as a precursor and as a useful way to learn about runtime performance, we will introduce merge sort here.

The merge sort algorithm is a classic algorithm developed over 60 years ago. It is still used widely in many of the most popular sorting libraries. It is relatively simple and efficient. It is a recursive algorithm that uses a divide and conquer approach. This involves breaking the problem into smaller sub-problems, recursively solving them, and then somehow combining the results. Merge sort is one of the most obvious demonstrations of the divide and conquer paradigm.

The merge sort algorithm consists of three simple steps:

1. Recursively sort the left half of the input array
2. Recursively sort the right half of the input array
3. Merge two sorted sub-arrays into one

A typical problem is sorting a list of numbers into a numerical order. Merge sort works by splitting the input into two halves and working on each half in parallel. We can illustrate this process schematically with the following diagram:

Here is the Python code for the merge sort algorithm:

```python
def mergeSort(A):
#base case if the input array is one or zero just return.
if len(A) > 1:
    # splitting input array
    print('splitting ', A )
    mid=len(A)//2
    left=A[:mid]
    right=A[mid:]
    #recursive calls to mergeSort for left and right subarrays
    mergeSort(left)
    mergeSort(right)
    #initalizes pointers for left(i) right(j) and output array (k)
    #3 initalization operations
    i = j = k = 0
    #Traverse and merges the sorted arrays
    while i < len(left) and j < len(right):
    #if left < right comparison operation
        if left[i] < right[j]:
        #if left < right Assignment operation
            A[k] = left[i]
            i=i+1
        else:
            #if right <= left assignment
            A[k]=right[j]
            j=j+1
            k=k+1
    while i< len(left):
    #Assignment operation
        A[k] = left[i]
        i=i+1
        k=k+1

    while j< len(right):
    # Assignment operation
        A[k] = right[j]
        j=j+1
        k=k+1

print('merging',A)
return(A)
```

We run this program for the following results:

```
In [2]: mergeSort([356,97,846,215])
splitting  [356, 97, 846, 215]
splitting  [356, 97]
merging    [356]
merging    [97]
merging    [97, 356]
splitting  [846, 215]
merging    [846]
merging    [215]
merging    [215, 846]
merging    [97, 215, 356, 846]
Out[2]: [97, 215, 356, 846]
```

The problem that we are interested in is how we determine the runtime performance, that is, what is the rate of growth in the time it takes for the algorithm to complete relative to the size of n? To understand this a bit better, we can map each recursive call onto a tree structure. Each node in the tree is a recursive call working on progressively smaller sub-problems:

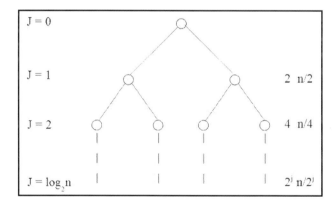

Each invocation of merge sort subsequently creates two recursive calls, so we can represent this with a binary tree. Each of the child nodes receives a subset of the input. Ultimately, we want to know the total time it takes for the algorithm to complete relative to the size of n. To begin with, we can calculate the amount of work and the number of operations at each level of the tree.

Focusing on the runtime analysis, at level one, the problem is split into two $n/2$ sub-problems; at level two, there are four $n/4$ subproblems, and so on. The question is, when does the recursion bottom out, that is, when does it reach its base case? This is simply when the array is either zero or one.

The number of recursive levels is exactly the number of times you need to divide n by two until you get a number that is at most one. This is precisely the definition of log2. Since we are counting the initial recursive call as level zero, the total number of levels is $\log_2 n + 1$.

Let's just pause to refine our definitions. So far, we have been describing the number of elements in our input by the letter n. This refers to the number of elements in the first level of the recursion, that is, the length of the initial input. We are going to need to differentiate between the size of the input at subsequent recursive levels. For this, we will use the letter m or specifically m_j for the length of the input at recursive level j.

Also, there are a few details we have overlooked, and I am sure you are beginning to wonder about. For example, what happens when $m/2$ is not an integer, or when we have duplicates in our input array? It turns out that this does not have an important impact on our analysis here; we will revisit some of the finer details of the merge sort algorithm in `Chapter 12`, *Design Techniques and Strategies*.

The advantage of using a recursion tree to analyze algorithms is that we can calculate the work done at each level of the recursion. How we define this work is simply by the total number of operations and this, of course, is related to the size of the input. It is important to measure and compare the performance of algorithms in a platform-independent way. The actual runtime will, of course, be dependent on the hardware on which it is run. Counting the number of operations is important because it gives us a metric that is directly related to an algorithm's performance, independent of the platform.

In general, since each invocation of merge sort is making two recursive calls, the number of calls is doubling at each level. At the same time, each of these calls is working on an input that is half of its parents. We can formalize this and say that for level j, where j is an integer $0, 1, 2 \ldots \log_2 n$, there are two sub-problems each of size $n/2^j$.

To calculate the total number of operations, we need to know the number of operations encompassed by a single merge of two sub-arrays. Let's count the number of operations in the previous Python code. What we are interested in is all the code after the two recursive calls have been made. Firstly, we have the three assignment operations. This is followed by three `while` loops. In the first loop, we have an if-else statement and within each of our two operations, a comparison followed by an assignment. Since there are only one of these sets of operations within the if-else statements, we can count this block of code as two operations carried out m times. This is followed by two `while` loops with an assignment operation each. This makes a total of $4m + 3$ operations for each recursion of merge sort.

Since m must be at least one, the upper bound for the number of operations is $7m$. It has to be said that this has no pretence at being an exact number. We could, of course, decide to count operations in a different way. We have not counted the increment operations or any of the housekeeping operations; however, this is not so important as we are more concerned with the rate of growth of the runtime with respect to n at high values of n.

This may seem a little daunting since each call of a recursive call itself spins off more recursive calls, and seemingly explodes exponentially. The key fact that makes this manageable is that as the number of recursive calls doubles, the size of each subproblem halves. These two opposing forces cancel out nicely, as we can demonstrate.

To calculate the maximum number of operations at each level of the recursion tree we simply multiply the number of subproblems by the number of operations in each subproblem as follows:

$$2^j \times 7(n/2^j) = 7n$$

Importantly, this shows that, because the 2^j cancels out the number of operations at each level is independent of the level. This gives us an upper bound to the number of operations carried out on each level, in this example, $7n$. It should be pointed out that this includes the number of operations performed by each recursive call on that level, not the recursive calls made on subsequent levels. This shows that the work is done, as the number of recursive calls doubles with each level, and is exactly counterbalanced by the fact that the input size for each sub-problem is halved.

To find the total number of operations for a complete merge sort, we simply multiply the number of operations on each level by the number of levels. This gives us the following:

$$7n(log_2 n + 1)$$

When we expand this out, we get the following:

$$7n log_2 n + 7$$

The key point to take from this is that there is a logarithmic component to the relationship between the size of the input and the total running time. If you remember from school mathematics, the distinguishing characteristic of the logarithm function is that it flattens off very quickly. As an input variable, x increases in size; the output variable y increases by smaller and smaller amounts.

For example, compare the log function to a linear function:

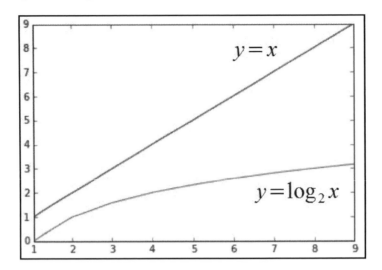

In the previous example, multiplying the $n\log_2 n$ component and comparing it to n^2:

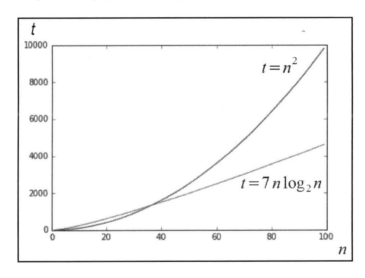

Notice how for very low values of n, the time to complete, t, is actually lower for an algorithm that runs in n2 time. However, for values above about 40, the log function begins to dominate, flattening the output until, at the comparatively moderate size $n = 100$, the performance is more than twice than that of an algorithm running in n^2 time. Notice also that the disappearance of the constant factor, $+7$, is irrelevant at high values of n.

The code used to generate these graphs is as follows:

```
import matplotlib.pyplotasplt
import math
x = list(range(1,100))
l=[]; l2=[]; a=1
plt.plot(x, [y*y for y in x])
plt.plot(x, [(7*y)*math.log(y,2) for y in x])
plt.show()
```

You will need to install the `matplotlib` library, if it is not installed already, for this to work. Details can be found at the following address; I encourage you to experiment with this list comprehension expression used to generate the plots. For example, we could add the following `plot` statement:

```
plt.plot(x, [(6*y)* math.log(y, 2) for y in x])
```

This gives the following output:

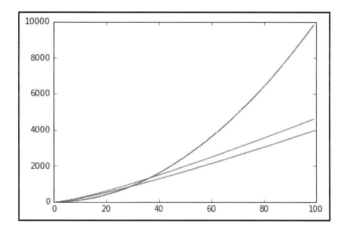

The preceding graph shows the difference between counting six operations or seven operations. We can see how the two cases diverge, and this is important when we are talking about the specifics of an application. However, what we are more interested in here is a way to characterize growth rates. We are not so much concerned with the absolute values, but how these values change as we increase n. In this way, we can see that the two lower curves have similar growth rates when compared to the top (x^2) curve. We say that these two lower curves have the same **complexity class**. This is a way to understand and describe different runtime behaviors. We will formalize this performance metric in the next section.

Asymptotic analysis

Asymptotic analysis of an algorithm refers to the computation of the running time of the algorithm. To determine which algorithm is better, given two algorithms, a simple approach can be to run both the programs, and the algorithm that takes the least time to execute for a given input is better than the other. However, it is possible that for a specific input, one algorithm performs better than other, whereas for any other input value that the algorithm may perform worse.

In asymptotic analysis, we compare two algorithms with respect to input size rather than the actual runtime, and we measure how the time taken increases with the increase in input size. This is depicted with the following code:

```python
# Linear search program to search an element, return the index position of
the #array
def searching(search_arr, x):
    for i in range(len(search_arr)):
        if search_arr [i] == x:
            return i
    return -1

search_ar= [3, 4, 1, 6, 14]
x=4

searching(search_ar, x)
print("Index position for the element x is :",searching(search_ar, x))

#outputs index position of the element x that is - 1
```

Assuming that the size of the array is n, and *T(n)* is the total number of key operations required to perform a linear search, the key operation in this example is the comparison. Let's consider the linear search as an example to understand the worst case, average-case, and best-case complexity:

- **Worst-case analysis**: We consider the upper-bound running time, that is, the maximum time to be taken by the algorithm. In the linear search, the worst case happens when the element to be searched is found in the last comparison or not found in the list. In this case, there will be a maximum number of comparisons and that will be the total number of elements in the array. Therefore, the worst-case time complexity is $\Theta(n)$.

- **Average-case analysis**: In this analysis, we consider all the possible cases where the element can be found in the list, and then, we compute the average running time complexity. For example, in the linear search, the number of comparisons at all the positions would be *1* if the element to be searched was found at *0th* index, and similarly, the number of comparisons would be 2, 3, and so forth, up to *n* respectively for elements found at *1, 2, 3, ... (n-1)* index positions. Thus the average time complexity can defined as `average-case complexity=` `(1+2+3...n)/n = n(n+1)/2.`

- **Best-case analysis**: Best-case running time complexity is the minimum time needed for an algorithm to run; it is the lower-bound running time. In a linear search, the best case would be if the element to be searched is found in the first comparison. In this example, it is clear that the best-case time complexity is not dependent upon how long the list is. So, the best-case time complexity would be *Θ(1)*.

Generally, we use worst-case analysis to analyze an algorithm as it provides us with the upper bound on the running time, whereas best-case anaylsis is the least important as it provides us with the lower bound—that is, a minimum time required for an algorithm. Furthermore, the computation of average-case analysis is very difficult.

To calculate each of these, we need to know the upper and lower bounds. We have looked at a way to represent an algorithm's runtime using mathematical expressions, essentially adding and multiplying operations. To use asymptotic analysis, we simply create two expressions, one each for the best and worst cases.

Big O notation

The letter O in big *O* notation stands for order, in recognition that rates of growth are defined as the order of a function. It measures the worst-case running time complexity, that is, the maximum time to be taken by the algorithm. We say that one function $T(n)$ is a big O of another function, $F(n)$, and we define this as follows:

$$T(n) = O(F(n) \; iff \; there \; exists \; constants, \; n_0 \; and \; c \; such \; that : \; T(n) <= c(F(n)) \; for \; all \; n >= n_0)$$

The function, $g(n)$, of the input size, n, is based on the observation that for all sufficiently large values of n, $g(n)$ is bounded above by a constant multiple of $f(n)$. The objective is to find the smallest rate of growth that is less than or equal to $f(n)$. We only care what happens at higher values of n. The variable $n0$ represents the threshold below which the rate of growth is not important. The function $T(n)$ represents the **tight upper bound** F(n). In the following plot, we can see that $T(n) = n^2 + 500 = O(n^2)$, with $C = 2$ and n_0 being approximately 23:

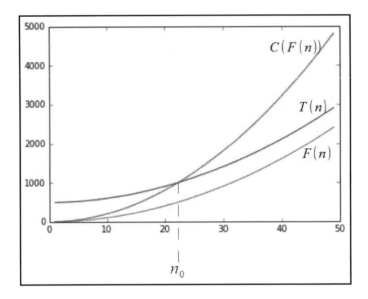

You will also see the notation $f(n) = O(g(n))$. This describes the fact that $O(g(n))$ is really a set of functions that includes all functions with the same or smaller rates of growth than $f(n)$. For example, $O(n^2)$ also includes the functions $O(n)$, $O(nlogn)$, and so on. Let's consider another example.

The big O time complexity for the function `f(x)= 19n log₂n +56` is $O(nlogn)$.

In the following table, we list the most common growth rates in order from lowest to highest. We sometimes call these growth rates the **time complexity** of a function, or the complexity class of a function:

Complexity class	Name	Example operations
$O(1)$	Constant	append, get item, set item.
$O(logn)$	Logarithmic	Finding an element in a sorted array.
$O(n)$	Linear	copy, insert, delete, iteration.

$nLogn$	Linear-logarithmic	Sort a list, merge-sort.
n^2	Quadratic	Find the shortest path between two nodes in a graph. Nested loops.
n^3	Cubic	Matrix multiplication.
2^n	Exponential	**Towers of Hanoi** problem, backtracking.

Composing complexity classes

Normally, we need to find the total running time of a number of basic operations. It turns out that we can combine the complexity classes of simple operations to find the complexity class of more complex, combined operations. The goal is to analyze the combined statements in a function or method to understand the total time complexity of executing several operations. The simplest way to combine two complexity classes is to add them. This occurs when we have two sequential operations. For example, consider the two operations of inserting an element into a list and then sorting that list. We can see that inserting an item occurs in $O(n)$ time and sorting is in $O(nlogn)$ time. We can write the total time complexity as $O(n + nlogn)$, that is, we bring the two functions inside the $O(...)$. We are only interested in the highest-order term, so this leaves us with just $O(nlogn)$.

If we repeat an operation, for example, in a `while` loop, then we multiply the complexity class by the number of times the operation is carried out. If an operation with time complexity $O(f(n))$ is repeated $O(n)$ times then we multiply the two complexities:

$$O(f(n) * O(n)) = O(nf(n))$$

For example, suppose the function `f(...)` has a time complexity of $O(n^2)$ and it is executed n times in a `while` loop, as follows:

```
for i in range(n):
        f(...)
```

The time complexity of this loop then becomes $O(n^2) * O(n) = O(n * n^2) = O(n^3)$. Here we are simply multiplying the time complexity of the operation by the number of times this operation executes. The running time of a loop is at most the running time of the statements inside the loop multiplied by the number of iterations. A single nested loop, that is, one loop nested inside another loop, will run in $n2$ time assuming both loops run n times, as demonstrated in the following example:

```
for i in range(0,n):
    for j in range(0,n)
            #statements
```

Each statement is a constant, c, executed *nn* times, so we can express the running time as the following:

$$cnn = cn2 = O(n2).$$

For consecutive statements within nested loops, we add the time complexities of each statement and multiply by the number of times the statement executed, for example:

```
n=500    #c0
#executes n times
for i in range(0,n):
    print(i)      #c1
    #executes n times
for i in range(0,n):
#executes n times
    for j in range(0,n):
        print(j)   #c2
```

This can be written as $c_0 + c_1 n + cn^2 = O(n^2)$.

We can define (base 2) logarithmic complexity, reducing the size of the problem by ½, in constant time. For example, consider the following snippet:

```
i=1
while i<=n:
    i=i*2
    print(i)
```

Notice that i is doubling on each iteration; if we run this with $n = 10$ we see that it prints out four numbers: 2, 4, 8, and 16. If we double n we see it prints out five numbers. With each subsequent doubling of n, the number of iterations is only increased by one. If we assume k iterations, we can write this as follows:

$$log_2(2^k) = log_2 n$$

$$k log_2 2 = log_2 n$$

$$k = log(n)$$

From this, we can conclude that the total time = $O(log(n))$.

Although big O is the most used notation involved in asymptotic analysis, there are two other related notations that should be briefly mentioned. They are Omega notation and Theta notation.

Omega notation (Ω)

Omega notation describes tight lower bound on algorithms, similar to big O notation which describes a tight upper bound. Omega notation computes the best-case running time complexity of the algorithm. It provides the highest rate of growth $T(n)$ which is less than or equal to the given algorithm. It can be computed as follows:

$$T(n) = \Omega(F(n) \; iff \; there \; exists \; constants, \; n_0 \; and \; c \; such \; that : \; 0 <= c(F(n)) <= T(n) \; for \; all \; n >= n_0)$$

Theta notation (Θ)

It is often the case where both the upper and lower bounds of a given function are the same and the purpose of Theta notation is to determine if this is the case. The definition is as follows:

$$T(n) = \theta(F(n) \; iff \; there \; exists \; constants, \; n_0 \; and \; c_1 \; and \; c_2 \; such \; that : \; 0 <= c_1(F(n)) <= T(n) <= c2(F(n)) \; for \; all \; n >= n_0)$$

Although Omega and Theta notations are required to completely describe growth rates, the most practically useful is big O notation and this is the one you will see most often.

Amortized analysis

Often we are not so interested in the time complexity of individual operations; we are more interested in the average running time of sequences of operations. This is called amortized analysis. It is different from average-case analysis, which we will discuss shortly, in that we make no assumptions regarding the data distribution of input values. It does, however, take into account the state change of data structures. For example, if a list is sorted, any subsequent find operations should be quicker. The amortized analysis considers the state change of data structures because it analyzes sequences of operations, rather than simply aggregating single operations.

Amortized analysis describes an upper bound on the runtime of the algorithm; it imposes an additional cost on each operation in the algorithm. The additional considered cost of a sequence may be cheaper as compared to the initial expensive operation.

When we have a small number of expensive operations, such as sorting, and lots of cheaper operations such as lookups, standard worst-case analysis can lead to overly pessimistic results, since it assumes that each lookup must compare each element in the list until a match is found. We should take into account that once we sort the list we can make subsequent find operations cheaper.

So far in our runtime analysis, we have assumed that the input data was completely random and have only looked at the effect the size of the input has on the runtime. There are two other common approaches to algorithm analysis; they are:

- Average-case analysis
- Benchmarking

Average-case analysis will find the average running time which is based on some assumptions regarding the relative frequencies of various input values. Using real-world data, or data that replicates the distribution of real-world data, is many times on a particular data distribution and the average running time is calculated.

Benchmarking is simply having an agreed set of typical inputs that are used to measure performance. Both benchmarking and average-time analysis rely on having some domain knowledge. We need to know what the typical or expected datasets are. Ultimately, we will try to find ways to improve performance by fine-tuning to a very specific application setting.

Let's look at a straightforward way to benchmark an algorithm's runtime performance. This can be done by simply timing how long the algorithm takes to complete given various input sizes. As we mentioned earlier, this way of measuring runtime performance is dependent on the hardware that it is run on. Obviously, faster processors will give better results, however, the relative growth rates as we increase the input size will retain characteristics of the algorithm itself rather than the hardware it is run on. The absolute time values will differ between hardware (and software) platforms; however, their relative growth will still be bound by the time complexity of the algorithm.

Let's take a simple example of a nested loop. It should be fairly obvious that the time complexity of this algorithm is $O(n^2)$ since for each n iterations in the outer loop there are also n iterations in the interloop. For example, our simple nested for loop consists of a simple statement executed on the inner loop:

```
def nest(n):
for i in range(n):
    for j in range(n):
        i+j
```

The following code is a simple test function that runs the `nest` function with increasing values of n. With each iteration, we calculate the time this function takes to complete using the `timeit.timeit` function. The `timeit` function, in this example, takes three arguments, a string representation of the function to be timed, a `setup` function that imports the `nest` function, and an `int` parameter that indicates the number of times to execute the main statement.

Since we are interested in the time the `nest` function takes to complete relative to the input size, n, it is sufficient, for our purposes, to call the `nest` function once on each iteration. The following function returns a list of the calculated runtimes for each value of n:

```
import timeit
def test2(n):
    ls=[]
    for n in range(n):
        t=timeit.timeit("nest(" + str(n) + ")", setup="from _main_ import
nest", number=1)
        ls.append(t)
    return ls
```

In the following code, we run the `test2` function and graph the results, together with the appropriately scaled n^2 function, for comparison, represented by the dashed line:

```
import matplotlib.pyplot as plt
n=1000
plt.plot(test2(n))
plt.plot([x*x/10000000 for x in range(n)])
```

This gives the following results:

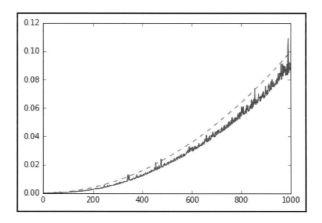

As we can see, this gives us pretty much what we expect. It should be remembered that this represents both the performance of the algorithm itself as well as the behavior of underlying software and hardware platforms, as indicated by both the variability in the measured runtime and the relative magnitude of the runtime. Obviously, a faster processor will result in faster runtimes, and also performance will be affected by other running processes, memory constraints, clock speed, and so on.

Summary

In this chapter, we have looked at a general overview of algorithm design. Importantly, we studied a platform-independent way to measure an algorithm's performance. We looked at some different approaches to algorithmic problems. We looked at a way to recursively multiply large numbers and also a recursive approach for merge sort. We learned how to use backtracking for exhaustive search and generating strings. We also introduced the idea of benchmarking and a simple platform-dependent way to measure runtime.

In the following chapters, we will revisit many of these ideas with reference to specific data structures. In the next chapter, we will discuss linked lists and other pointer structures.

4
Lists and Pointer Structures

We have discussed **lists** in Python, and these are convenient and powerful. Normally, most of the time, we use Python's built-in list implementation to store any data. However, in this chapter, we will be understanding how lists work and will be studying list internals.

Python's list implementation is quite powerful and can encompass several different use cases. The concept of a node is very important in lists. We shall discuss them in this chapter and will be referring to them throughout the book. Thus, we suggest readers study the content of this chapter carefully.

The focus of this chapter will be the following:

- Understanding pointers in Python
- Understanding the concept and implementation of nodes
- Implementing singly, doubly, and circularly linked lists

Technical requirements

Executing the programs based on the concepts discussed in this chapter will help you to better understand them. We have provided the source codes of all the programs and concepts in the chapter. We also provide the complete source code files on GitHub at the following link: `https://github.com/PacktPublishing/Hands-On-Data-Structures-and-Algorithms-with-Python-Second-Edition/tree/master/Chapter04`.

We assume that you have already installed Python on your system.

Beginning with an example

Let's remind you about the concept of pointers as we will be dealing with them in this chapter. To begin with, imagine that you have a house that you want to sell. Lacking time, you contact an agent to find interested buyers. So, you pick up your house and take it over to the agent, who will, in turn, carry the house to anybody who may want to buy it. Ludicrous, you say? Now imagine that you have a few Python functions that work with images. So, you pass high-resolution image data between your functions.

Of course, you don't carry your house around. What you do is write the address of the house down on a piece of scrap paper and hand it over to the agent. The house remains where it is, but the note containing the directions to the house is passed around. You might even write it down on several pieces of paper. Each one is small enough to fit in your wallet, but they all point to the same house.

As it turns out, things are not very different in Python land. Those large image files remain in one single place in memory.

What you do is create variables that hold the locations of those images in memory. These variables are small and can easily be passed around between different functions.

That is the big benefit of pointers—they allow you to point to a potentially large segment of memory with just a simple memory address.

Support for pointers exists in your computer's hardware, where it is known as indirect addressing.

In Python, you don't manipulate pointers directly, unlike in some other languages, such as C or Pascal. This has led some people to think that pointers aren't used in Python. Nothing could be further from the truth. Consider this assignment in the Python interactive shell:

```
>>> s = set()
```

We would normally say that s is a variable of the **set** type. That is, s is a set. However, this is not strictly true; the variable s is rather a reference (a *safe* pointer) to a set. The set constructor creates a set somewhere in memory and returns the memory location where that set starts. This is what gets stored in s. Python hides this complexity from us. We can safely assume that s is a set and that everything works fine.

Arrays

An array is a sequential list of data. Being sequential means that each element is stored right after the previous one in memory. If your array is really big and you are low on memory, it could be impossible to find large enough storage to fit your entire array. This will lead to problems.

Of course, the flip side of the coin is that arrays are very fast. Since each element follows on from the previous one in memory, there is no need to jump around between different memory locations. This can be a very important point to take into consideration when choosing between a list and an array in your own real-world applications.

We have already discussed arrays in `Chapter 2`, *Python Data Types and Structures*. We looked at the array data type and discussed various operations that could be performed on it.

Pointer structures

Contrary to arrays, pointer structures are lists of items that can be spread out in memory. This is because each item contains one or more links to other items in the structure. The types of these links are dependent on the type of structures we have. If we are dealing with linked lists, then we will have links to the next (and possibly previous) items in the structure. In the case of a tree, we have parent-child links as well as sibling links.

There are several benefits to pointer structures. First of all, they don't require sequential storage space. Secondly, they can start small and grow arbitrarily as you add more nodes to the structure. However, this flexibility in pointers comes at a cost. We need additional space to store the address. For example, if you have a list of integers, each node is going to take up space by storing an integer, as well as an additional integer for storing the pointer to the next node.

Nodes

At the heart of lists (and several other data structures) is the concept of a node. Before we go any further, let us consider this idea for a while.

To begin with, let us consider an example. We shall create a few strings:

```
>>> a = "eggs"
>>> b = "ham"
>>> c = "spam"
```

Now you have three variables, each with a unique name, a type, and a value. At the moment, there is no way to show the relationships between these variables. Nodes allow us to show how these variables relate to each other. A node is a container of data, together with one or more links to other nodes. A link is a pointer.

A simple type of node is one that has only a link to the next node. As we know about the pointers, the string is not actually stored in the node, but rather there is a pointer to the actual string. Consider the example in the following diagram, in which there are two nodes. The first node has a pointer to the string (**eggs**) stored in the memory and another pointer that stores the address of another node:

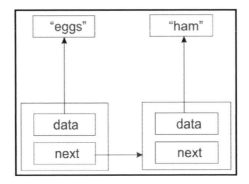

Thus, the storage requirement for this simple node is two memory addresses. The data attributes of the nodes are pointers to the strings **eggs** and **ham**.

Finding endpoints

We have created three nodes—one containing **eggs**, one **ham**, and another **spam**. The **eggs** node points to the **ham** node, which in turn points to the **spam** node. But what does the **spam** node point to? Since this is the last element in the list, we need to make sure its next member has a value that makes this clear.

If we make the last element point to nothing, then we make this fact clear. In Python, we will use the special value **None** to denote nothing. Consider the following diagram. Node **B** is the last element in the list, and thus it is pointing to **None**:

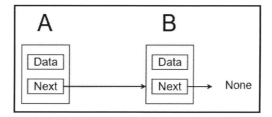

The last node has its next point pointing to **None**. As such, it is the last node in the chain of nodes.

Node class

Here is a simple node implementation of what we have discussed so far:

```
class Node:

    def __init__ (self, data=None):
        self.data = data
        self.next = None
```

The **Next** pointer is initialized to None, meaning that unless you change the value of **Next**, the node is going to be an endpoint. This is a good idea, so that we do not forget to terminate the list properly.

You can add other things to the node class as you see fit. Just make sure that you keep in mind the distinction between nodes and data. If your node is going to contain customer data, then create a Customer class and put all the data there.

One thing you may want to do is implement the _str_ method so that it calls the _str_ method of the contained object is called when the node object is passed to print:

```
def _str_ (self):
    return str(data)
```

Other node types

As we have already discussed a node that has a pointer to the next node to link the data items, however, it is probably the simplest type of node. Further, depending on our requirements, we can create a number of other types of nodes.

Sometimes we want to go from node **A** to node **B**, but at the same time we may need to go from node **B** to node **A**. In that case, we add a **Previous** pointer in addition to the **Next** pointer:

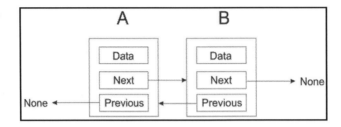

As you can see from the preceding diagram, we have created the **Previous** pointer in addition to the data and the **Next** pointer. It is also important to note that the **Next** pointer to **B** is **None**, and the **Previous** pointer in node **A** is also **None**—that is to indicate that we have reached the boundary of our list at both endpoints. The first node **A**'s previous pointer points to **None** since it has no predecessor, just as the last item **B**'s **Next** pointer points to **None** because it has no successor node.

Introducing lists

The list is an important and popular data structure. There are three kinds of the list—singly linked list, doubly linked list, and circular linked list. We will discuss these data structures in more detail in this chapter. We will also be discussing various important operations such as the `append` operation, `delete` operation, and the `traversing` and `searching` operations that can be performed on these lists in subsequent subsections.

Singly linked lists

A singly linked list is a list with only one pointer between two successive nodes. It can only be traversed in a single direction; that is, you can go from the first node in the list to the last node, but you cannot move from the last node to the first node.

We can actually use the node class that we created earlier to implement a very simple singly linked list. For example, we create three nodes n1, n2, and n3 that stores three strings:

```
>>> n1 = Node('eggs')
>>> n2 = Node('ham')
>>> n3 = Node('spam')
```

Next, we link the nodes together so that they form a chain:

```
>>> n1.next = n2
>>> n2.next = n3
```

To traverse the list, you could do something like the following. We start by setting the `current` variable to the first item in the list, and then we traverse the whole list through a loop as shown in the following code:

```
current = n1
while current:
    print(current.data)
    current = current.next
```

In the loop, we print out the current element after which we set `current` to point to the next element in the list. We keep doing this until we have reached the end of the list.

There are, however, several problems with this simplistic list implementation:

- It requires too much manual work by the programmer
- It is too error prone (this is a consequence of the first point)
- Too much of the inner workings of the list is exposed to the programmer

We are going to address all these issues in the following sections.

Singly linked list class

A list is a separate concept from a node. We start by creating a very simple class to hold our list. We start with a constructor that holds a reference to the very first node in the list (that is `tail` in the following code). Since this list is initially empty, we will start by setting this reference to `None`:

```
class SinglyLinkedList:
    def __init__ (self):
        self.tail = None
```

The append operation

The first operation that we need to perform is to append items to the list. This operation is sometimes called an insert operation. Here we get a chance to hide away the `Node` class. The user of our list class should really never have to interact with `Node` objects. These are purely for internal use.

The first shot at an `append()` method may look like this:

```
class SinglyLinkedList:
    # ...
    def append(self, data):
        # Encapsulate the data in a Node
        node = Node(data)
        if self.tail == None:
            self.tail = node
        else:
            current = self.tail
            while current.next:
                current = current.next
            current.next = node
```

We encapsulate data in a node so that it has the next pointer attribute. From here, we check if there are any existing nodes in the list (that is, whether `self.tail` points to a `Node` or not). If there is `None`, we make the new node the first node of the list; otherwise, we find the insertion point by traversing the list to the last node, updating the next pointer of the last node to the new node.

Consider the following example code to append three nodes:

```
>>> words = SinglyLinkedList()
>>> words.append('egg')
>>> words.append('ham')
>>> words.append('spam')
```

List traversal will work as we discussed before. You will get the first element of the list from the list itself, and then traverse the list through the `next` pointer:

```
>>> current = words.tail
>>> while current:
        print(current.data)
        current = current.next
```

A faster append operation

There is a big problem with the append method in the previous section: it has to traverse the entire list to find the insertion point. This may not be a problem when there are just a few items in the list, but it will be a big problem when the list is long, as we would need to traverse the whole list to add an item every time. Each append will be slightly slower than the previous one. The current implementation for the append operation is slowed down by `O(n)`, which is not desirable in the case of a long list.

To fix this, we store not only a reference to the first node in the list but also a reference to the last node. That way, we can quickly append a new node at the end of the list. The worst-case running time of the append operation is now reduced from O(n) to O(1). All we have to do is make sure the previous last node points to the new node that is about to be appended to the list. Here is our updated code:

```
class SinglyLinkedList:
    def init (self):
        # ...
        self.tail = None
    def append(self, data):
        node = Node(data)
        if self.head:
            self.head.next = node
            self.head = node
        else:
            self.tail = node
            self.head = node
```

Take note of the convention being used. The point at which we append new nodes is through `self.head`. The `self.tail` variable points to the first node in the list.

Getting the size of the list

We would like to be able to get the size of the list by counting the number of nodes. One way we could do this is by traversing the entire list and increasing a counter as we go along:

```
def size(self):
 count = 0
 current = self.tail
 while current:
     count += 1
     current = current.next
 return count
```

This works fine. However, list traversal is potentially an expensive operation that we should avoid wherever we can. So instead, we shall opt for another rewrite of the method. We add a size member to the `SinglyLinkedList` class, initializing it to 0 in the constructor. Then we increment the size by one in the append method:

```
class SinglyLinkedList:
    def init (self):
        # ...
```

```
        self.size = 0
    def append(self, data):
        # ...
        self.size += 1
```

Because we are now only reading the size attribute of the node object, and not using a loop to count the number of nodes in the list, we reduce the worst-case running time from `O(n)` to `O(1)`.

Improving list traversal

If you will notice in the earlier of the list traversal, where we are exposing the node class to the client/user. However, it is desirable that the client node should not interact with the node object. We need to use `node.data` to get the contents of the node and `node.next` to get the next node. We can access the data by creating a method that returns a generator. It looks as follows:

```
def iter(self):
    current = self.tail
    while current:
        val = current.data
        current = current.next
        yield val
```

Now, list traversal is much simpler and looks a lot better as well. We can completely ignore the fact that there is anything called a node outside of the list:

```
for word in words.iter():
    print(word)
```

Notice that since the `iter()` method yields the data member of the node, our client code doesn't need to worry about that at all.

Deleting nodes

Another common operation that you will perform on a list is to delete nodes. This may seem simple, but we first have to decide how to select a node for deletion. Is it going to be determined by the index number or by the data the node contains? Here, we will choose to delete a node depending on the data it contains.

The following is a diagram of a special case considered when deleting a node from the list:

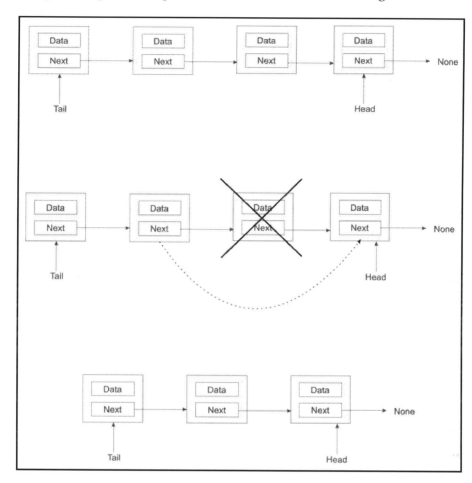

When we want to delete a node that is between two other nodes, all we have to do is we make the previous node point to the successor of its next node that is to be deleted. That is, we simply cut the node to be deleted out of the chain and point directly to the next node as shown in the preceding diagram.

Here is what the implementation of the delete() method may look like:

```
def delete(self, data):
    current = self.tail
    prev = self.tail
    while current:
        if current.data == data:
```

```
                    if current == self.tail:
                        self.tail = current.next
                    else:
                        prev.next = current.next
                    self.count -= 1
                    return
                prev = current
                current = current.next
```

The `delete` operation to remove a node has the time complexity `O(n)`.

List search

We may also need a way to check whether a list contains an item. This method is fairly easy to implement thanks to the `iter()` method we previously wrote. Each pass of the loop compares the current data to the data being searched. If a match is found, `True` is returned, or else `False` is returned:

```
def search(self, data):
    for node in self.iter():
        if data == node:
            return True
    return False
```

Clearing a list

We may need to clear a list quickly; there is a very simple way to do it. We can clear a list by simply clearing the pointer head and tail by setting them to `None`:

```
def clear(self):
    """ Clear the entire list. """
    self.tail = None
    self.head = None
```

Doubly linked lists

We have discussed the singly linked list and the important operation that can be performed on it. Now, we will be focusing on the topic of a doubly linked list in this section.

A doubly linked list is quite similar to the singly linked list in the sense that we use the same fundamental concept of string nodes together, as we did in a singly linked list. The only difference between a singly linked list and a doubly linked list is that in a singly linked list, there is only one link between each successive node, whereas, in a doubly linked list, we have two pointers—a pointer to the next node and a pointer to the previous node. See the following diagram of a *node*; there is a pointer to the next node and the previous node, which are set to None as there is no node attached to this node. Consider the following diagram:

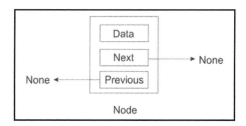

A node in a singly linked list can only determine the next node associated with it. However, there is no way or link to go back from this referenced node. The direction of flow is only one way.

In a doubly linked list, we solve this issue and include the ability not only to reference the next node but also to reference the previous node. Consider the following example diagram to understand the nature of the linkages between two successive nodes. Here, node **A** is referencing node **B**; in addition, there is also a link back to node **A**:

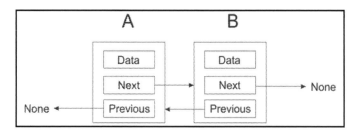

With the existence of two pointers that point to the next and previous nodes, doubly linked lists become equipped with certain capabilities.

Doubly linked lists can be traversed in any direction. A node in a doubly linked list can be easily referred to its previous node whenever required without having a variable to keep track of that node. However, in a singly linked list, it may be difficult to move back to the start or beginning of the list in order to make some changes at the start of the list, which is very easy now in the case of a doubly linked list.

A doubly linked list node

The Python code to create a doubly linked list node includes its initializing methods, the prev pointer, the next pointer, and the data instance variables. When a node is newly created, all these variables default to None:

```
class Node(object):
    def __init__ (self, data=None, next=None, prev=None):
        self.data = data
        self.next = next
        self.prev = prev
```

The prev variable has a reference to the previous node, while the next variable keeps the reference to the next node, and the data variable stores the data.

Doubly linked list class

The doubly linked list class captures the data on which our functions will be operating. For the size method, we set the count instance variable to 0; it can be used to keep track of the number of items in the linked list. head and tail will point to the head and tail of the list when we begin to insert nodes into the list. Consider the following Python code for creating a class:

```
class DoublyLinkedList(object):
    def init (self):
        self.head = None
        self.tail = None
        self.count = 0
```

> We adopt a new convention where self.head points to the beginner node of the list and self.tail points to the latest node added to the list. This is contrary to the convention we used in the singly linked list. There are no fixed rules as to the naming of the head and tail node pointers.

Doubly linked lists also require functionalities that return the size of the list, insert items into the list, and also delete nodes from the list. We will be discussing and providing important functionalities and code on the doubly linked list in the following subsections. Let's start with the append operation.

Append operation

The `append` operation is used to add an element at the end of a list. It is important to check whether the `head` of the list is `None`. If it is `None`, it means that the list is empty, or else the list has some nodes and a new node will be appended to the list. If a new node is to be added to the empty list, it should have the `head` pointing to the newly created node, and the tail of the list should also point at this newly created node through `head`. By the end of these series of steps, the head and tail will now be pointing to the same node. The following diagram illustrates the `head` and `tail` pointers of the doubly linked list when a new node is added to an empty list:

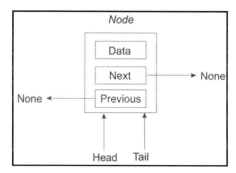

The following code is used to append an item to the doubly linked list:

```
def append(self, data):
    """ Append an item to the list. """
    new_node = Node(data, None, None)
    if self.head is None:
        self.head = new_node
        self.tail = self.head
    else:
        new_node.prev = self.tail
        self.tail.next = new_node
        self.tail = new_node
        self.count += 1
```

The If part of the preceding program is for adding a node to the empty node; the else part of the preceding program will be executed if the list is not empty. If the new node is to be added to a list, the new node's previous variable is to be set to the tail of the list:

```
new_node.prev = self.tail
```

The tail's next pointer (or variable) has to be set to the new node:

```
self.tail.next = new_node
```

Lastly, we update the tail pointer to point to the new node:

```
self.tail = new_node
```

Since an append operation increases the number of nodes by one, we increase the counter by one:

```
self.count += 1
```

A visual representation of the append operation to an existing list is shown in the following diagram:

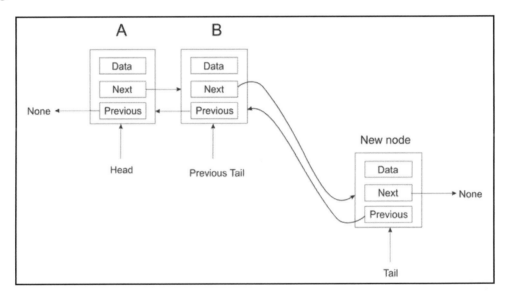

The delete operation

The deletion operation is easier in the doubly linked list compared to the singly linked list.

Unlike a singly linked list, where we needed to keep track of the previously encountered node any time we traverse the whole length of the list, the doubly linked list avoids that whole step. This is made possible by the use of the previous pointer.

The `delete` operation in a doubly linked list can encounter the following four scenarios:

- The search item to be deleted is not found in the list
- The search item to be deleted is located at the start of the list
- The search item to be deleted is found at the tail end of the list
- The search item to be deleted is located in the middle of the list

The node to be deleted is identified by matching the data instance variable with the data that is passed to the method. If the data matches the data variable of a node, that matching node will be deleted. Following is the complete code to delete a node from the doubly linked list. We'll discuss each part of this code step by step:

```python
def delete(self, data):
    """ Delete a node from the list. """
    current = self.head
    node_deleted = False
    if current is None:         #Item to be deleted is not found in the list
        node_deleted = False
    elif current.data == data:  #Item to be deleted is found at starting
of list
        self.head = current.next
        self.head.prev = None
        node_deleted = True
    elif self.tail.data == data:   #Item to be deleted is found at the end
of list.
        self.tail = self.tail.prev
        self.tail.next = None
        node_deleted = True
    else:
        while current:          #search item to be deleted, and delete that
node
            if current.data == data:
                current.prev.next = current.next
                current.next.prev = current.prev
                node_deleted = True
            current = current.next
    if node_deleted:
        self.count -= 1
```

Initially, we create a `node_deleted` variable to denote the deleted node in the list and this is initialized to `False`. The `node_deleted` variable is set to `True` if a matching node is found and subsequently removed. In the delete method, the `current` variable is initially set to the `head` of the list (that is, it points to the `self.head` of the list). See the following code fragment:

```
def delete(self, data):
    current = self.head
    node_deleted = False
    ...
```

Next, we use a set of `if...else` statements to search various parts of the list to find out the node with the specified data that is to be deleted.

First of all, we search for the data to be deleted at the `head` node and if the data is matched at the `head` node, this node would be deleted. Since `current` is pointing at `head`, if `current` is `None`, it means that the list is empty and has no nodes to find the node to be deleted. The following is its code fragment:

```
if current is None:
    node_deleted = False
```

However, if `current` (which now points to head) contains the data being searched for, it means that we found the data to be deleted at the `head` node, then `self.head` is marked to point to the `current` node. Since there is no node behind `head` now, `self.head.prev` is set to `None`. Consider the following code snippet for this:

```
elif current.data == data:
    self.head = current.next
    self.head.prev = None
    node_deleted = True
```

Similarly, if the node that is to be deleted is found at the `tail` end of the list, we delete the last node by setting its previous node pointing to `None`. This is the third possible scenario in the `delete` operation in a doubly linked list that searches for the node to be deleted might be found at the end of the list. The `self.tail` is set to point to `self.tail.prev`, and `self.tail.next` is set to `None` as there is no node afterward. Consider the following code fragment for this:

```
elif self.tail.data == data:
    self.tail = self.tail.prev
    self.tail.next = None
    node_deleted = True
```

Lastly, we search for the node to be deleted by looping through the whole list of the nodes. If the data that is to be deleted is matched with a node, that node will be deleted. To delete a node, we make the previous node of the `current` node to point to the current's next node using the code `current.prev.next = current.next`. After that step, we make the current's next node to point to the previous node of the `current` node using `current.next.prev = current.prev`. Consider the following code snippet for this:

```
else
    while current:
        if current.data == data:
            current.prev.next = current.next
            current.next.prev = current.prev
            node_deleted = True
        current = current.next
```

To better understand the concept of a delete operation in a doubly linked list, consider the following example diagram. In the following diagram, there are three nodes, **A**, **B**, and **C**. To delete node **B** in the middle of the list, we will essentially make **A** point to node **C** as its next node, while making **C** point to **A** as its previous node:

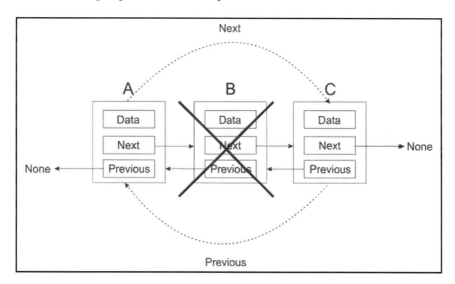

After such an operation, we end up with the following list:

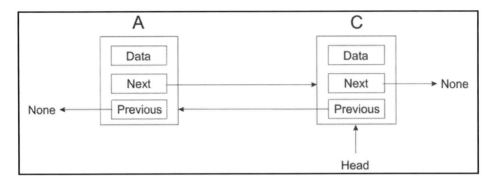

Finally, the `node_delete` variable is then checked to find out if a node is actually deleted or not. If any node is deleted then we decrease the count variable by 1, and this keeps track of the total number of nodes in the list. See the following code fragment that decrements the count variable by 1 in case any node is deleted:

```
if node_deleted:
    self.count -= 1
```

List search

The search for an item in a doubly linked list is similar to the way we did it in the singly linked list. We use the `iter()` method to check the data in all the nodes. As we run a loop through all the data in the list, each node is matched with the data passed in the `contain` method. If we find the item in the list, `True` is returned, denoting that the item is found, otherwise `False` is returned, which means the item was not found in the list. The Python code for this is as follows:

```
def contain(self, data):
    for node_data in self.iter():
        if data == node_data:
        return True
    return False
```

The append operation in a doubly linked list has running time complexity `O(1)` and the delete operation has the complexity `O(n)`.

Circular lists

A circular linked list is a special case of a linked list. In a circular linked list, the endpoints are connected to each other. It means that the last node in the list points back to the first node. In other words, we can say that in circular linked lists all the nodes point to the next node (and the previous node in the case of a doubly linked list) and there is no end node, thus no node will point to Null. Circular lists can be based on both singly and doubly linked lists. In the case of a doubly linked circular list, the first node points to the last node and the last node points back to the first node. Consider the following diagram for the circular linked list, based on a singly linked list where the last node **C** is again connected to the first node **A**, thus making a circular list:

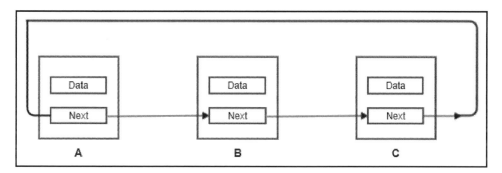

The following diagram shows the concept of the circular linked list based on a doubly linked list where the last node **C** is again connected to the first node **A** through the next pointer. The node **A** is also connected to the node **C** through, previous pointer, thus making a circular list:

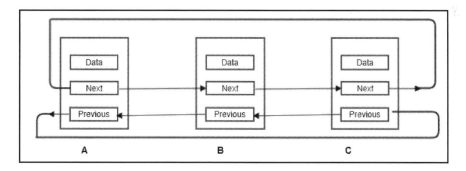

Here, we are going to look at an implementation of a singly linked circular list. It should be straightforward to implement a doubly linked circular list once we understand the basic concepts.

We can reuse the node class that we created in the subsection—singly linked lists. As a matter of fact, we can reuse most parts of the `SinglyLinkedList` class as well. So we are going to focus on the methods where the circular list implementation differs from the normal singly linked list.

Appending elements

To append an element to the circular list in a singly linked list, we have to just include a new functionality so that the newly added or appended node points back to the `tail` node. This is demonstrated in the following code. There is one extra line as compared to the singly linked list implementation, which is shown in bold font:

```
def append(self, data):
    node = Node(data)
    if self.head:
        self.head.next = node
        self.head = node
    else:
        self.head = node
        self.tail = node

    self.head.next = self.tail
    self.size += 1
```

Deleting an element in a circular list

To delete a node in a circular list, it looks like we can do it similarly to how we did in the case of the append operation—simply make sure that head points to the `tail`. There is just a single line that needs to change in the delete operation. It is only when we remove the `tail` node that we need to make sure that the `head` node is updated to point to the new tail node. This would give us the following implementation (the bold font code line is an addition to the delete operation implementation in the singly linked list):

```
def delete(self, data):
    current = self.tail
    prev = self.tail
    while current:
        if current.data == data:
            if current == self.tail:
                self.tail = current.next
                self.head.next = self.tail
            else:
                prev.next = current.next
```

```
        self.size -= 1
        return
    prev = current
    current = current.next
```

However, there is a serious problem with this code. In the case of a circular list, we cannot loop until `current` becomes `None`, since the current node will never point to the `None` in case of circular linked lists. If you delete an existing node, you won't see this, but try deleting a nonexistent node and you will get stuck in an indefinite loop.

We thus need to find a different way to control the `while` loop. We cannot check whether `current` has reached `head`, because then it will never check the last node. But we could use `prev`, since it lags behind `current` by one node. However, there is a special case. The very first loop iteration, `current`, and `prev`, will point to the same node, namely the tail node. We want to ensure that the loop runs here since we need to take the one node list into consideration. The updated delete method now looks as follows:

```
def delete(self, data):
    current = self.tail
    prev = self.tail
    while prev == current or prev != self.head:
        if current.data == data:
            if current == self.tail:
                self.tail = current.next
                self.head.next = self.tail
            else:
                prev.next = current.next
                self.size -= 1
            return
        prev = current
        current = current.next
```

Iterating through a circular list

To traverse the circular linked list, it is very convenient as we don't need to look for the starting point. We can start anywhere, and we just need to carefully stop traversing when we reach the same node again. We can use the same `iter()` method, which we discussed at the start of this chapter. It should work for our circular list; the only difference is that we have to mention an exit condition when we are iterating through the circular list, or otherwise the program will get stuck in a loop and it will run indefinitely. We can make an exit condition by using a counter variable. Consider the following example code:

```
words = CircularList()
words.append('eggs')
```

```
words.append('ham')
words.append('spam')
counter = 0

for word in words.iter():
    print(word)
    counter += 1
    if counter > 1000:
        break
```

Once we have printed out 1,000 elements, we break out of the loop.

Summary

In this chapter, we looked at linked lists. We studied the concepts that underlie lists, such as nodes and pointers to other nodes. We implemented the major operations that occur in these types of lists and saw how the worst-case running times compare.

In the next chapter, we are going to look at two other data structures that are usually implemented using lists—stacks and queues.

5
Stacks and Queues

In this chapter, we are going to build upon the skills we learned in the last chapter in order to create special list implementations. We are still sticking to linear structures. We will get into the details of more complex data structures in the coming chapters.

In this chapter, we are going to understand the concepts of stacks and queues. We will also implement these data structures in Python using various methods such as `lists` and `node`.

In this chapter, we will cover the following:

- Implementing stacks and queues using various methods
- Some real-life example applications of stacks and queues

Technical requirements

You should have a computer system on which Python is installed. All the programs based on the concepts discussed in this chapter are provided in the book as well as the GitHub repository at the following link: `https://github.com/PacktPublishing/Hands-On-Data-Structures-and-Algorithms-with-Python-Second-Edition/tree/master/Chapter05`.

Stacks

A stack is a data structure that stores data, similar to a stack of plates in a kitchen. You can put a plate on the top of the stack, and when you need a plate, you take it from the top of the stack. The last plate that was added to the stack will be the first to be picked up from the stack. Similarly, a stack data structure allows us to store and read data from one end, and the element which is added last is picked up first. Thus, a stack is a **last in, first out (LIFO)** structure:

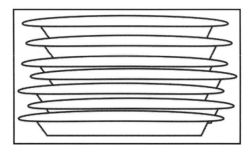

The preceding diagram depicts a stack of plates. Adding a plate to the pile is only possible by leaving that plate on top of the pile. To remove a plate from the pile of plates means to remove the plate that is on top of the pile.

There are two primary operations that are performed on stacks—push and pop. When an element is added to the top of the stack, it is pushed onto the stack. When an element is to be picked up from the top of the stack, it is popped off the stack. Another operation that is used sometimes is peek, which makes it possible to see the element on top of the stack without popping it off.

Stacks are used for a number of things. One very common usage for stacks is to keep track of the return address during function calls. Let's imagine that we have the following program:

```python
def b():
    print('b')

def a():
    b()

a()
print("done")
```

When the program execution gets to the call to a(), the following happens:

1. It first pushes the address of the current instruction onto the stack, then jumps to the definition of a
2. Inside function a(), the function b() is called
3. And, the return address of the function b() is pushed onto the stack
4. Once the execution of the instructions in b() and the function are complete, the return address is popped off the stack, which takes us back to function a()
5. When all the instructions in function a are completed, the return address is again popped off from the stack, which takes us back to the main function and the print statement

Stacks are also used to pass data between functions. Consider the following example. Say you have the following function call somewhere in your code:

```
somefunc(14, 'eggs', 'ham', 'spam')
```

What happens internally is that the values passed by the functions 14, 'eggs', 'ham', and 'spam' will be pushed onto the stack, one at a time, as shown in the following diagram:

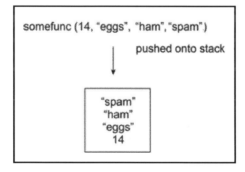

When the code calls jump to the definition of the function, the values for a, b, c, d will be popped off the stack. The spam element will be popped off first and assigned to d, then ham will be assigned to c, and so on:

```
def somefunc(a, b, c, d):
    print("function executed")
```

Stack implementation

Stacks can be implemented in Python using node. We start off by creating a `node` class, as we did in the previous chapter with lists:

```
class Node:
    def __init__(self, data=None):
        self.data = data
        self.next = None
```

As we discussed, a node holds data and a reference to the next item in a list. Here, we are going to implement a stack instead of a list; however, the same principle of nodes works here—nodes are linked together through references.

Now let us look at the `stack` class. It starts off in a similar way to a singly linked list. We will need two things to implement a stack using nodes:

1. We first need to know the node which is at the top of the stack so that we will be able to apply the `push` and `pop` operations through this node.
2. We would also like to keep track of the number of nodes in the stack, so we add a `size` variable to the stack class. Consider the following code snippet for the stack class:

```
class Stack:
    def __init__(self):
        self.top = None
        self.size = 0
```

Push operation

The `push` operation is an important operation on a stack; it is used to add an element at the top of the stack. We implement the push functionality in Python to understand how it works. At first, we check if the stack already has some items in it or it is empty when we wish to add a new node in the stack.

If the stack already has some elements, then we have to do two things:

1. The new node must have its next pointer pointing to the node that was at the top earlier.

2. We put this new node at the top of the stack by pointing `self.top` to the newly added node. See the two instructions in the following diagram:

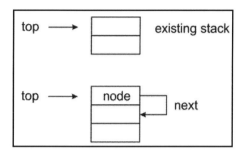

If the existing stack is empty, and the new node to be added is the first element, we need to make this node the top node of the element. Thus, `self.top` will point to this new node. See the following diagram:

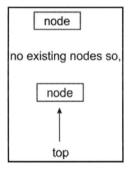

The following is globally the complete implementation of the `push` operation in `stack`:

```
def push(self, data):
    node = Node(data)
    if self.top:
        node.next = self.top
        self.top = node
    else:
        self.top = node
    self.size += 1
```

Pop operation

Now, we need another important function of the stack, and that is the `pop` operation. It reads the topmost element of the stack and removes it from the stack. The `pop` operation returns the topmost element of the stack and returns `None` if the stack is empty.

To implement the `pop` operation on a stack:

1. First, check if the stack is empty. The `pop` operation is not allowed on an empty stack.

2. If the stack is not empty, it can be checked if the top node has its **next** attribute pointing to some other node. It means the stack has elements, and the topmost node is pointing to the next node in the stack. To apply the `pop` operation, we have to change the top pointer. The next node should be at the top. We do this by pointing `self.top` to `self.top.next`. See the following diagram to understand this:

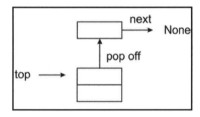

3. When there is only one node in the stack, the stack will be empty after the pop operation. We have to change the top pointer to `None`. See the following diagram:

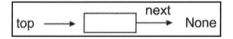

4. Removing such a node results in `self.top` pointing to `None`:

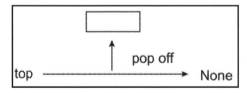

5. We also decrement the size of the stack by 1 if the stack is not empty. Here is the complete code for the `pop` operation for `stack` in Python:

```python
def pop(self):
    if self.top:
        data = self.top.data
        self.size -= 1
        if self.top.next:
            self.top = self.top.next
        else:
            self.top = None
        return data
    else:
        return None
```

Peek operation

There is another important operation that can be applied on stacks—the `peek` method. This method returns the top element from the stack without deleting it from the stack. The only difference between `peek` and `pop` is that the `peek` method just returns the topmost element; however, in the case of a `pop` method, the topmost element is returned and also that element is deleted from the stack.

The pop operation allows us to look at the top element without changing the stack. This operation is very straightforward. If there is a top element, return its data; otherwise, return `None` (thus, the behavior of `peek` matches that of `pop`):

```python
def peek(self):
    if self.top
        return self.top.data
    else:
        return None
```

Bracket-matching application

Now let us look at an example application showing how we can use our stack implementation. We are going to write a little function that will verify whether a statement containing brackets— (, [, or {—is balanced, that is, whether the number of closing brackets matches the number of opening brackets. It will also ensure that one pair of brackets really is contained in another:

```python
def check_brackets(statement):
    stack = Stack()
```

```
            for ch in statement:
                if ch in ('{', '[', '('):
                    stack.push(ch)
                if ch in ('}', ']', ')'):
                    last = stack.pop()
                if last is '{' and ch is '}':
                    continue
                elif last is '[' and ch is ']':
                    continue
                elif last is '(' and ch is ')':
                    continue
                else:
                    return False
        if stack.size > 0:
            return False
        else:
            return True
```

Our function parses each character in the statements passed to it. If it gets an open bracket, it pushes it onto the stack. If it gets a closing bracket, it pops the top element off the stack and compares the two brackets to make sure their types match, (should match), [should match], and { should match }. If they don't, we return `False`; otherwise, we continue parsing.

Once we reach the end of the statement, we need to do one last check. If the stack is empty, then it is fine and we can return `True`. But if the stack is not empty, then we have an opening bracket that does not have a matching closing bracket and we will return `False`. We can test the bracket-matcher with the following code:

```
sl = (
    "{(foo)(bar)}[hello](((this)is)a)test",
    "{(foo)(bar)}[hello](((this)is)atest",
    "{(foo)(bar)}[hello](((this)is)a)test))"
)
for s in sl:
    m = check_brackets(s)
    print("{}: {}".format(s, m))
```

Only the first of the three statements should match. And when we run the code, we get the following output:

```
% ./stack.py
{(foo)(bar)}[hello](((this)is)a)test: True
{(foo)(bar)}[hello](((this)is)atest: False
{(foo)(bar)}[hello](((this)is)a)test)): False
%
```

The output of the preceding code is `True`, `False`, and `False`.

 In summary, the `push` and `pop` operations of the stack data structure attract a complexity of *O(1)*. The stack data structure is simple; however, it is used to implement many functionalities in real-world applications. The back and forward buttons in the browser are implemented using the stacks. Stacks are also used to implement the undo and redo functionalities in word processors.

Queues

Another special type of list is the queue data structure. The queue data structure is very similar to the regular queue you are accustomed to in real life. If you have stood in line at an airport or to be served your favorite burger at your neighborhood shop, then you should know how things work in a queue.

Queues are very fundamental and an important concept to grasp since many other data structures are built on them.

A queue works as follows. The first person to join the queue usually gets served first, and everyone will be served in the order of how they joined the queue. The acronym FIFO best explains the concept of a queue. **FIFO** stands for **first in, first out**. When people are standing in a queue waiting for their turn to be served, service is only rendered at the front of the queue. The only time people exit the queue is when they have been served, which only occurs at the very front of the queue. See the following diagram, where people are standing in the queue, and the person in the front would be served first:

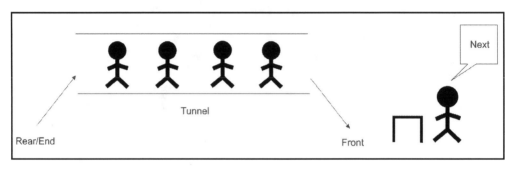

To join the queue, participants must stand behind the last person in the queue. This is the only legal or permitted way the queue accepts new entrants. The length of the queue does not matter.

We shall provide various implementations of a queue, but this will revolve around the same concept of FIFO. The item added first will be read first. We shall call the operation to add an element to the queue as `enqueue`. When we delete an element from the queue, we shall call this a `dequeue` operation. Whenever an element is enqueued, the length or size of the queue increments by 1. Conversely, dequeuing items reduces the number of elements in the queue by 1.

To demonstrate the two operations, the following table shows the effects of adding and removing elements from a queue:

Queue operation	Size	Contents	Operation results
`Queue()`	0	`[]`	Queue object created, which is empty.
`Enqueue` Packt	1	`['Packt']`	One item *Packt* is added to queue.
`Enqueue` Publishing	2	`['Publishing', 'Packt']`	One more item *Publishing* is added to the queue.
`Size()`	2	`['Publishing', 'Packt']`	Return the number of items in the queue, which is 2 in this example.
`Dequeue()`	1	`['Publishing']`	The *Packt* item is dequeued and returned. (This item was added first, so it is removed first.)
`Dequeue()`	0	`[]`	The *Publishing* item is dequeued and returned. (This is the last item added, so it is returned last.)

List-based queues

Queues can be implemented using various methods such as `list`, `stack`, and `node`. We shall discuss the implementation of queues using all these methods one by one. Let's start by implementing a queue using Python's `list` class. This is to help us quickly learn about queues. The operations that must be performed on the queue are encapsulated in the `ListQueue` class:

```
class ListQueue:
    def __init__(self):
        self.items = []
        self.size = 0
```

In the initialization method, `__init__`, the `items` instance variable is set to `[]`, which means the queue is empty when created. The size of the queue is also set to `zero`. The `enqueue` and `dequeue` are important methods in queues, and we will discuss them in the next subsections.

The enqueue operation

The `enqueue` operation adds an item to the queue. It uses the `insert` method of the `list` class to insert items (or data) at the front of the list. See the following code for the implementation of the `enqueue` method:

```
def enqueue(self, data):
    self.items.insert(0, data)    # Always insert items at index 0
    self.size += 1                # increment the size of the queue by 1
```

It is important to note how we implement insertions in queues using list. The concept is that we add the items at index 0 in a list; it is the first position in an array or list. To understand the concept of how the queue works when we add items at index 0 in a list, consider the following diagram. We start with an empty list. Initially, we add an item 1 at index 0. Next, we add an item 2 at index 0; it will shift the previously added item to the next index.

Next, when we again add a new item 3 to the list at index 0, all the items already added to the list are shifted, as shown in the following figure. Similarly, when we add item 4 at index 0, all the items are shifted in the list:

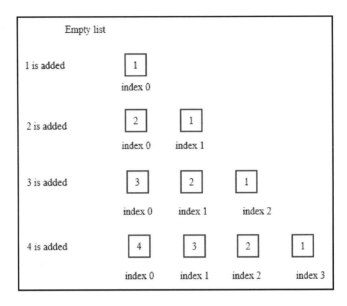

Thus, in our implementation of a queue using a Python list, the array index 0 is the only place where new data elements are inserted into the queue. The insert operation will shift existing data elements in the list by one position up and then insert the new data in the space created at index 0.

To make our queue reflect the addition of the new element, the size is increased by 1:

```
self.size += 1
```

 We could have used Python's shift method on the list as another way of implementing the insert at 0.

The dequeue operation

The `dequeue` operation is used to delete items from the queue. This method returns the topmost item from the queue and deletes it from the queue. Here is the implementation of the `dequeue` method:

```
def dequeue(self):
    data = self.items.pop()     # delete the topmost item from the queue
    self.size -= 1              # decrement the size of the queue by 1
    return data
```

The Python `list` class has a method called `pop()`. The `pop` method does the following:

1. Deletes the last item from the list
2. Returns the deleted item from the list back to the user or code that called it

The last item in the list is popped and saved in the `data` variable. In the last line of the method, the data is returned.

Consider the following figure as our queue implementation, where three elements are added—1, 2, and 3. To perform a `dequeue` operation, the node with data 1 is removed from the front of the queue as it was added first:

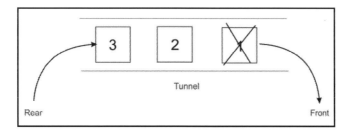

The resulting elements in the queue are shown as follows:

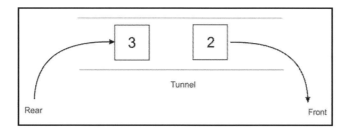

The enqueue operation is very inefficient due to one reason. The method has to first shift all the elements by one space. Imagine there are 1 million elements in a list which need to be shifted around any time a new element is being added to the queue. This will make the enqueue process very slow for large lists.

Stack-based queues

Queues can also be implemented using two stacks. We initially set two instance variables to create an empty queue upon initialization. These are the stacks that will help us to implement a queue. The stacks, in this case, are simply Python lists that allow us to call push and pop methods on them, which eventually allow us to get the functionality of enqueue and dequeue operations. Here is the Queue class:

```
class Queue:
    def __init__(self):
        self.inbound_stack = []
        self.outbound_stack = []
```

The inbound_stack is only used to store elements that are added to the queue. No other operation can be performed on this stack.

Enqueue operation

The enqueue method is to add items to the queue. This method is very simple and only receives the data to append to the queue. This data is then passed to the append method of the inbound_stack in the queue class. Further, the append method is used to mimic the push operation, which pushes elements to the top of the stack. The following code is the implementation of enqueue using the stack in Python:

```
def enqueue(self, data):
    self.inbound_stack.append(data)
```

To enqueue data onto the inbound_stack, the following code does the job:

```
queue = Queue()
queue.enqueue(5)
queue.enqueue(6)
queue.enqueue(7)
print(queue.inbound_stack)
```

A command-line output of the `inbound_stack` inside the queue is as follows:

```
[5, 6, 7]
```

Dequeue operation

The `dequeue` operation is used to delete the elements from the queue in the order of items added. New elements added to our queue end up in the `inbound_stack`. Instead of removing elements from the `inbound_stack`, we shift our attention to another stack, that is, `outbound_stack`. We shall delete the elements from our queue only through the `outbound_stack`.

To understand how `outbound_stack` can be used to delete the items from the queue, let us consider the following example.

Initially, our `inbound_stack` was filled with the elements **5**, **6**, and **7**, as shown in the following diagram:

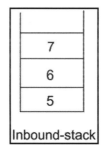

We first check if the `outbound_stack` is empty or not. As it is empty at the start, we move all the elements of the `inbound_stack` to the `outbound_stack` using the `pop` operation on the stack. Now the `inbound_stack` becomes empty and the `outbound_stack` keeps the elements. We show this in the following diagram for more clarity:

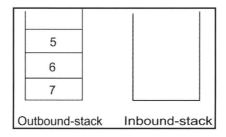

Now, if the `outbound_stack` is not empty, we proceed to remove the items from the queue using the `pop` operation. In the preceding figure, when we apply the `pop` operation on `outbound_stack`, we get the element 5, which is correct as it was added first and should be the first element to be popped off from the queue. This leaves the `outbound_stack` with only two elements:

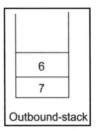

Here is the implementation of the `dequeue` method for the queue:

```
def dequeue(self):
    if not self.outbound_stack:
        while self.inbound_stack:
            self.outbound_stack.append(self.inbound_stack.pop())
    return self.outbound_stack.pop()
```

The `if` statement first checks whether the `outbound_stack` is empty or not. If it is not empty, we proceed to remove the element at the front of the queue using the `pop` method, shown as follows:

```
return self.outbound_stack.pop()
```

If the `outbound_stack` is empty instead, all the elements in the `inbound_stack` are moved to the `outbound_stack` before the front element in the queue is popped out:

```
while self.inbound_stack:
    self.outbound_stack.append(self.inbound_stack.pop())
```

The `while` loop will continue to be executed as long as there are elements in the `inbound_stack`.

The `self.inbound_stack.pop()` statement will remove the latest element that was added to the `inbound_stack` and immediately passes the popped data to the `self.outbound_stack.append()` method call.

Let us consider an example code to understand the operations on the queue. We firstly use the queue implementation to add three items in the queue,that is, 5, 6, and 7. Next, we apply dequeue operations to remove items from the queue. Here is the code :

```
queue = Queue()
queue.enqueue(5)
queue.enqueue(6)
queue.enqueue(7)
print(queue.inbound_stack)
queue.dequeue()
print(queue.inbound_stack)
print(queue.outbound_stack)
queue.dequeue()
print(queue.outbound_stack)
```

The output for the preceding code is as follows:

```
[5, 6, 7]
[]
[7, 6]
[7]
```

The preceding code snippet firstly adds elements to a queue and prints out the elements within the queue. Next, the dequeue method is called, after which a change in the number of elements is observed when the queue is printed out again.

 Implementing a queue with two stacks is very important and questions about this are often posed during interviews.

Node-based queues

Using a Python list to implement a queue is a good start to get a feel for how queues work. It is also possible for us to implement our own queue data structure by utilizing pointer structures.

A queue can be implemented using a doubly linked list, and insertion and deletion operations on this data structure, and that has a time complexity of O(1).

The definition for the node class remains the same as the Node we defined when we discussed in the doubly linked lists. A doubly linked list can be treated as a queue if it enables a FIFO kind of data access, where the first element added to the list is the first to be removed.

Queue class

The queue class is very similar to that of the doubly linked list class and the Node class to adding a node in a doubly linked list:

```
class Node(object):
    def __init__(self, data=None, next=None, prev=None):
        self.data = data
        self.next = next
        self.prev = prev

class Queue:
    def __init__(self):
        self.head = None
        self.tail = None
        self.count = 0
```

Initially, the self.head and self.tail pointers are set to None upon creation of an instance of the queue class. To keep a count of the number of nodes in Queue, the count instance variable is also maintained here and initially set to 0.

The enqueue operation

Elements are added to a Queue object via the enqueue method. The elements or data are added through nodes. The enqueue method code is very similar to the append operation of the doubly linked list which we discussed in Chapter 4, *Lists and Pointer Structures*.

The enqueue operation creates a node from the data passed to it and appends it to the tail of the queue, and points both self.head and self.tail to the newly created node if the queue is empty. The total count of elements in the queue is increased by the line self.count += 1. If the queue is not empty, the new node's previous variable is set to the tail of the list, and the tail's next pointer (or variable) is set to the new node. Lastly, we update the tail pointer to point to the new node. This is shown in the following code:

```
def enqueue(self, data):
    new_node = Node(data, None, None)
    if self.head is None:
        self.head = new_node
        self.tail = self.head
    else:
        new_node.prev = self.tail
        self.tail.next = new_node
        self.tail = new_node

    self.count += 1
```

The dequeue operation

The other operation that makes our doubly linked list behave as a queue is the `dequeue` method. This method removes the node at the front of the queue. To remove the first element pointed to by `self.head`, an `if` statement is used:

```
def dequeue(self):
    current = self.head
        if self.count == 1:
            self.count -= 1
            self.head = None
            self.tail = None
        elif self.count > 1:
            self.head = self.head.next
            self.head.prev = None
            self.count -= 1
```

`current` is initialized by pointing it to `self.head`. If `self.count` is 1, then it means only one node is in the list and invariably the queue. Thus, to remove the associated node (pointed to by `self.head`), the `self.head` and `self.tail` variables are set to `None`.

If the queue has many nodes, then the head pointer is shifted to point to the next node after `self.head`.

After the `if` statement is executed, the method returns the node that was pointed to by the `head`. Also, the variable `self.count` is decremented by 1 in both of these conditions, that is, when the count is initially 1 and more than 1.

Equipped with these methods, we have implemented a queue, borrowing heavily from the idea of a doubly linked list.

Remember also that the only things transforming our doubly linked list into a queue are the two methods, namely, `enqueue` and `dequeue` methods.

Application of queues

Queues can be used to implement a variety of functionalities in many real computer-based applications. For instance, instead of providing each computer on a network with its own printer, a network of computers can be made to share one printer by queuing what each printer wants to print. When the printer is ready to print, it will pick one of the items (usually called jobs) in the queue to print out. It will print the command from the computer that has given the command first and in the order of the commands given by different computers.

Operating systems also queue processes to be executed by the CPU. Let's create an application that makes use of a queue to create a bare-bones media player.

Media player queues

The most music player software allows users to add songs to a playlist. Upon hitting the play button, all the songs in the main playlist are played one after the other. Sequential playing of the songs can be implemented with queues because the first song to be queued is the first song that is to be played. This aligns with the FIFO acronym. We will implement our own playlist queue to play songs in the FIFO manner.

Our media player queue will only allow for the addition of tracks and a way to play all the tracks in the queue. In a full-blown music player, threads would be used to improve how the queue is interacted with, while the music player continues to be used to select the next song to be played, paused, or even stopped.

The track class will simulate a musical track:

```python
from random import randint
class Track:
    def __init__(self, title=None):
        self.title = title
        self.length = randint(5, 10)
```

Each track holds a reference to the title of the song and also the length of the song. The length of the song is a random number between 5 and 10. The random module in Python provides the randint function to enable us to generate the random numbers. The class represents any MP3 track or file that contains music. The random length of a track is used to simulate the number of seconds it takes to play a song or track.

To create a few tracks and print out their lengths, we do the following:

```python
track1 = Track("white whistle")
track2 = Track("butter butter")
print(track1.length)
print(track2.length)
```

The output of the preceding code is as follows:

```
6
7
```

Your output may be different depending on the random length generated for the two tracks.

Now, let's create our queue. Using inheritance, we simply inherit from the queue class:

```
import time
class MediaPlayerQueue(Queue):

    def __init__(self):
        super(MediaPlayerQueue, self).__init__()
```

A call is made to properly initialize the queue by making a call to super. This class is essentially a queue that holds a number of track objects in a queue. To add tracks to the queue, an add_track method is created:

```
def add_track(self, track):
    self.enqueue(track)
```

The method passes a track object to the enqueue method of the queue super class. This will, in effect, create a Node using the track object (as the node's data) and point either the tail, if the queue is not empty, or both head and tail, if the queue is empty, to this new node.

Assuming the tracks in the queue are played sequentially from the first track added to the last (FIFO), then the play function has to loop through the elements in the queue:

```
def play(self):
    while self.count > 0:
        current_track_node = self.dequeue()
        print("Now playing {}".format(current_track_node.data.title))
        time.sleep(current_track_node.data.length)
```

The self.count keeps count of when a track is added to our queue and when tracks have been dequeued. If the queue is not empty, a call to the dequeue method will return the node (which houses the track object) at the front of the queue. The print statement then accesses the title of the track through the data attribute of the node. To further simulate the playing of a track, the time.sleep() method halts program execution till the number of seconds for the track has elapsed:

```
time.sleep(current_track_node.data.length)
```

The media player queue is made up of nodes. When a track is added to the queue, the track is hidden in a newly created node and associated with the data attribute of the node. That explains why we access a node's track object through the data property of the node which is returned by the call to dequeue:

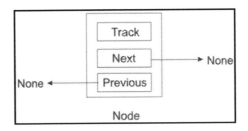

You can see that, instead of our node object just storing just any data, it stores tracks in this case.

Let's take our music player for a spin:

```
track1 = Track("white whistle")
track2 = Track("butter butter")
track3 = Track("Oh black star")
track4 = Track("Watch that chicken")
track5 = Track("Don't go")
```

We create five track objects with random words as titles:

```
print(track1.length)
print(track2.length)
>> 8
>> 9
```

The output should be different from what you get on your machine due to the random length.

Next, an instance of the MediaPlayerQueue class is created:

```
media_player = MediaPlayerQueue()
```

The tracks will be added and the output of the `play` function should print out the tracks being played in the same order in which we queued them:

```
media_player.add_track(track1)
media_player.add_track(track2)
media_player.add_track(track3)
media_player.add_track(track4)
media_player.add_track(track5)
media_player.play()
```

The output of the preceding code is as follows:

```
>>Now playing white whistle
>>Now playing butter butter
>>Now playing Oh black star
>>Now playing Watch that chicken
>>Now playing Don't go
```

Upon execution of the program, it can be seen that the tracks are played in the order in which they were queued. When playing the track, the system also pauses for the number of seconds equal to that of the length of the track.

Summary

In this chapter, we used our knowledge of linking nodes together to create other data structures, namely `stacks` and `queues`. We have seen how these data structures closely mimic stacks and queues in the real world. Concrete implementations, together with their varying types, were explored. We later applied the concepts of stacks and queues to write real-life programs.

We shall consider trees in the next chapter. The major operations of a tree will be discussed, and likewise the different spheres in which to apply their data structure.

6
Trees

A **tree** is a hierarchical form of data structure. In the case of other data structures such as lists, queues, and stacks that we have discussed till now, the items are stored in a sequential way. However, in the case of a tree data structure, there is a *parent-child* relationship between the items. The top of the tree's data structure is known as a **root node**. This is the ancestor of all other nodes in the tree.

Tree data structures are very important owing to their use in various important applications. Trees are used for a number of things, such as parsing expressions, searches, storing data, manipulating data, sorting, priority queues, and so on. Certain document types, such as XML and HTML, can also be represented in a tree form. We shall look at some of the uses of trees in this chapter.

In this chapter, we will cover the following topics:

- Terms and definitions of trees
- Binary trees and binary search trees
- Tree traversal
- Ternary search tree

Technical requirements

All of the source code discussed in this chapter is provided in the GitHub repository for this book at `https://github.com/PacktPublishing/Hands-On-Data-Structures-and-Algorithms-with-Python-3.x-Second-Edition/tree/master/Chapter06`.

Terminology

Let's consider some terminology associated with tree data structures.

To understand trees, we need to first understand the basic concepts related to them. A tree is a data structure in which data is organized in a hierarchical form. The following diagram contains a typical tree consisting of character nodes lettered **A** through to **M**:

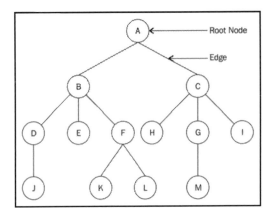

Here is a list of terms associated with a tree:

- **Node**: Each circled letter in the preceding diagram represents a node. A node is any data structure that actually stores the data.
- **Root node**: The root node is the first node from which all other nodes in the tree are attached. In every tree, there is always one unique root node. The root node in our example tree is node A.
- **Sub-tree**: A sub-tree of a tree is a tree with its nodes being a descendant of some other tree. For example, nodes F, K, and L form a sub-tree of the original tree consisting of all the nodes.
- **Degree**: The total number of children of the given node is called the **degree of that node**. A tree consisting of only one node has a degree of 0. The degree of node A in the preceding diagram is 2, the degree of node B is 3, the degree of node C is 3, and similarly, the degree of node G is 1.
- **Leaf node**: The leaf node does not have any children, and is the terminal node of the given tree. The degree of the leaf node is always 0. In the preceding diagram, the nodes J, E, K, L, H, M, and I are all leaf nodes.

- **Edge**: The connection among any given two nodes in the tree is called an **edge**. The total number of edges in a given tree will be a maximum of one less than the total nodes in the tree. An example edge is shown in the preceding sample tree structure.

- **Parent**: A node in the tree which has a further sub-tree is the parent node of that sub-tree. For example, node B is the parent of nodes D, E, and F, and node F is the parent of nodes K and L.

- **Child**: This is a node connected to its parent, and it is the node that is a descendant of that node. For example, nodes B and C are children of node A, while the nodes H, G, and I are the children of node C.

- **Sibling**: All nodes with the same parent are siblings. For example, nodes B and C are siblings, and, similarly, nodes D, E, and F are also siblings.

- **Level**: The root node of the tree is considered to be at level 0. The children of the root node are considered at level 1, and the children of the nodes at level 1 are considered at level 2, and so on. For example, the root node is at level 0, nodes B and C are at level 1, and nodes D, E, F, H, G, and I are at level 2.

- **Height of a tree**: The total number of the nodes in the longest path of the tree is the height of a tree. For example, in the preceding example tree, the height of the tree is 4 as the longest paths, `A-B-D-J` or `A-C-G-M` or `A-B-F-K`, all have a total number of 4 nodes each.

- **Depth**: The depth of a node is the number of edges from the root of the tree to that node. In the preceding tree example, the depth of node H is 2.

We shall begin our treatment of trees by considering the node in a tree and abstracting a class.

Tree nodes

In linear data structures, data items are stored in a sequential order, one after another, whereas nonlinear data structures store data items in a non-linear order, where a data item can be connected to more than one data item. All of the data items in the linear data structures can be traversed in one pass, whereas this is not possible in the case of a non-linear data structure. The trees are the non-linear data structure; they store the data differently from other linear data structures such as *arrays*, *lists*, *stacks*, and *queues*.

In the tree data structure, the nodes are arranged in a *parent-child* relationship. There should not be any cycle among the nodes in trees. The tree structure has nodes to form a hierarchy, and a tree that has no node is called an **empty tree**.

First, we will discuss one of most important and special kinds of trees available, that is, the *binary tree*. A binary tree is a collection of nodes, where the nodes in the tree can have zero, 1, or 2 child nodes. A simple binary tree has a maximum of two children, that is, the left child and the right child. For example, in the following binary tree example, there is a root node that has two children (left child, right child):

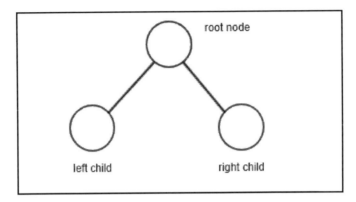

A tree is called a **full binary tree** if all the nodes of a binary tree have either zero or two children, and if there is no node that has 1 child. A binary tree is called a **complete binary tree** if it is completely filled, with a possible exception at the bottom level, which is filled from left to right.

Just like in our previous implementations, a node is a container for data and holds references to other nodes. In a binary tree node, these references are to the left and the right children. Let's look at the following code for building a binary tree node class in Python:

```python
class Node:
    def __init__(self, data):
        self.data = data
        self.right_child = None
        self.left_child = None
```

To test this class, we must first create four nodes—n1, n2, n3, and n4:

```python
n1 = Node("root node")
n2 = Node("left child node")
n3 = Node("right child node")
n4 = Node("left grandchild node")
```

Next, we connect the nodes to each other according to the property of a binary tree. We let n1 be the root node, with n2 and n3 as its children. Finally, we take n4 as the left child to n2. Take a look at the following diagram to see how we connect these nodes to each other:

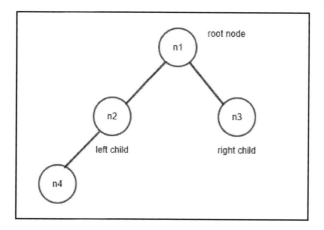

The next code snippet should be following in order to connect the nodes to each other according to the preceding diagram:

```
n1.left_child = n2
n1.right_child = n3
n2.left_child = n4
```

Here, we have set a very simple tree structure of four nodes. The first important operation that we would like to perform on trees is traversal. To understand traversing, let's traverse the left sub-tree of this binary tree. We will start from the root node, print out the node, and move down the tree to the next left node. We keep doing this until we have reached the end of the left sub-tree, like so:

```
current = n1
while current:
    print(current.data)
    current = current.left_child
```

The output of traversing the preceding code block is as follows:

root node
left child node
left grandchild node

Tree traversal

The method to visit all the nodes in a tree is called **tree traversal**. This can be done either **depth-first search (DFS)** or **breadth-first search (BFS)**. We will discuss these two methods in the subsequent subsections.

Depth-first traversal

In depth-first traversal, we traverse the tree, starting from the root, and go deeper into the tree as much as possible on each child, and then continue to traverse to the next sibling. We use the recursive approach for tree traversal. There are three forms of depth-first traversal, namely, in-order, pre-order, and post-order.

In-order traversal and infix notation

In-order tree traversal works as follows. First of all, we check if the current node is null or empty. If it is not empty, we traverse the tree. In in-order tree traversal, we follow these steps:

1. We start traversing the left sub-tree and call the `inorder` function recursively
2. Next, we visit the root node
3. Finally, we traverse the right sub-tree and call the `inorder` function recursively

So, in a nutshell, in in-order tree traversal, we visit the nodes in the tree in the order of (left sub-tree, root, right sub-tree).

Let's consider an example to understand in-order tree traversal:

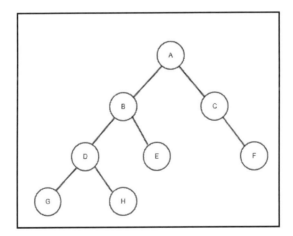

In the example binary tree for in-order traversal, first, we recursively visit the left sub-tree of the root node **A**. The left sub-tree of node **A** has node **B** as root, so we again go to the left sub-tree of the root node **B**, that is, node **D**. We recursively go to the left sub-tree of root node **D** so that we get the left child with root node **D**. So, first, we visit the left child, that is, **G**, then visit the root node, **D**, and then visit the right child, **H**.

Next, we visit node **B** and then visit node **E**. In this manner, we have visited the left sub-tree with the root node **A**. So, next, we visit the root node **A**. After that, we will visit the right sub-tree with root node **A**. Here, we go to the left sub-tree with root node **C**, which is null, so next we visit node **C**, and then we visit the right child of node **C**, that is, node **F**.

Therefore, the in-order traversal for this example tree is G–D–H–B–E–A–C–F.

The Python implementation of a recursive function to return an `inorder` listing of nodes in a tree is as follows:

```
def inorder(self, root_node):
    current = root_node
    if current is None:
        return
    self.inorder(current.left_child)
    print(current.data)
    self.inorder(current.right_child)
```

We visit the node by printing the visited node. In this case, we first recursively call the `inorder` function with `current.left_child`, then we visit the root node, and finally we recursively call the `inorder` function with `current.right_child` once more.

The **infix** notation (also known as reverse Polish notation) is a commonly used notation to express arithmetic expressions where the operators are placed in-between the operands. It is common to use this way of representing an arithmetic expression since this is the way we are normally taught in schools. For example, the operator is inserted (infixed) between the operands, as in 3 + 4. When necessary, parentheses can be used to build a more complex expression, such as (4 + 5) * (5 - 3).

An expression tree is a special kind of **binary tree** that can be used to represent arithmetic expressions. This in-order traversal of an expression tree produce the infix notation. For example, consider the following expression tree:

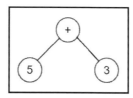

The in-order traversal of the preceding expression tree gives us the infix notation, that is, (5 + 3).

Pre-order traversal and prefix notation

Pre-order tree traversal works as follows. First of all, we check if the current node is null or empty. If it is not empty, we traverse the tree. The pre-order tree traversal works as follows:

1. We start traversing with the root node
2. Next, we traverse the left sub-tree and call the `preorder` function with the left sub-tree recursively
3. Next, we visit the right sub-tree and call the `preorder` function with the right sub-tree recursively

So, to traverse a tree in pre-order mode, we visit the tree in the order of root node, the left sub-tree, and the right sub-tree node.

Consider the following example tree to understand pre-order traversal:

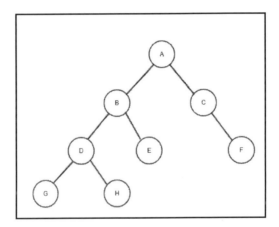

In the preceding example of a binary tree, first, we visit root node **A**. Next, we go to the left sub-tree of root node **A**. The left sub-tree of node **A** has node **B** as the root, so we visit this root node and the go to the left sub-tree of root node **B**, that is, node **D**. We then visit node **D** and go to the left sub-tree of root node **D**, and then we visit the left child, **G**, which is the sub-tree of root node **D**. Next, we visit the right child of the sub-tree with root node **D**, that is, node **H**. Next, we visit the right child of the sub-tree with root node **B**, that is, node **E**. So, in this manner, we have visited root node **A** and the left sub-tree with root node **A**. Now, we will visit the right sub-tree of root node **A**. Here, we visit the root node **C**, and then we go to the left sub-tree with root node **C**, which is null, so next, we visit the right child of node **C**, that is, node **F**.

The pre-order traversal for this example tree would be A–B–D–G–H–E–C–F.

The recursive function for `pre-order` tree traversal is as follows:

```
def preorder(self, root_node):
    current = root_node
    if current is None:
        return
    print(current.data)
    self.preorder(current.left_child)
    self.preorder(current.right_child)
```

Prefix notation is commonly referred to as Polish notation. In this notation, the operator comes before its operands. Prefix notation is well known to LISP programmers. For example, the arithmetic expression to add two numbers, 3 and 4, would be shown as `+ 3 4`. Since there is no ambiguity of precedence, parentheses are not required: `* + 4 5 - 5 3`.

Let's consider another example, that is, the `(3 +4) * 5` . This can also be represented as `* (+ 3 4) 5` in prefix notation.

The pre-order traversal of an expression tree results in the prefix notation of the arithmetic expression. For example, consider the following expression tree:

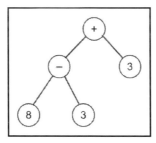

The preorder traversal of the preceding tree will give the expression in prefix notation as `+- 8 3 3`.

Post-order traversal and postfix notation

`Post-order` tree traversal works as follows. First of all, we check if the current node is null or empty. If it is not empty, we traverse the tree. `Post-order` tree traversal works as follows:

1. We start traversing the left sub-tree and call the `postorder` function recursively

2. Next, we traverse the right sub-tree and call the postorder function recursively
3. Finally, we visit the root node

So. in a nutshell, regarding `post-order` tree traversal, we visit the nodes in the tree in the order of left sub-tree, right sub-tree, and finally the root node.

Consider the following example tree to understand post-order tree traversal:

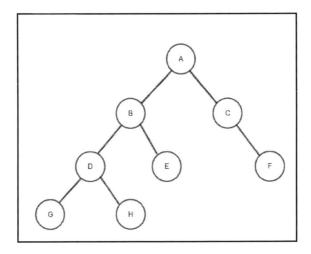

In the preceding diagram, we first visit the left sub-tree of root node **A** recursively. We get to the last left subtree, that is, root node D, and then we visit the left node of it, which is node **G**. Then, we visit the right child, **H**, and then we visit the root node **D**. Following the same rule, we next visit the right child of node **B**, that is, node **E**. Then, we visit node **B**. Following on from this, we traverse the right sub-tree of node **A**. Here, we first reach the last right sub-tree and visit node **F**, and then we visit node **C**. Finally, we visit root node **A**.

The postorder traversal for this example tree would be G-H-D-E-B-F-C-A.

The implementation of the `post-order` method for tree traversal is as follows:

```
def postorder(self, root_node):
    current = root_node
    if current is None:
        return
    self.postorder(current.left_child)
    self.postorder(current.right_child)

    print(current.data)
```

Postfix or **reverse Polish notation** (**RPN**) places the operator after its operands, as in 3 4 +. As is the case with Polish notation, there is no further confusion over the precedence of operators, so parentheses are never needed: 4 5 + 5 3 − *.

The post-order traversal of the following expression tree will give the postfix notation of the arithmetic expression:

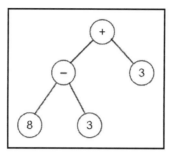

The postfix notation for the preceding expression tree is 8 3 −3 +.

Breadth-first traversal

Breadth-first traversal starts from the root of the tree and then visits every node on the next level of the tree. Then, we move to the next level in the tree, and so on. This kind of tree traversal is breadth-first as it broadens the tree by traversing all the nodes in a level before going deep into the tree.

Let's consider the following example tree and traverse it by using the breadth-first traversal method:

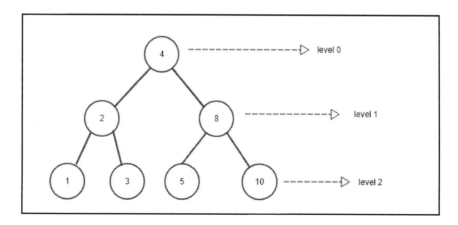

In the preceding diagram, we start by visiting the root node at **level 0**, that is, the node with a value of **4**. We visit this node by printing out its value. Next, we move to **level 1** and visit all the nodes on this level, which are the nodes with the values **2** and **8**. Finally, we move to the next level in the tree, that is, **level 3**, and we visit all the nodes at this level. The nodes at this level are **1, 3, 5**, and **10**.

Thus, the breadth-first tree traversal for this tree is as follows—**4, 2, 8, 1, 3, 5**, and **10**.

This mode of traversal is implemented using a queue data structure. Starting with the root node, we push it into a queue. The node at the front of the queue is accessed (dequeued) and either printed or stored for later use. The left node is added to the queue followed by the right node. Since the queue is not empty, we repeat this process.

The Python implementation of this algorithm will enqueue the root node **4**, dequeue it, and visit the node. Next, nodes **2** and **8** are enqueued as they are the left and right nodes at the next level, respectively. Node **2** is dequeued so that it can be visited. Next, its left and right nodes, that is, nodes **1** and **3**, are enqueued. At this point, the node at the front of the queue is **8**. We dequeue and visit node **8**, after which we enqueue its left and right nodes. This process continues until the queue is empty.

The Python implementation of breadth-first traversal is as follows:

```
from collections import deque
class Tree:
    def breadth_first_traversal(self):
        list_of_nodes = []
        traversal_queue = deque([self.root_node])
```

We enqueue the root node and keep a list of the visited nodes in the `list_of_nodes` list. The `dequeue` class is used to maintain a queue:

```
while len(traversal_queue) > 0:
    node = traversal_queue.popleft()
    list_of_nodes.append(node.data)
    if node.left_child:
        traversal_queue.append(node.left_child)

    if node.right_child:
        traversal_queue.append(node.right_child)
return list_of_nodes
```

If the number of elements in `traversal_queue` is greater than zero, the body of the loop is executed. The node at the front of the queue is popped off and appended to the `list_of_nodes` list. The first `if` statement will `enqueue` the left child node if the `node` provided with a left node exists. The second `if` statement does the same for the right child node.

The `list_of_nodes` list is returned in the last statement.

Binary trees

A binary tree is one in which each node has a maximum of two children. The nodes in the binary tree are organized in the form of left sub-tree and right sub-tree. If the tree has a root, R, and two sub-trees, that is, left sub-tree `T1`, and right sub-tree `T2`, then their roots are called `left successor` and `right successor`, respectively.

The following diagram is an example of a binary tree with five nodes:

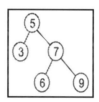

Here are the following observations that we have made regarding the preceding diagram:

- Each node holds a reference to a right and left node if the nodes do not exist
- The root node is denoted with **5**
- The root node has two sub-trees, where the left sub-tree has one node, that is, a node with a value of **3**, and the right sub-tree has three nodes with the values **7, 6,** and **9**
- The node with a value of **3** is a left successor node, whereas the node with a value of **7** is the right successor

A regular binary tree has no other rules as to how elements are arranged in the tree. It should only satisfy the condition that each node should have a maximum of two children.

Binary search trees

A **binary search tree** (BST) is a special kind of binary tree. It is one of the most important and commonly used data structures in computer science applications. A binary search tree is a tree that is structurally a binary tree, and stores data in its nodes very efficiently. It provides very fast search operations, and other operations such as insertion and deletion are also very easy and convenient.

A binary tree is called a binary search tree if the value at any node in the tree is greater than the values in all the nodes of its left sub-tree, and less than or equal to the values of all the nodes of the right sub-tree. For example, if **K1**, **K2**, and **K3** are key values in a tree of three nodes (as shown in the following diagram), then it should satisfy the following conditions:

1. The key values of $K2 <= K1$
2. The key values $K3 > K1$

The following diagram depicts this:

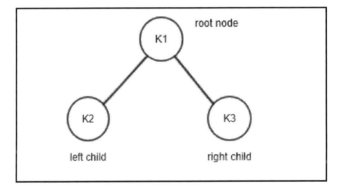

Let's consider another example so that we have a better understanding of binary search trees. Consider the following tree:

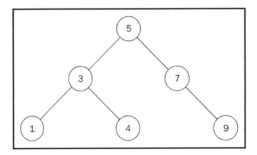

This is an example of a BST. In this tree, all of the nodes in the left sub-tree are less than or equal to the value of that node. Also, all of the nodes in the right sub-tree of this node are greater than that of the parent node.

Testing our tree for the properties of a BST, we notice that all of the nodes in the left sub-tree of the root node have a value less than 5. Likewise, all the nodes in the right sub-tree have a value that is greater than 5. This property applies to all the nodes in a BST, with no exceptions.

Considering another example of a binary tree, let's see if it is a binary search tree or not. Despite the fact that the following diagram looks similar to the previous diagram, it does not qualify as a BST as node **7** is greater than the root node **5**; however, it is located to the left of the root node. Node **4** is to the right sub-tree of its parent node **7**, which is incorrect. Thus, the following diagram is not a binary search tree:

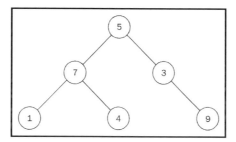

Binary search tree implementation

Let's begin the implementation of a BST in Python. We need to keep track of the root node of the tree, so we start by creating a `Tree` class that holds a reference to the root node:

```
class Tree:
    def __init__(self):
        self.root_node = None
```

That's all that is needed to maintain the state of a tree. Let's examine the main operations on the tree in the next section.

Binary search tree operations

The operations that can be performed on a binary search tree are `insert`, `delete`, finding `min`, finding `max`, `searching`, and so on. We will discuss them in subsequent subsections.

Finding the minimum and maximum nodes

The structure of the binary search tree makes searching a node that has a maximum or a minimum value very easy.

To find a node that has the smallest value in the tree, we start traversal from the root of the tree and visit the left node each time until we reach the end of the tree. Similarly, we traverse the right sub-tree recursively until we reach the end to find the node with the biggest value in the tree.

For example, consider the following diagram; we move down from node **6** to **3** and then from node **3** to **1** to find the node with the smallest value. Similarly, to find the maximum value node from the tree, we go down from the root to the right-hand side of the tree, then go from node **6** to node **8** and then node **8** to node **10** to find the node with the largest value. Here is an example BST tree:

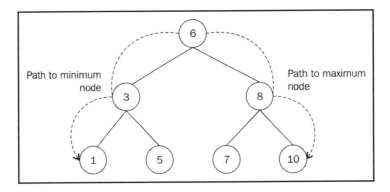

This concept of finding the minimum and maximum nodes applies to sub-trees, too. Thus, the minimum node in the sub-tree with root node **8** is node **7**. Similarly, the node that has the maximum value within that sub-tree is **10**.

The Python implementation of the method that returns the minimum node is as follows:

```
def find_min(self):
    current = self.root_node
    while current.left_child:
        current = current.left_child

    return current
```

The `while` loop continues to get the left node and visits it until the last left node points to `None`. It is a very simple method.

Similarly, the following is the code of the method that returns the maximum node:

```
def find_max(self):
    current = self.root_node
    while current.right_child:
        current = current.right_child

    return current
```

The running time complexity to find the minimum or maximum value in a BST is O(*h*), where h is the height of the tree.

There are essentially two other operations, that is, insert and delete, and they are very important for BST. It is important to ensure that we maintain the property of the BST tree while applying these operations on the tree.

Inserting nodes

One of the most important operations to implement on a binary search tree is to insert data items in the tree. As we have already discussed, regarding the properties of the binary search tree, for each node in the tree, the left child nodes should contain the data less than their own value and the right child nodes should have data greater than their value. So, we have to ensure that the property of the binary search tree satisfies whenever we insert an item in the tree.

For example, let's create a binary search tree by inserting data items **5, 3, 7,** and **1** in the tree. Consider the following:

1. **Insert 5:** We start with the first data item, **5**. To do this, we will create a node with its data attribute set to **5**, since it is the first node.
2. **Insert 3:** Now, we want to add the second node with value **3** so that data value **3** is compared with the existing node value, **5**, of the root node:

Since the node value **3** is less than **5**, it will be placed in the left sub-tree of node **5**. Our BST will look as follows:

The tree satisfies the BST rule, where all the nodes in the left sub-tree are less than the parent.

3. **Insert 7:** To add another node of value **7** to the tree, we start from the root node with value **5** and make a comparison:

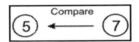

Since **7** is greater than **5**, the node with value **7** is placed to the right of this root.

4. **Insert 1:** Let's add another node with value **1**. Starting from the root of the tree, we make a comparison between **1** and **5**:

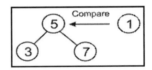

This comparison shows that **1** is less than **5**, so we go to the left node of **5**, which is the node with a value of **3**:

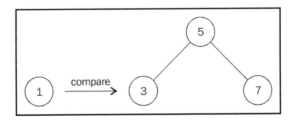

When we compare **1** with **3**, since **1** is less than **3**, we move a level below node **3** and to its left. However, there is no node there. Therefore, we create a node with the value **1** and associate it with the left pointer of node **3** to obtain the following structure. Here, we have the final binary search tree of **4** nodes:

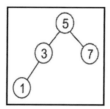

We can see that this example contains only integers or numbers. So, if we need to store the string data in the binary search tree, in this case strings would be compared alphabetically. And, if we want to store our own custom data types inside a BST, we will have to make sure that our class supports ordering.

The Python implementation of the `insert` method to add the nodes in the BST is given as follows:

```
def insert(self, data):
    node = Node(data)
    if self.root_node is None:
        self.root_node = node
    else:
        current = self.root_node
        parent = None
    while True:
        parent = current
        if node.data < parent.data:
            current = current.left_child
            if current is None:
                parent.left_child = node
                return
        else:
            current = current.right_child
            if current is None:
                parent.right_child = node
                return
```

Now, let's understand each of the instructions of this `insert` function, step by step. We will begin with a function declaration:

```
def insert(self, data):
```

By now, you will be used to the fact that we encapsulate the data in a node. This way, we hide away the `node` class from the client code, who only needs to deal with the tree:

```
node = Node(data)
```

A first check will be done to find out whether we have a root node. If we don't, the new node becomes the root node (we cannot have a tree without a root node):

```
if self.root_node is None:
    self.root_node = node
else:
```

As we walk down the tree, we need to keep track of the current node we are working on, as well as its parent. The `current` variable is always used for this purpose:

```
current = self.root_node
parent = None
while True:
    parent = current
```

Here, we must perform a comparison. If the data held in the new node is less than the data held in the current node, then we check whether the current node has a left child node. If it doesn't, this is where we insert the new node. Otherwise, we keep traversing:

```
if node.data < current.data:
    current = current.left_child
    if current is None:
        parent.left_child = node
        return
```

Now, we need to take care of the greater than or equal case. If the current node doesn't have a right child node, then the new node is inserted as the right child node. Otherwise, we move down and continue looking for an insertion point:

```
else:
    current = current.right_child
    if current is None:
        parent.right_child = node
        return
```

Insertion of a node in a BST takes `O(h)`, where `h` is the height of the tree.

Deleting nodes

Another important operation on a BST is the `deletion` or `removal` of nodes. There are three scenarios that we need to cater for during this process. The node that we want to remove might have the following:

- **No children**: If there is no leaf node, directly remove the node
- **One child**: In this case, we swap the value of that node with its child, and then delete the node
- **Two children**: In this case, we first find the in-order successor or predecessor, swap the value with it, and then delete that node

The first scenario is the easiest to handle. If the node about to be removed has no children, we simply remove it from its parent:

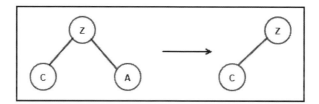

In the preceding example, node **A** has no children, so we will simply delete it from its parent, that is, node **Z**.

On the other hand, when the node we want to remove has one child, the parent of that node is made to point to the child of that particular node. Let's take a look at the following diagram, where we want to delete node **6** who has one child, that is, node **5**:

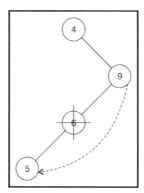

In order to delete node **6**, which has node **5** as its only child, we point the left pointer of node **9** to node **5**. Here, we need to ensure that the child and parent relationship follows the properties of a binary search tree.

A more complex scenario arises when the node we want to delete has two children. Consider the following example tree, where we want to delete node **9**, which has two children:

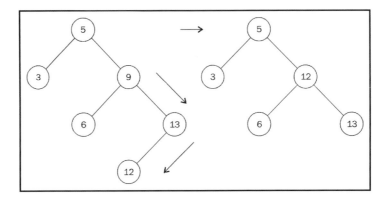

We cannot simply replace node **9** with either node **6** or **13**. What we need to do is find the next biggest descendant of node **9**. This is node **12**. To get to node **12**, we move to the right node of node **9**. Then, we move left to find the leftmost node. Node **12** is called the in-order successor of node **9**. The second step resembles the move to find the maximum node in a sub-tree.

We replace the value of node **9** with the value **12** and remove node **12**. Upon removing node **12**, we end up with a simpler form of node removal that was addressed previously. Node 12 has no children, so we apply the rule for removing nodes without children accordingly.

Our node class does not have a reference to a parent. As such, we need to use a helper method to search and return the node with its parent node. This method is similar to the search method:

```
def get_node_with_parent(self, data):
    parent = None
    current = self.root_node
    if current is None:
        return (parent, None)
    while True:
        if current.data == data:
            return (parent, current)
```

```
        elif current.data > data:
            parent = current
            current = current.left_child
        else:
            parent = current
            current = current.right_child

    return (parent, current)
```

The only difference is that before we update the current variable inside the loop, we store its parent with `parent = current`. The method to do the actual removal of a node begins with this search:

```
def remove(self, data):
    parent, node = self.get_node_with_parent(data)

    if parent is None and node is None:
        return False

    # Get children count
    children_count = 0

    if node.left_child and node.right_child:
        children_count = 2
    elif (node.left_child is None) and (node.right_child is None):
        children_count = 0
    else:
        children_count = 1
```

We pass the parent and the found nodes to `parent` and `node`, respectively with the `parent, node = self.get_node_with_parent(data)` line. It is important to know the number of children that the node has that we want to delete, and we do so in the `if` statement.

After we know the number of children a node has that we want to delete, we need to handle various conditions in which a node can be deleted. The first part of the `if` statement handles the case where the node has no children:

```
if children_count == 0:
    if parent:
        if parent.right_child is node:
            parent.right_child = None
        else:
            parent.left_child = None
    else:
        self.root_node = None
```

In cases where the node to be deleted has only one child, the `elif` part of the `if` statement does the following:

```
elif children_count == 1:
    next_node = None
    if node.left_child:
        next_node = node.left_child
    else:
        next_node = node.right_child

    if parent:
        if parent.left_child is node:
            parent.left_child = next_node
        else:
            parent.right_child = next_node
    else:
        self.root_node = next_node
```

The `next_node` is used to keep track of that single node. which is the child of the node that is to be deleted. We then connect `parent.left_child` or `parent.right_child` to `next_node`.

Lastly, we handle the condition where the node we want to delete has two children:

```
    ...
    else:
        parent_of_leftmost_node = node
        leftmost_node = node.right_child
        while leftmost_node.left_child:
            parent_of_leftmost_node = leftmost_node
            leftmost_node = leftmost_node.left_child

        node.data = leftmost_node.data
```

In finding the in-order successor, we move to the right node with `leftmost_node = node.right_child`. As long as a left node exists, `leftmost_node.left_child` will evaluate to `True` and the `while` loop will run. When we get to the leftmost node, it will either be a leaf node (meaning that it will have no child node) or have a right child.

We update the node that's about to be removed with the value of the in-order successor with `node.data = leftmost_node.data`:

```
if parent_of_leftmost_node.left_child == leftmost_node:
    parent_of_leftmost_node.left_child = leftmost_node.right_child
else:
    parent_of_leftmost_node.right_child = leftmost_node.right_child
```

The preceding statement allows us to properly attach the parent of the leftmost node with any child node. Observe how the right-hand side of the equals sign stays unchanged. This is because the in-order successor can only have a right child as its only child.

The `remove` operation takes $O(h)$, where h is the height of the tree.

Searching the tree

A binary search tree is a tree data structure in which all the nodes follow the property that all the nodes in the left sub-tree of a node have lower key values, and have greater key values in its right sub-tree. Thus, searching for an element with a given key value is quite easy. Let's consider an example binary search tree that has nodes **1**, **2**, **3**, **4**, **8**, **5**, and **10**, as shown in the following diagram:

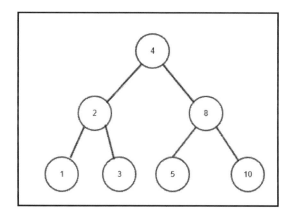

In the preceding tree, if we wish to search for a node with a value of **5**, then we start from the root node and compare it with the root. As node **5** is a greater value compared to root node value **4**, we move to the right sub-tree. In the right sub-tree, we have node **8** as the root node; we compare node **5** with node **8**. As the node to be searched has a smaller value than node **8**, we move to the left sub-tree. When we move to the left sub-tree, we compare the left sub-tree node **5** with the required node with value **5**. This is a match, so we return `"item found"`.

Here is the implementation of the `searching` method in a binary search tree:

```
def search(self, data):
    current = self.root_node
    while True:
        if current is None:
            return None
```

```
        elif current.data is data:
            return data
        elif current.data > data:
            current = current.left_child
        else:
            current = current.right_child
```

In the preceding code, we will return the data if it was found, or None if the data wasn't found. We start searching from the root node. Next, if the data item to be searched for doesn't exist in the tree, we return None to the client code. We might also have found the data—in that case, we return the data.

If the data we are searching for is less than that of the current node, we go down the tree to the left. Furthermore, in the else part of the code, we check if the data we are looking for is greater than the data held in the current node, which means that we go down the tree to the right.

Finally, we can write some client code to test how the BST works. We must create a tree and insert a few numbers between 1 and 10. Then, we search for all the numbers in that range. The ones that exist in the tree get printed:

```
tree = Tree()
tree.insert(5)
tree.insert(2)
tree.insert(7)
tree.insert(9)
tree.insert(1)

for i in range(1, 10):
    found = tree.search(i)
    print("{}: {}".format(i, found))
```

Benefits of a binary search tree

A binary search tree is a better choice compared to arrays and linked lists. A BST is fast for most operations such as searching, insertion, and deletion, whereas arrays provide fast searching, but are comparatively slow in insertion and deletion operations. In a similar fashion, linked lists are efficient in performing insertion and deletion operations, but are slower when performing the search operation. The best-case running time complexity for searching an element from a binary search tree is O(log n), and the worst-case time complexity is O(n), whereas both best-case and worst-case time complexity for searching in lists is O(n).

The following table provides a comparison of the array, linked list, and binary search tree data structures:

Properties	Array	Linked list	BST
Data structure	Linear.	Linear.	Non-linear.
Ease of use	Easy to create and use. Average-case complexity for search, insert, and delete is `O(n)`.	Insertion and deletion is fast, especially with the doubly linked list.	Access of elements, insertion, and deletion is fast with the average-case complexity of `O(log n)`.
Access Complexity	Easy to access elements. Complexity is `O(1)`.	Only sequential access is possible, so slow. Average and worst-case complexity is `O(n)`.	Access is fast, but slow when the tree is unbalanced, with the worst-case complexity of `O(n)`.
Search complexity	Average and worst-case complexity is `O(n)`.	It is slow due to sequential searching. Average and worst-case complexity is `O(n)`.	Worst-case complexity for searching is `O(n)`.
Insertion complexity	Insertion is slow. Average and worst-case complexity is `O(n)`.	Average and worst-case complexity is `O(1)`.	The worst-case complexity for insertion is `O(n)`.
Deletion complexity	Deletion is slow. Average and worst-case complexity is `O(n)`.	Average and worst-case complexity is `O(1)`.	The worst-case complexity for deletion is `O(n)`.

Let's consider an example to understand when the binary search tree is a good choice to store the data. Let's assume that we have the following data nodes—**5, 3, 7, 1, 4, 6**, and **9**. If we use a list to store this data, the worst-case scenario will require us to search through the entire list of seven elements for finding the item. So, it will require seven comparisons to search for item **9** in this data node:

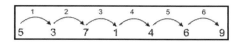

However, if we use a binary search tree to store these values, as shown in the following diagram, in the worst-case scenario, we would require three comparisons to search for item **9**:

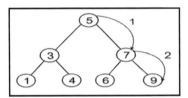

However, it is important to note that the efficiency of searching also depends on how we built the binary search tree. If the tree hasn't been constructed properly, it can be slow. For example, if we had inserted the elements into the tree in the order {1, 3, 4, 5, 6, 7,9}, as shown in the following diagram, then the tree would not be more efficient than the list:

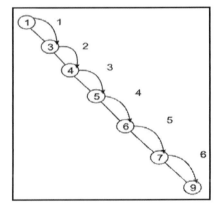

Thus, choosing a self-balancing tree helps to improve the `search` operation. Here, we should note that the binary search tree is a better choice in most of the cases; however, we should try to balance the tree.

Balancing trees

We have seen in the previous section that if nodes are inserted into a tree in a sequential order, it becomes slow and behaves more or less like a list; that is, each node has exactly one child node. To improve the performance of the tree data structure, we generally like to reduce the height of the tree as much as possible to balance the tree by filling up each row in the tree. This process is called **balancing the tree**.

There are different types of self-balancing trees, such as red-black trees, AA trees, and scapegoat trees. These balance the tree during each operation that modifies the tree, such as insert or delete. There are also external algorithms that balance a tree. The benefits of these are that you don't need to balance the tree on every single operation and can leave balancing to the point where you need it.

Expression trees

An arithmetic expression is represented by a combination of operators and operands where the operators can be unary or binary. An arithmetic expression can also be represented using a **binary tree**, which is called an expression tree. This tree structure can also be used to parse arithmetic and boolean expressions. In an expression tree, all the leaf nodes contain the operands and non-leaf nodes contain the operators. We should also note that the expression tree will have one of its sub-trees (right sub-tree or left sub-tree) empty in the case of a unary operator.

For example, the expression tree for 3 + 4 would look as follows:

For a slightly more complex expression, (4 + 5) * (5-3), we would get the following:

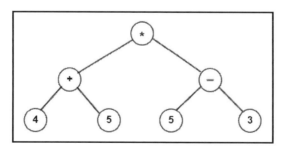

The arithmetic expression can be expressed using three notations (that is, infix, postfix, and prefix), as discussed in the previous section on tree traversal. Due to this, it becomes easy to evaluate an expression tree for the given arithmetic expression. The reverse Polish notation provides faster calculations. We will show you how to construct the expression tree for the given postfix notation in the following subsection.

Parsing a reverse Polish expression

Now, we are going to build up a tree for an expression written in postfix notation. Then, we will calculate the result. We will use a simple tree implementation. To keep it simple, since we are going to grow the tree by merging smaller trees, we only need a tree node implementation:

```
class TreeNode:
    def __init__(self, data=None):
        self.data = data
        self.right = None
        self.left = None
```

In order to build the tree, we are going to enlist the items with the help of a stack. Let's just create an arithmetic expression and set up our stack:

```
expr = "4 5 + 5 3 - *".split()
stack = Stack()
```

Since Python is a language that tries hard to have sensible defaults, its `split()` method splits on whitespace by default. (If you think about it, this is most likely what you would expect.) The result is going to be that `expr` is a list with the values 4, 5, +, 5, 3, −, and *.

Each element of the `expr` list is going to be either an operator or an operand. If we get an operand, then we embed it in a tree node and push it onto the stack. If we get an operator, on the other hand, then we embed the operator into a tree node and pop its two operands into the node's left and right children. Here, we have to take care to ensure that the first pop goes into the right child; otherwise, we will have problems with subtraction and division.

Here is the code to build the tree:

```
for term in expr:
    if term in "+-*/":
        node = TreeNode(term)
        node.right = stack.pop()
        node.left = stack.pop()
    else:
        node = TreeNode(int(term))
    stack.push(node)
```

Notice that we perform a conversion from `string` to `int` in the case of an operand. You could use `float()` instead, if you wish to support floating point operands.

At the end of this operation, we should have one single element in the stack, and that holds the full tree. If we want to evaluate the expression, we would build the following little function:

```
def calc(node):
    if node.data is "+":
        return calc(node.left) + calc(node.right)
    elif node.data is "-":
        return calc(node.left) - calc(node.right)
    elif node.data is "*":
        return calc(node.left) * calc(node.right)
    elif node.data is "/":
        return calc(node.left) / calc(node.right)
    else:
        return node.data
```

In the preceding code, we pass in a node to the function. If the node contains an operand, then we simply return that value. If we get an operator, then we perform the operation that the operator represents on the node's two children. However, since one or more of the children could also contain either operators or operands, we call the `calc()` function recursively on the two child nodes (bearing in mind that all the children of every node are also nodes).

Now, we just need to pop the root node off the stack and pass it into the `calc()` function. Then, we should have the result of the calculation:

```
root = stack.pop()
result = calc(root)
print(result)
```

Running this program should yield the result 18, which is the result of `(4 + 5) * (5 - 3)`.

Heaps

A heap data structure is a specialization of a tree in which the nodes are ordered in a specific way. Heaps are divided into `max` heaps and `min` heaps.

In a max heap, each parent node value must always be greater than or equal to its children. It follows that the root node must be the greatest value in the tree. Consider the following diagram for the max heap, where all the nodes have greater values compared to their children:

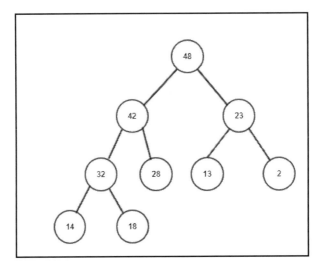

In a min heap, each parent node must be less than or equal to both its children. As a consequence, the root node holds the lowest value. Consider the following diagram for the min heap, where all the nodes have smaller values compared to their children:

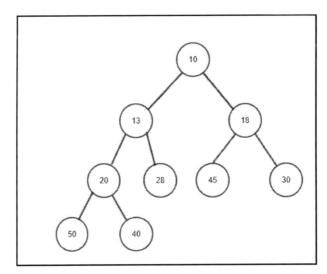

Heaps are used for a number of different things. For one, they are used to implement priority queues. There is also a very efficient sorting algorithm, called **heap sort**, that uses heaps. We are going to study these in depth in subsequent chapters.

Ternary search tree

A ternary tree is a data structure where each node of the tree can contain up to 3 children. It is different compared to the binary search tree in the sense that a node in a binary tree can have a maximum of 2 children, whereas a node in the ternary tree can have a maximum of 3 children. The ternary tree data structure is also considered a special case of the trie data structure. In trie data structure, each node contains 26 pointers to its children when we use trie data structure to store strings in contrast to the ternary search tree data structure, where we have 3 pointers to its children.

The ternary search tree can be represented as follows:

- Each node stores a character in it
- It has the equal pointer that points to a node that stores a value equal to the current node
- It has the left pointer that points to a node that stores a value smaller than the current node
- It has the right pointer that points to a node that stores a value greater than the current node
- Each node has a flag variable that keeps track of whether that node is the end of a string or not

To better understand the ternary search tree data structure, we will demonstrate it through an example where we insert the strings **PUT**, **CAT**, **SIT**, **SING**, and **PUSH** to an empty ternary tree, as shown in the following diagram:

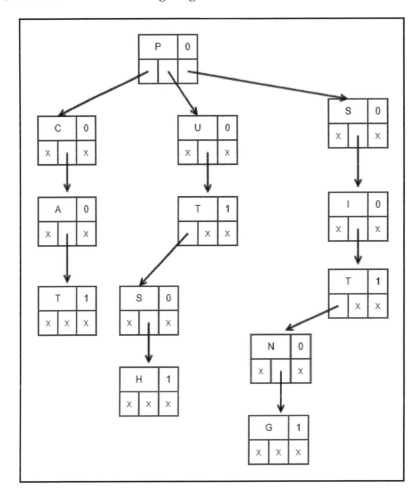

Inserting a value into a ternary search tree is quite similar to how we do it in a binary search tree. In the ternary search tree, we follow these steps to insert a string in the ternary search tree:

1. Since the tree is empty initially, we start by creating the root node with the first character, **P**, and then we create another node for the character **U**, and finally the character **T**.

2. Next, we wish to add the word **CAT**. First, we compare the first character **C** with the root node character, **P**. Since it does not match, and it is smaller than the root node, we create a new node for the character **C** on the left-hand side of the root node. Furthermore, we create the nodes for characters **A** and **T**.

3. Next, we add a new word, **SIT**. First, we compare the first character, **S**, with the root node character, **P**. Since it does not match, and character **S** is greater than character **P**, we create a new node on the right-hand side for the character **S**. Furthermore, we create nodes for characters **I** and **T**.

4. Next, we insert a new word, **SING**, into the ternary search tree. We start by comparing the first character, **S**, to the root node. Since it does not match, and the character **S** is greater than the root node **P**, we look at the next character to the right-hand side, that is, **S**. Here, the character matches, so we compare the next character, which is **I**; this also matches. Next, we compare the character **N**, to the character **T** in the tree. Here, the characters do not match, so we move to the left-hand side of node **T**. Here, we create a new node for the character **N**. Furthermore, we create another new node for the character **G**.

5. Then, we add a new node, **PUSH**, in the ternary search tree. First, we compare the first character of the word, that is, **P**, to the root node. Since it matches, we look at the next character in the ternary tree. Here, the character **U** also matches with the next character of the word. So, we look at the next character of the word, that is, **S**. It doesn't match with the next character in the tree, which is **T**. Therefore, we create a new node for the character **S** to the left-hand side of node **T** since character **S** is smaller than **T**. Next, we create another node for the next character, **H**.

Take note that each node in the ternary tree keeps track of which node is the leaf node or non-leaf node via the use of a flag variable.

Ternary search trees are very efficient for strings searching for related applications such as when we wish to search all of the strings that start with a given prefix, or when we wish to search for a phone number that starts with given specific numbers, spell checks, and so on.

Summary

In this chapter, we looked at tree data structures and their uses. We studied binary trees in particular, which is a subtype of tree where each node has two children at most. We also looked at how a binary tree can be used as a searchable data structure with a BST. The breadth-first and depth-first search traversal modes were also implemented in Python by using queue recursion.

We also looked at how a binary tree can be used to represent an arithmetic or a Boolean expression. We then built an expression tree to represent an arithmetic expression. Afterward, we showed you how to use a stack to parse an expression written in RPN, build up the expression tree, and finally traverse it to get the result of the arithmetic expression.

Finally, we mentioned heaps, a specialization of a tree structure. We have tried to at least lay down the theoretical foundation for the heap in this chapter so that we can go on to implement heaps for different purposes in upcoming chapters.

In the next chapter, we will be discussing the details of hash tables and symbol tables.

7
Hashing and Symbol Tables

We have previously looked at **arrays** and **lists**, where items are stored in sequence and accessed by index number. Index numbers work well for computers. They are integers so they are fast and easy to manipulate. However, they don't always work so well for us. For example, if we have an address book entry, let's say at index number 56, that number doesn't tell us much. There is nothing to link a particular contact with number 56. It is difficult to retrieve an entry from the list using the index value.

In this chapter, we are going to look at a data structure that is better suited to this kind of problem: a dictionary. A dictionary uses a keyword instead of an index number, and it stores data in (key, value) pairs. So, if that contact was called *James*, we would probably use the keyword *James* to locate the contact. That is, instead of accessing the contact by calling *contacts [56]*, we would use *contacts* james.

Dictionaries are a widely used data structure, often built using hash tables. As the name suggests, hash tables rely on a concept called **hashing**. A hash table data structure stores the data in key/value pairs, where keys are obtained by applying a hash function to it. It stores the data in a very efficient way so that retrieval can be very fast. We will discuss all the related issues in this chapter.

We will cover the following topics in this chapter:

- Hashing
- Hash tables
- Different functions with elements

Technical requirements

There is no additional technical requirement, except for the fact that Python needs to be installed on the system. Here is the GitHub link for the source code discussed in this chapter: `https://github.com/PacktPublishing/Hands-On-Data-Structures-and-Algorithms-with-Python-Second-Edition/tree/master/Chapter07`.

Hashing

Hashing is a concept in which, when we give data of an arbitrary size to a function, we get a small simplified value. This function is called a **hash function**. Hashing uses a hash function that maps the given data to another range of data, so that a new range of data can be used as an index in the hash table. More specifically, we will use hashing to convert strings into integers. In our discussions in this chapter, we are using strings to convert into integers, however, it can be any other data type which can be converted into integers. Let's look at an example to better understand the concept. We want to hash the expression `hello world`, that is, we want to get a numeric value that we could say *represents* the string.

We can obtain the unique ordinal value of any character by using the `ord()` function. For example, the `ord('f')` function gives 102. Further, to get the hash of the whole string, we could just sum the ordinal numbers of each character in the string. See the following code snippet:

```
>>> sum(map(ord, 'hello world'))
1116
```

The obtained numeric value, `1116`, for the whole `hello world` string is called the **hash of the string**. Consider the following diagram to see the ordinal value of each character in the string that results in the hash value `1116`:

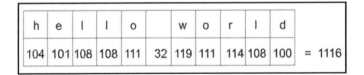

The preceding approach is used to obtain the hash value for a given string and seems to work fine. However, note that we could change the order of the characters in the string and we would have got the same hash; see the following code snippet where we get the same hash value for the world hello string:

```
>>> sum(map(ord, 'world hello'))
1116
```

Again, there would be the same hash value for the gello xorld string, as the sum of the ordinal values of the characters for this string would be the same since g has an ordinal value that is one less than that of h, and x has an ordinal value that is one greater than that of w. See the following code snippet:

```
>>> sum(map(ord, 'gello xorld'))
1116
```

Look at the following diagram, where we can observe that the hash value for this string is again, 1116:

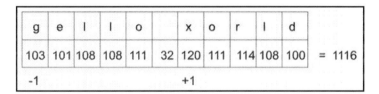

Perfect hashing functions

A **perfect hashing function** is the one by which we get a unique hash value for a given string (it can be any data type, here it is a string as we are limiting the discussion to strings for now). In practice, most of the hashing functions are imperfect and face collisions. This means that a hash function gives the same hash value to more than one string; that is undesirable because a perfect hash function should return a unique hash value to a string. Normally, hashing functions need to be very fast, so trying to create a function that gives us a unique hash value for each string is normally not possible. Hence, we accept this fact and we know that we may get some collisions, that is, two or more strings may have the same hash value. Therefore, we try to find a strategy to resolve the collisions rather than trying to find a perfect hash function.

To avoid the collisions of the previous example, we could, for example, add a multiplier, so that the ordinal value of each character is multiplied by a value that continuously increases as we progress in the string. Next, the hash value of the string is obtained by adding the multiplied ordinal value of each character. To better understand the concept, refer to the following diagram:

h	e	l	l	o		w	o	r	l	d	
104	101	108	108	111	32	119	111	114	108	100	= 1116
1	2	3	4	5	6	7	8	9	10	11	
104	202	324	432	555	192	833	888	1026	1080	1100	= 6736

In the preceding diagram, the ordinal value of each character is progressively multiplied by a number. Note that the last row is the result of multiplying the values; row two has the ordinal values of each character; row three shows the multiplier value; and, in row four, we get values by multiplying the values of row two and three so that 104 x 1 equals 104. Finally, we add all of these multiplied values to get the hash value of the hello world string, that is, 6736.

The implementation of this concept is shown in the following function:

```
def myhash(s):
    mult = 1
    hv = 0
    for ch in s:
        hv += mult * ord(ch)
        mult += 1
    return hv
```

We can test this function on the strings that we used earlier, shown as follows:

```
for item in ('hello world', 'world hello', 'gello xorld'):
    print("{}: {}".format(item, myhash(item)))
```

Running this program, we get the following output:

```
% python hashtest.py

hello world: 6736
world hello: 6616
gello xorld: 6742
```

We can see that, this time, we get different hash values for these three strings. Still, this is not a perfect hash. Let's try the strings, ad and ga:

```
% python hashtest.py

ad: 297
ga: 297
```

We still get the same hash value for two different strings. Therefore, we need to devise a strategy for resolving such collisions. We shall look at that shortly, but first, we will study an implementation of a hash table.

Hash tables

A **hash table** is a data structure where elements are accessed by a keyword rather than an index number, unlike in **lists** and **arrays**. In this data structure, the data items are stored in key/value pairs similar to dictionaries. A hash table uses a hashing function in order to find an index position where an element should be stored and retrieved. This gives us fast lookups since we are using an index number that corresponds to the hash value of the key.

Each position in the hash table data structure is often called a **slot** or **bucket** and can store an element. So, each data item in the form of (key, value) pairs would be stored in the hash table at a position that is decided by the hash value of the data. For example, the hashing function maps the input string names to a hash value; the hello world string is mapped to a hash value of 92, which finds a slot position in the hash table. Consider the following diagram:

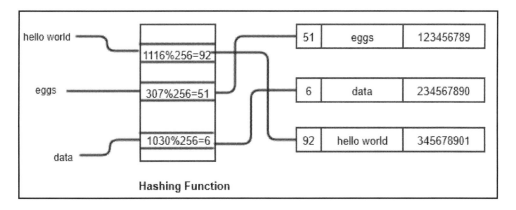

To implement the hash table, we start by creating a class to hold hash table items. These need to have a key and a value since our hash table is a {key-value} store:

```
class HashItem:
    def __init__(self, key, value):
        self.key = key
        self.value = value
```

This gives us a very simple way to store items. Next, we start working on the hash table class itself. As usual, we start off with a constructor:

```
class HashTable:
    def __init__(self):
        self.size = 256
        self.slots = [None for i in range(self.size)]
        self.count = 0
```

The hash table uses a standard Python list to store its elements. Let's set the size of the hash table to 256 elements to start with. Later, we will look at strategies for how to grow the hash table as we begin filling it up. We will now initialize a list containing 256 elements in the code. These are the positions where the elements are to be stored—the slots or buckets. So, we have 256 slots to store elements in the hash table. Finally, we add a counter for the number of actual hash table elements we have:

0	1	2	......	255
empty	empty	empty	......	empty

used slots = 0

It is important to note the difference between the size and count of a table. The size of a table refers to the total number of slots in the table (used or unused). The count of the table refers to the number of slots that are filled, meaning the number of actual (key-value) pairs that have been added to the table.

Now, we have to decide on adding our hashing function to the table. We can use the same hash function that returns the sum of ordinal values for each character in the strings with a slight change. Since our hash table has 256 slots, that means we need a hashing function that returns a value in the range of 1 to 256 (the size of the table). A good way of doing it is to return the remainder of dividing the hash value by the size of the table since the remainder would surely be an integer value between 0 and 255.

As the hashing function is only meant to be used internally by the class, we put an underscore (_) at the beginning of the name to indicate this. This is a normal Python convention for indicating that something is meant for internal use. Here is the implementation of the hash function:

```
def _hash(self, key):
    mult = 1
    hv = 0
    for ch in key:
        hv += mult * ord(ch)
        mult += 1
    return hv % self.size
```

For the time being, we are going to assume that keys are strings. We shall discuss how one can use non-string keys later. For now, the _hash() function is going to generate the hash value for a string.

Storing elements in a hash table

To store the elements in the hash table, we add them to the table with the put() function and retrieve them with the get() function. First, we will look at the implementation of the put() function. We start by embedding the key and the value into the HashItem class and then compute the hash value of the key.

Here is the implementation of the put function to store the elements in the hash table:

```
def put(self, key, value):
    item = HashItem(key, value)
    h = self._hash(key)
```

Once we know the hash value of the key, it will be used to find the position where the element should be stored in the hash table. Hence, we need to find an empty slot. We start at the slot that corresponds to the hash value of the key. If that slot is empty, we insert our item there.

However, if the slot is not empty and the key of the item is not the same as our current key, then we have a collision. It means that we have a hash value for the item that is the same as some previously stored item in the table. This is where we need to figure out a way to handle a conflict.

For example, in the following diagram, the **hello world** key string is already stored in the table, and there is a collision when a new string, `world hello`, gets the same hash value of `92`. Take a look at the following diagram:

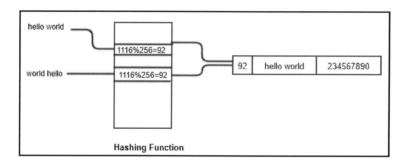

One way of resolving this kind of collision is to find another free slot from the position of the collision; this collision resolution process is called **open addressing**. We can do this by linearly looking for the next available slot by adding 1 to the previous hash value where we get the collision. We can resolve this conflict by adding 1 to the sum of the ordinal values of each character in the key string, which is further divided by the size of the hash table to obtain the hash value. This systematic way of visiting each slot is a linear way of resolving collisions and is called **linear probing**.

Let's consider an example as shown in the following diagram to better understand how we resolve this collision. The hash value for the `eggs` key string is `51`. Now, there is a collision because we have already used this location to store data. Therefore, we add 1 in the hash value that is computed by the sum of the ordinal values of each character of the string to resolve the collision. Hence, we obtain a new hash value for this key string to store the data—location `52`. See the following diagram and code snippet for this implementation:

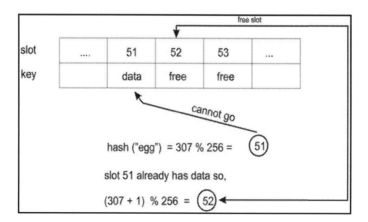

Now, consider the following code:

```
while self.slots[h] is not None:
    if self.slots[h].key is key:
        break
    h = (h + 1) % self.size
```

The preceding code is to check whether the slot is empty, then get the new hash value using the method described. If the slot is empty, to store the new element (that means the slot contained None previously), then we increase the count by one. Finally, we insert the item into the list at the required position:

```
if self.slots[h] is None:
    self.count += 1
self.slots[h] = item
```

Retrieving elements from the hash table

To retrieve the elements from the hash table, the value stored corresponding to the key would be returned. Here, we will discuss the implementation of the retrieval method—the get() method. This method would return the value stored in the table corresponding to the given key.

First of all, we compute the hash of the given key corresponding to the value that is to be retrieved. Once we have the hash value of the key, we look up the hash table at the position of the hash value. If the key item is matched with the stored key value at that location, the corresponding value is retrieved. If that does not match, then we add 1 to the sum of the ordinal values of all the characters in the string, similar to what we did at the time of storing the data, and we look at the newly obtained hash value. We keep looking until we get our key element or we check all the slots in the hash table.

Consider an example to understand the concept in the following diagram in four steps:

1. We compute the hash value for the given key string, "egg", which turns out to be 51. Then, we compare this key with the stored key value at location 51, but it does not match.
2. As the key does not match, we compute a new hash value.
3. We look up the key at the location of the newly created hash value, which is 52; we compare the key string with the stored key value and, here, it matches, as shown in the following diagram.

4. The stored value is returned corresponding to this key value in the hash table. See the following diagram:

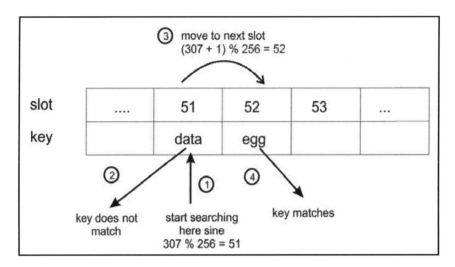

To implement this retrieval method that is, the `get()` method, we start by calculating the hash of the key. Next, we look up at the computed hash value in the table. If there is a match, we return the corresponding stored value. Otherwise, we keep looking at the new hash value location computed as described. Here is the implementation of the `get()` method:

```
def get(self, key):
    h = self._hash(key)     # computer hash for the given key
    while self.slots[h] is not None:
        if self.slots[h].key is key:
            return self.slots[h].value
        h = (h+ 1) % self.size
    return None
```

Finally, we return `None` if the key was not found in the table. Another good alternative may be to raise an exception in case the key does not exist in the table.

Testing the hash table

To test our hash table, we create `HashTable` and store a few elements in it, then try to retrieve them. We will also try to `get()` a key that does not exist. We also use the two strings, `ad` and `ga`, which had the collision and returned the same hash value by our hashing function. To properly evaluate the work of the hash table, we throw this collision as well, just to see that the collision is properly resolved. See the example code, as follows:

```
ht = HashTable()
    ht.put("good", "eggs")
    ht.put("better", "ham")
    ht.put("best", "spam")
    ht.put("ad", "do not")
    ht.put("ga", "collide")

    for key in ("good", "better", "best", "worst", "ad", "ga"):
        v = ht.get(key)
        print(v)
```

Running the preceding code returns the following:

```
% python hashtable.py

eggs
ham
spam
None
do not
collide
```

As you can see, looking up the `worst` key returns `None`, since the key does not exist. The `ad` and `ga` keys also return their corresponding values, showing that the collision between them is properly handled.

Using [] with the hash table

Using the `put()` and `get()` methods doesn't look very convenient to use. However, we would have preferred to be able to treat our hash table as a list, as it would be easier to use. For example, we would like to be able to use `ht["good"]` instead of `ht.get("good")` for the retrieval of elements from the table.

This can be easily done with the special methods, __setitem__() and __getitem__(). See the following code for this:

```
def __setitem__(self, key, value):
    self.put(key, value)

def __getitem__(self, key):
    return self.get(key)
```

Now, our test code would be like the following:

```
ht = HashTable()
ht["good"] = "eggs"
ht["better"] = "ham"
ht["best"] = "spam"
ht["ad"] = "do not"
ht["ga"] = "collide"

for key in ("good", "better", "best", "worst", "ad", "ga"):
    v = ht[key]
    print(v)

print("The number of elements is: {}".format(ht.count))
```

Notice that we also print the number of elements already stored in the hash table using the count variable.

Non-string keys

In most cases in real-time applications, generally, we need to use strings for the keys. However, if necessary, you could use any other Python types. If you create your own class that you want to use as a key, you will need to override the special __hash__() function for that class, so that you get reliable hash values.

Note that you would still have to calculate the modulo (%) of the hash value and the size of the hash table to get the slot. That calculation should happen in the hash table and not in the key class since the table knows its own size (the key class should not know anything about the table that it belongs to).

Growing a hash table

In our example, we fixed the hash table size to 256. It is obvious that, when we add the elements to the hash table, we would begin to fill up the empty slots, and at some point, all of the slots would be filled up and the hash table will be full. To avoid such a situation, we can grow the size of the table when it is starting to get full.

To grow the size of the hash table, we compare the size and the count in the table. `size` is the total number of the slots and `count` denotes the number of slots that contains elements. So, if `count` is equal to `size`, that means we have filled up the table. The load factor of the hash table is generally used to expand the size of the table; that gives us an indication of how many available slots of the table have been used. The load factor of the hash table is computed by dividing the number of **used** slots by the **total** number of slots in the table. It is defined as follows:

$$\text{load factor} = \frac{n}{k}$$

n is the number of used slots
k is the total number of slots

As the load factor value approaches 1, it means that the table is going to be filled, and we need to grow the size of the table. It is better to grow the size of the table before it gets almost full, as the retrieval of elements from the table becomes slow when the table fills up. A value of 0.75 for the load factor may be a good value to grow the size of the table.

The next question is how much we should increase the size of the table. One strategy would be to simply double the size of the table.

Open addressing

The collision resolution mechanism we used in our example was linear probing, which is an example of an open addressing strategy. Linear probing is simple since we use a fixed number of slots. There are other open addressing strategies as well, however, they all share the idea that there is an array of slots. When we want to insert a key, we check whether the slot already has an item or not. If it does, we look for the next available slot.

If we have a hash table that contains 256 slots, then 256 is the maximum number of elements in that hash. Moreover, as the load factor increases, it will take longer to find the insertion point for the new element.

Because of these limitations, we may prefer to use a different strategy to resolve collisions, such as chaining.

Chaining

Chaining is another method to handle the problem of collision in hash tables. It solves this problem by allowing each slot in the hash table to store a reference to many items at the position of a collision. So, at the index of a collision, we are allowed to store many items in the hash table. Observe the following diagram—there is a collision for the strings, **hello world** and **world hello**. In the case of chaining, both items are allowed to store at the location of the **92** hash value using a **list**. Here is the example diagram to show collision resolution using chaining:

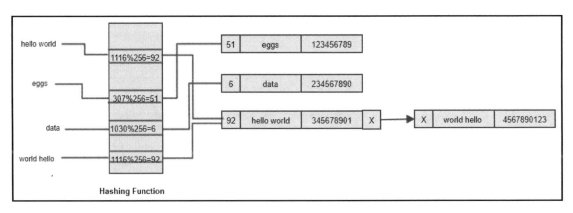

In chaining, the slots in the hash table are initialized with empty lists:

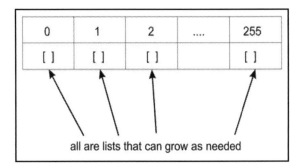

When an element is inserted, it will be appended to the list that corresponds to that element's hash value. That is, if you have two elements that both have a hash value of `1075`, both of these elements would be added to the list that exists in the `1075%256=51` slot of the hash table:

The preceding diagram shows a list of entries with hash value `51`.

Chaining then avoids conflict by allowing multiple elements to have the same hash value. Hence, there is no limit on the number of elements that can be stored in a hash table, whereas, in the case of linear probing, we had to fix the size of the table, which we need to later grow when the table is filled up, depending upon the load factor. Moreover, the hash table can hold more values than the number of available slots, since each slot holds a list that can grow.

However, there is a problem in chaining—it becomes inefficient when a list grows at a particular hash value location. As a particular slot has many items, searching them can get very slow since we have to do a linear search through the list until we find the element that has the key we want. This can slow down retrieval, which is not good, since hash tables are meant to be efficient. The following diagram demonstrates a linear search through list items until we find a match:

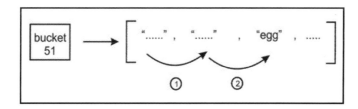

So, there is a problem of slow retrieval of items when a particular position in a hash table has many entries. This problem can be resolved using another data structure in place of using a list that can perform fast searching and retrieval. There is a nice choice of using **binary search trees** (BSTs), which provide fast retrieval, as we discussed in the previous chapter.

We could simply put an (initially empty) BST in each slot as shown in the following diagram:

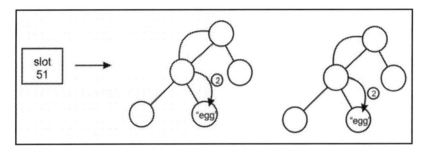

In the preceding diagram, the 51 slot holds a BST, which we use to store and retrieve the data items. But we would still have a potential problem—depending on the order in which the items were added to the BST, we could end up with a search tree that is as inefficient as a list. That is, each node in the tree has exactly one child. To avoid this, we would need to ensure that our BST is self-balancing.

Symbol tables

Symbol tables are used by compilers and interpreters to keep track of the symbols that have been declared and to keep information about them. Symbol tables are often built using hash tables since it is important to efficiently retrieve a symbol from the table.

Let's look at an example. Suppose we have the following Python code:

```
name = "Joe"
age = 27
```

Here, we have two symbols, name and age. They belong to a namespace, which could be __main__, but it could also be the name of a module if you placed it there. Each symbol has a value; for example, the name symbol has the value, Joe, and the age symbol has the value, 27. A symbol table allows the compiler or the interpreter to look up these values. So, the name and age symbols become keys in the hash table. All of the other information associated with them become the value of the symbol table entry.

It's not only variables that are symbols, but functions and classes are also treated as symbols, and they will also be added to the symbol table so that, when any one of them needs to be accessed, they are accessible from the symbol table. For example, the greet() function and two variables are stored in the symbol table in the following diagram:

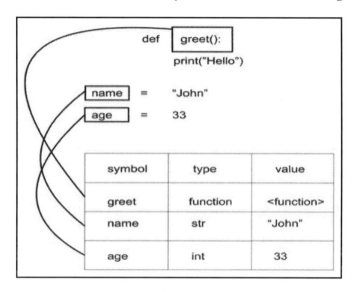

In Python, each module that is loaded has its own symbol table. The symbol table is given the name of that module. This way, modules act as namespaces. We can have multiple symbols of the same name as long as they exist in different symbol tables, and we can access them through the appropriate symbol table. See the following example, showing multiple symbol tables in a program:

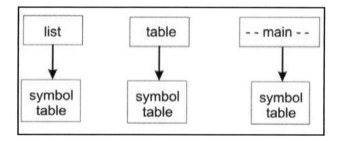

Summary

In this chapter, we looked at hash tables. We looked at how to write a hashing function to turn string data into integer data. Then, we looked at how we can use hashed keys to quickly and efficiently look up the value that corresponds to a key.

Further, we looked at the difficulties in the implementation of hash tables due to collisions in hash values. This led us to look at collision resolution strategies, so we discussed two important collision resolution methods, which are linear probing and chaining.

In the last section of this chapter, we studied symbol tables, which are often built using hash tables. Symbol tables allow a compiler or an interpreter to look up a symbol (such as a variable, function, or class) that has been defined and retrieve all information about it.

In the next chapter, we will talk about graphs and other algorithms.

8
Graphs and Other Algorithms

In this chapter, we will discuss concepts related to the graphs. The concept of graphs comes from a branch of mathematics called **graph theory**. Graphs are used to solve a number of computing problems. Graphs are a non-linear data structure. This structure represents data by connecting a set of nodes or vertices along their edges. It is quite a different data structure compared to what we have looked at so far, and operations on graphs (for example, traversal) may be unconventional. We will be discussing many concepts related to graphs in this chapter. In addition, we will also be discussing priority queues and heaps later in the chapter.

By the end of this chapter, you should be able to do the following:

- Understand what graphs are
- Know the types of graphs and their constituents
- Know how to represent a graph and traverse it
- Get a fundamental idea of what priority queues are
- Be able to implement a priority queue
- Be able to determine the ith smallest element in a list

Technical requirements

All source code discussed in this chapter is provided in the GitHub repository at the following link: `https://github.com/PacktPublishing/Hands-On-Data-Structures-and-Algorithms-with-Python-Second-Edition/tree/master/Chapter08`.

Graphs

A graph is a set of vertices and edges that form connections between the vertices. In a more formal approach, a graph **G** is an ordered pair of a set *V* of vertices and a set **E** of edges, given as `G = (V, E)` in formal mathematical notation.

An example of a graph is given here:

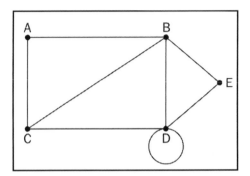

Let's discuss some of the important definitions of a graph:

- **Node or vertex**: A point or node in a graph is called a vertex, which is usually represented in a graph by a dot. In the preceding diagram, the vertices or nodes are **A**, **B**, **C**, **D**, and **E**.
- **Edge**: This is a connection between two vertices. The line connecting **A** and **B** is an example of an edge in the preceding graph.
- **Loop**: When an edge from a node is incident on itself, that edge forms a loop.
- **Degree of a vertex**: The total number of edges that are incident on a given vertex is called the degree of that vertex. For example, the degree of the **B** vertex in the previous diagram is 4.
- **Adjacency**: This refers to the connection(s) between any two nodes; thus, if there is a connection between any two vertices or nodes, then they are said to be adjacent to each other. For example, the **C** node is adjacent to the **A** node because there is an edge between them.

- **Path**: A sequence of vertices and edges between any two nodes represents a path from the **A** vertex to the **B** vertex. For example, **CABE** represents a path from the C node to the E node.
- **Leaf vertex** (also called *pendant vertex*): A vertex or node is called a leaf vertex or pendant vertex if it has exactly one degree.

Directed and undirected graphs

Graphs are represented by the edges between the nodes. The connecting edges can be considered directed or undirected. If the connecting edges in a graph are undirected, then the graph is called an undirected graph, and if the connecting edges in a graph are directed, then it is called a directed graph. An undirected graph simply represents edges as lines between the nodes. There is no additional information about the relationship between the nodes, other than the fact that they are connected. For example, in the following diagram, we demonstrate an undirected graph of four nodes, **A**, **B**, **C**, and **D**, which are connected using edges:

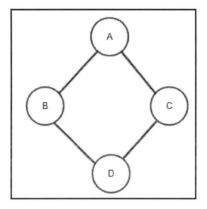

In a directed graph, the edges provide the information on the direction of connection between any two nodes in a graph. If an edge from node **A** to **B** is said to be directed, then the edge (**A**, **B**) would not be equal to the edge (**B**, **A**). The directed edges are drawn as lines with arrows, which will point in whichever direction the edge connects the two nodes. For example, in the following diagram, we show a directed graph where many nodes are connected using directed edges:

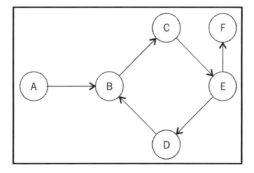

The arrow of an edge determines the flow of direction. One can only move from **A** to **B**, as shown in the preceding diagram—not **B** to **A**. In a directed graph, each node (or vertex) has an indegree and an outdegree. Let's have a look at what these are:

- **Indegree**: The total number of edges that come into a vertex in the graph is called the indegree of that vertex. For example, in the previous diagram, the **E** node has 1 indegree, due to edge **CE** coming into the **E** node.
- **Outdegree**: The total number of edges that goes out from a vertex in the graph is called the outdegree of that vertex. For example, the **E** node in the previous diagram has an outdegree of 2, as it has two edges, **EF** and **ED**, going out of that node.
- **Isolated vertex**: A node or vertex is called an isolated vertex when it has a degree of zero.
- **Source vertex**: A vertex is called a source vertex if it has an indegree of zero. For example, in the previous diagram, the **A** node is the source vertex.
- **Sink vertex**: A vertex is a sink vertex if that has an outdegree of zero. For example, in the previous diagram, the **F** node is the sink vertex.

Weighted graphs

A weighted graph is a graph that has a numeric weight associated with the edges in the graph. It can be either a directed or an undirected graph. This numerical value can possibly be used to indicate distance or cost, depending upon the purpose of the graph. Let's consider an example. The following graph indicates different ways to get from the **A** node to the **D** node. You can either go straight from **A** to **D**, or choose to pass through **B** and **C**, considering that the associated weight with each edge is the amount of time, in minutes, for the journey to the next node:

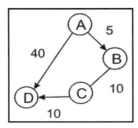

In this example, **AD** and **ABCD** represent two different paths. A path is simply a sequence of edges that you pass through between two nodes. Following these paths, you see that the **AD** journey takes **40** minutes, whereas the **ABCD** journey takes **25** minutes. If the only concern is time, then it would be better to travel along the **ABCD** path, even though it may be a longer route. The point to take away here is that edges can be directed and may hold other information (for example, time taken, distance to be traveled, and so on).

We can implement our graphs in a similar manner to what we have done with other data structures, such as linked lists. With graphs, it makes sense to see edges as objects, just as nodes. Just like nodes, edges can also contain extra information that makes it necessary to follow a particular path. The edges in the graphs can be represented using the links between different nodes; if there is a directed edge in the graph, we can implement it with an arrow pointing from one node to another, which is easy to represent in the node class by using `next` or `previous`, `parent`, or `child`.

Graph representations

Graphs can be represented with two main forms while implementing them in Python. One way is to use an adjacency list, and the other is to use an adjacency matrix. Let's consider an example, shown in the following diagram, to develop both types of representation for graphs:

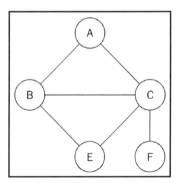

Adjacency lists

An adjacency list stores all the nodes, along with other nodes that are directly connected to them in the graph. Two nodes, A and B, in a graph G, are said to be adjacent if there is a direct connection between them. A `list` data structure in Python is used to represent a graph. The `indices` of the list can be used to represent the nodes or vertices in the graph.

At each index, the adjacent nodes to that vertex are stored. For example, consider the following adjacency list corresponding to the sample graph shown previously:

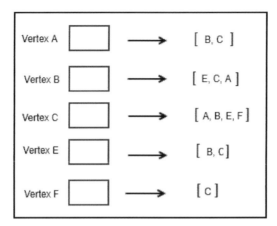

The numbers in the box represent the vertices. The 0 index represents the A vertex of the graph, with its adjacent nodes being B and C. The 1 index represents the B vertex of the graph, with its adjacent nodes of E, C, and A. Similarly, the other vertices, C, E, and F, of the graph are represented at the indices of 2, 3, and 4 with their adjacent nodes, as shown in the previous diagram.

Using a list for the representation is quite restrictive, because we lack the ability to directly use the vertex labels. Therefore, a dictionary data structure is more suitable to represent the graph. To implement the same preceding graph using a dictionary data structure, we can use the following statements:

```
graph = dict()
graph['A'] = ['B', 'C']
graph['B'] = ['E','C', 'A']
graph['C'] = ['A', 'B', 'E','F']
graph['E'] = ['B', 'C']
graph['F'] = ['C']
```

Now we can easily establish that the **A** vertex has the adjacent vertices of **B** and **C**. The **F** vertex has the **C** vertex as its only neighbor. Similarly, the **B** vertex has adjacent vertices of **E**, **B**, and **A**.

Adjacency matrices

Another approach by which a graph can be represented is by using an adjacency matrix. A matrix is a two-dimensional array. The idea here is to represent the cells with a 1 or 0, depending on whether two vertices are connected by an edge or not. We demonstrate an example graph, along with its corresponding adjacency matrix, in the following diagram:

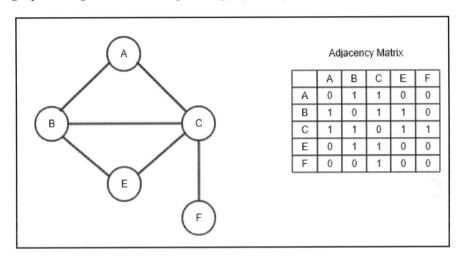

An adjacency matrix can be implemented using the given an adjacency list. To implement the adjacency matrix, let's take the previous dictionary-based implementation of the graph. Firstly, we have to obtain the key elements of the adjacency matrix. It is important to note that these matrix elements are the vertices of the graph. We can get the key elements by sorting the keys of the graph. The code snippet for this is as follows:

```
matrix_elements = sorted(graph.keys())
cols = rows = len(matrix_elements)
```

Next, the length of the keys of the graph is used to provide the dimensions of the adjacency matrix, which are stored in `cols` and `rows`, and the values in the `cols` and `rows` are equal. We then create an empty adjacency matrix of the right size for the number of `cols` by `rows`, filling it with zeros. The `edges_list` variable will store the tuples that form the edges in the graph. For example, an edge between the A and B nodes will be stored as `(A, B)`. The code snippet to initialize an empty adjacency matrix is as follows:

```
adjacency_matrix = [[0 for x in range(rows)] for y in range(cols)]
edges_list = []
```

The multidimensional array is filled using a nested `for` loop:

```
for key in matrix_elements:
    for neighbor in graph[key]:
        edges_list.append((key, neighbor))
```

The neighbors of a vertex are obtained by `graph[key]`. The key, in combination with the `neighbor`, is then used to create the tuple stored in `edges_list`.

The output of the preceding Python code for storing the edges of the graph is as follows:

```
>>> [('A', 'B'), ('A', 'C'), ('B', 'E'), ('B', 'C'), ('B', 'A'), ('C',
'A'),
    ('C', 'B'), ('C', 'E'), ('C', 'F'), ('E', 'B'), ('E', 'C'),
    ('F', 'C')]
```

The next step in implementing the adjacency matrix is to fill it, using 1 to denote the presence of an edge in the graph. This can be done with the `adjacency_matrix[index_of_first_vertex][index_of_second_vertex] = 1` statement. The full code snippet that marks the presence of edges of the graph is as follows

```
for edge in edges_list:
    index_of_first_vertex = matrix_elements.index(edge[0])
    index_of_second_vertex = matrix_elements.index(edge[1])
    adjacency_matrix[index_of_first_vertex][index_of_second_vertex] = 1
```

The `matrix_elements` array has its `rows` and `cols`, starting from A to all other vertices with indices of 0 to 5. The `for` loop iterates through our list of tuples and uses the `index` method to get the corresponding index where an edge is to be stored.

The output of the preceding code is the adjacency matrix for the sample graph shown previously. The adjacency matrix produced looks like the following:

```
>>>
[0, 1, 1, 0, 0]
[1, 0, 0, 1, 0]
[1, 1, 0, 1, 1]
[0, 1, 1, 0, 0]
[0, 0, 1, 0, 0]
```

At row 1 and column 1, the 0 represents the absence of an edge between A and A. Similarly, at column 2 and row 3, there is a value of 1 that denotes the edge between the C and B vertices in the graph.

Graph traversals

A graph traversal means to visit all the vertices of the graph, while keeping track of which nodes or vertices have already been visited and which ones have not. A graph traversal algorithm is efficient if it traverses all the nodes of the graph in the minimum possible time. A common strategy of graph traversal is to follow a path until a dead end is reached, then traverse back up until there is a point where we meet an alternative path. We can also iteratively move from one node to another in order to traverse the full graph, or part of it. Graph traversal algorithms are very important in answering many fundamental problems—they can be useful to determine how to reach from one vertex to another in a graph, and which path from the A to B vertices in the graph is better than other paths. In the next section, we will discuss two important graph traversal algorithms: **breadth-first search (BFS)** and **depth-first search (DFS)**.

Breadth-first traversal

Breadth-first traversal algorithms work breadth-wise in the graph. A queue data structure is used to store the information of vertices that are to be visited in the graph. We begin with the starting node, the **A** node. Firstly, we visit that node, and then we look up all of its neighboring, or adjacent, vertices. We first visit these adjacent vertices one by one, while adding their neighbors to the list of vertices that are to be visited. We follow this process until we have visited all the vertices of the graph, ensuring that no vertex is visited twice.

Let's consider an example to better understand breadth-first traversal for graphs, using the following diagram:

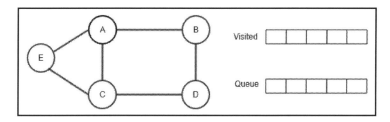

In the preceding diagram, we have a graph of five nodes on the left, and on the right, a queue data structure to store the vertices to be visited. We start visiting the first node, **A**, and then add all its adjacent vertices, **B**, **C**, and **E**, to the queue. Here, it is important to note that there are multiple ways of adding the adjacent nodes to the queue, since there are three nodes, **B**, **C**, and **E**, that can be added in the queue as either **BCE**, **CEB**, **CBE**, **BEC**, or **ECB**, each of which would give us different tree traversal results.

All of these possible solutions to the graph traversal are correct, but in this example, we will add the nodes in alphabetical order. The **A** node is visited as shown:

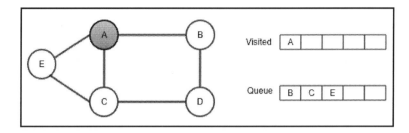

Once we have visited the **A** vertex, next, we visit its first adjacent vertex, **B**, and add those adjacent vertices that are not already added in the queue or not visited. In this case, we have to add the **D** vertex to the queue:

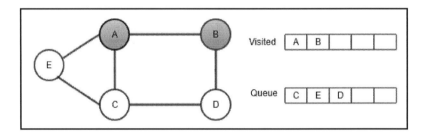

Now, after visiting the **B** vertex, we visit the next vertex from the queue—the **C** vertex. And again, add those of its adjacent vertices that have not already been added in the queue. In this case, there are no unrecorded vertices left, so there is no need to do anything:

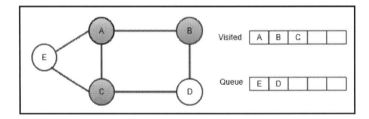

After visiting the **C** vertex, we visit the next vertex from the queue, the **E** vertex:

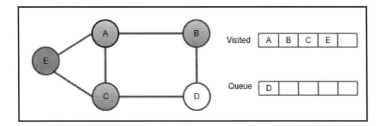

Similarly, after visiting the **E** vertex, we visit the **D** vertex in the last step:

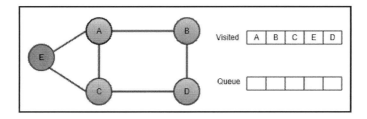

Therefore, the BFS algorithm for traversing the preceding graph visits the vertices in the order of **A-B-C-E-D**. This is one of the possible solutions to the BFS traversal for the preceding graph, but we can get many possible solutions, depending on how we add the adjacent nodes to the queue.

To learn the implementation of this algorithm in Python, let's consider another example of an undirected graph. Consider the following diagram as a graph:

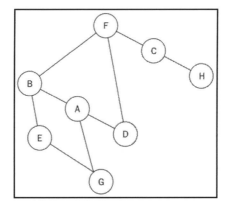

The adjacency list for the graph is as follows:

```
graph = dict()
graph['A'] = ['B', 'G', 'D']
graph['B'] = ['A', 'F', 'E']
graph['C'] = ['F', 'H']
graph['D'] = ['F', 'A']
graph['E'] = ['B', 'G']
graph['F'] = ['B', 'D', 'C']
graph['G'] = ['A', 'E']
graph['H'] = ['C']
```

To traverse this graph using the breadth-first algorithm, we will employ the use of a queue. The algorithm creates a list to store the vertices that have been visited as the traversal process proceeds. We shall start our traversal from the A node.

The A node is queued and added to the list of visited nodes. Afterward, we use a `while` loop to effect traversal of the graph. In the `while` loop, the A node is dequeued. Its unvisited adjacent nodes, B, G, and D, are sorted in alphabetical order and queued up. The queue will now contain the B, D, and G nodes. These nodes are also added to the list of visited nodes. At this point, we start another iteration of the `while` loop, because the queue is not empty, which also means that we are not really done with the traversal.

The B node is dequeued. Out of its adjacent nodes, A, F, and E, node A has already been visited. Therefore, we only queue the E and F nodes in alphabetical order. The E and F nodes are then added to the list of visited nodes.

Our queue now holds the following nodes at this point—D, G, E, and F. The list of visited nodes contains A, B, D, G, E, and F.

The D node is dequeued, but all of its adjacent nodes have been visited, so we simply dequeue it. The next node at the front of the queue is G. We dequeue the G node, but we also find out that all its adjacent nodes have been visited, because they are in the list of visited nodes. So, the G node is also dequeued. We dequeue the E node too, because all of its nodes have also been visited. The only node in the queue now is the F node.

The F node is dequeued, and we realize that out of its adjacent nodes, B, D, and C, only C has not been visited. We then enqueue the C node and add it to the list of visited nodes. Then, the C node is dequeued. C has the adjacent nodes of F and H, but F has already been visited, leaving the H node. The H node is enqueued and added to the list of visited nodes.

Finally, the last iteration of the `while` loop will lead to the H node being dequeued. Its only adjacent node, C, has already been visited. Once the queue is completely empty, the loop breaks.

The output of the traversal the graph in the diagram is A, B, D, G, E, F, C, and H.

The code for a BFS is as follows:

```python
from collections import deque

def breadth_first_search(graph, root):
    visited_vertices = list()
    graph_queue = deque([root])
    visited_vertices.append(root)
    node = root

    while len(graph_queue) > 0:
        node = graph_queue.popleft()
        adj_nodes = graph[node]

        remaining_elements =
            set(adj_nodes).difference(set(visited_vertices))
        if len(remaining_elements) > 0:
            for elem in sorted(remaining_elements):
                visited_vertices.append(elem)
                graph_queue.append(elem)

    return visited_vertices
```

When we want to find out whether a set of nodes are in the list of visited nodes, we use the `remaining_elements = set(adj_nodes).difference(set(visited_vertices))` statement. This uses the `set` object's `difference` method to find the nodes that are in `adj_nodes`, but not in `visited_vertices`.

In the worst-case scenario, each vertex or node and the edge will be traversed, thus the time complexity of the BFS algorithm is $O(|V| + |E|)$, where $|V|$ is the number of vertices or nodes, while $|E|$ is the number of edges in the graph.

Depth-first search

As the name suggests, the DFS algorithm traverses the depth of any particular path in the graph before traversing its breadth. As such, child nodes are visited first before sibling nodes. The `stack` data structure is used to implement the DFS algorithm.

We start by visiting the A node, and then we look at the neighbors of the A vertex, then a neighbor of that neighbor, and so on. Let's consider the following graph in the context of DFS:

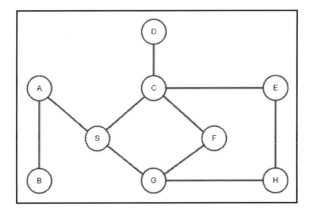

After visiting the **A** vertex, we visit one of its neighbors, **B**, as shown:

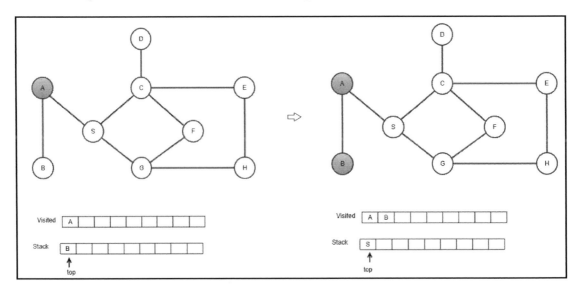

After visiting the **B** vertex, we look at another neighbor of **A**, that is, **S**, as there is no vertex connected to **B** which can be visited. Next, we look for the neighbors of the **S** vertex, which are the **C** and **G** vertices. We visit **C** as follows:

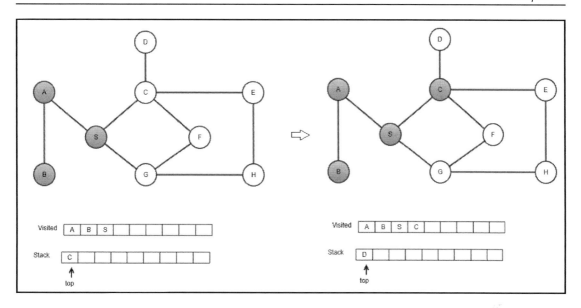

After visiting the **C** node, we visit its neighboring vertices, **D** and **E**:

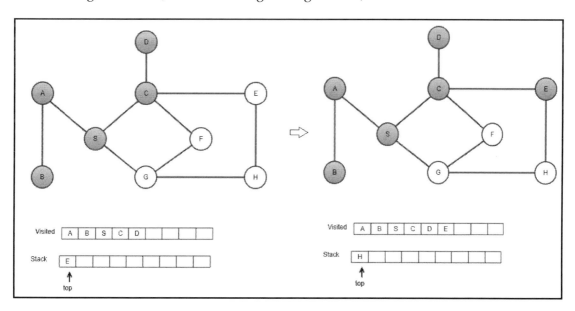

Similarly, after visiting the **E** vertex, we visit the **H** and **F** vertices, as shown in the following graphs:

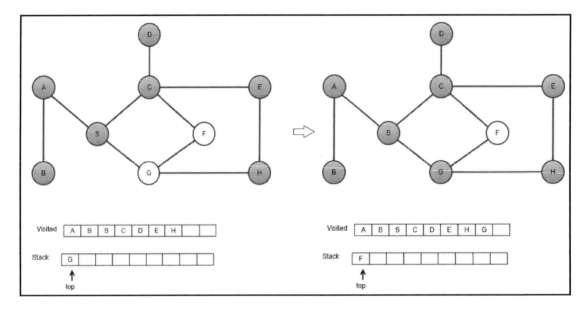

Finally, we visit the **F** node:

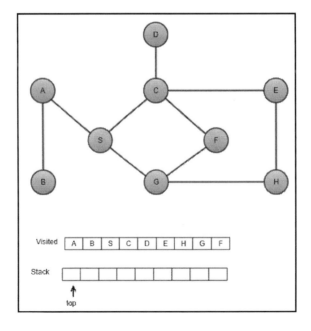

The output of the DFS traversal is **A-B-S-C-D-E-H-G-F**.

To implement the DFS, we start with the adjacency list of the given graph. Here is the adjacency list of the preceding graph:

```
graph = dict()
    graph['A'] = ['B', 'S']
    graph['B'] = ['A']
    graph['S'] = ['A','G','C']
    graph['D'] = ['C']
    graph['G'] = ['S','F','H']
    graph['H'] = ['G','E']
    graph['E'] = ['C','H']
    graph['F'] = ['C','G']
    graph['C'] = ['D','S','E','F']
```

The implementation of the DFS algorithm begins by creating a list to store the visited nodes. The `graph_stack` stack variable is used to aid the traversal process. We are using a regular Python list as a stack. The starting node, called `root`, is passed with the graph's adjacency matrix, graph. `root` is pushed onto the stack. `node = root` holds the first node in the stack:

```
def depth_first_search(graph, root):
    visited_vertices = list()
    graph_stack = list()

    graph_stack.append(root)
    node = root
```

The body of the `while` loop will be executed, provided the stack is not empty. If `node` is not in the list of visited nodes, we add it. All adjacent nodes to `node` are collected by `adj_nodes = graph[node]`. If all the adjacent nodes have been visited, we pop that node from the stack and set `node` to `graph_stack[-1]`. `graph_stack[-1]` is the top node on the stack. The `continue` statement jumps back to the beginning of the `while` loop's test condition.

```
while len(graph_stack) > 0:
    if node not in visited_vertices:
        visited_vertices.append(node)
    adj_nodes = graph[node]
    if set(adj_nodes).issubset(set(visited_vertices)):
        graph_stack.pop()
        if len(graph_stack) > 0:
            node = graph_stack[-1]
        continue
    else:
```

```
                remaining_elements =
                set(adj_nodes).difference(set(visited_vertices))

        first_adj_node = sorted(remaining_elements)[0]
        graph_stack.append(first_adj_node)
        node = first_adj_node
    return visited_vertices
```

If, on the other hand, not all the adjacent nodes have been visited, then the nodes that are yet to be visited are obtained by finding the difference between the `adj_nodes` and `visited_vertices` with the `remaining_elements = set(adj_nodes).difference(set(visited_vertices))` statement.

The first item within `sorted(remaining_elements)` is assigned to `first_adj_node`, and pushed onto the stack. We then point the top of the stack to this node.

When the `while` loop exists, we will return `visited_vertices`.

We will now explain the working of the source code by relating it to the previous example. The **A** node is chosen as our starting node. **A** is pushed onto the stack and added to the `visisted_vertices` list. In doing so, we mark it as having been visited. The `graph_stack` stack is implemented with a simple Python list. Our stack now has A as its only element. We examine the **A** node's adjacent nodes, **B** and **S**. To test whether all the adjacent nodes of **A** have been visited, we use the `if` statement:

```
if set(adj_nodes).issubset(set(visited_vertices)):
    graph_stack.pop()
    if len(graph_stack) > 0:
        node = graph_stack[-1]
    continue
```

If all the nodes have been visited, we pop the top of the stack. If the `graph_stack` stack is not empty, we assign the node on top of the stack to `node`, and start the beginning of another execution of the body of the `while` loop. The `set(adj_nodes).issubset(set(visited_vertices))` statement will evaluate to `True` if all the nodes in `adj_nodes` are a subset of `visited_vertices`. If the `if` statement fails, it means that some nodes remain to be visited. We obtain that list of nodes with `remaining_elements = set(adj_nodes).difference(set(visited_vertices))`.

Referring to the diagram, the **B** and **S** nodes will be stored in `remaining_elements`. We will access the list in alphabetical order as follows:

```
first_adj_node = sorted(remaining_elements)[0]
graph_stack.append(first_adj_node)
node = first_adj_node
```

We sort `remaining_elements` and return the first node to `first_adj_node`. This will return **B**. We push the **B** node onto the stack by appending it to the `graph_stack`. We prepare the **B** node for access by assigning it to `node`.

On the next iteration of the `while` loop, we add the **B** node to the list of `visited nodes`. We discover that the only adjacent node to **B**, which is **A**, has already been visited. Because all the adjacent nodes of **B** have been visited, we pop it off the stack, leaving **A** as the only element on the stack. We return to **A** and examine whether all of its adjacent nodes have been visited. The **A** node now has **S** as the only unvisited node. We push **S** to the stack and begin the whole process again.

The output of the traversal is `A-B-S-C-D-E-H-G-F`.

DFS find applications in solving maze problems, finding connected components, and finding the bridges of a graph, among others.

Other useful graph methods

It is very often that we need to use graphs for finding a path between two nodes. Sometimes, it is necessary to find all the paths between nodes, and in some situations, we might need to find the shortest path between nodes. For example, in routing applications, we generally use various algorithms to determine the shortest path from the source node to the destination node. For an unweighted graph, we would simply determine the path with the lowest number of edges between them. If a weighted graph is given, we have to calculate the total weight of passing through a set of edges.

Thus, in a different situation, we may have to find the longest or shortest path using different algorithms.

Priority queues and heaps

A priority queue is a data structure which is similar to the queue and stack data structures that stores data along with the priority associated with it. In the priority queue, the item with the highest priority is served first. Priority queues are often implemented using a heap, since it is very efficient for this purpose; however, it can be implemented using other data structures. It is a modified queue that returns the items in the order of highest priority, whereas the queue returns the items in the order that the items were added. The priority queue is used in many applications, such as CPU scheduling.

Let's consider an example to demonstrate the importance of priority queues over regular queues. Assume that, in a store, customers queue in a line where service is rendered only at the front of the queue. Each customer will spend some time in the queue before getting served. If the units of time spent by four customers in the queue are 4, 30, 2, and 1 respectively, then the average time spent in the queue becomes (4 + 34 + 36 + 37)/4, which is 27.75. However, if we associate the priority condition with the data stored in the queue, then we can give more priority to the customer that spends the least time. In this situation, the customers will be served in the order of time spent by the customers, that is, in the order of 1, 2, 4, then 30. Thus, the average waiting time would be (1 + 3 + 7 + 37)/4, which now equals 12—a better average waiting time. Clearly, there is merit to serving the customers by the least time spent. This method of selecting the next item by priority, or some other criterion, is the basis for creating priority queues. Priority queues are mostly implemented using heaps.

A heap is a data structure that satisfies a heap property. A heap property states that there must be a certain relationship between a parent node and its child nodes. This property must apply throughout the entire heap.

In a min heap, the relationship between parent and children is that the value at the parent must always be less than or equal to its children. As a consequence of this, the lowest element in the heap must be the root node.

In a max heap, on the other hand, the parent is greater than or equal to its child or its children. It follows from this that the largest value makes up the root node.

The heaps are binary trees, and although we are going to use a binary tree, we will actually use a list to represent it. The heap stores a complete binary tree. A complete binary tree is one in which each row must be fully filled before starting to fill the next row, as shown in the following diagram:

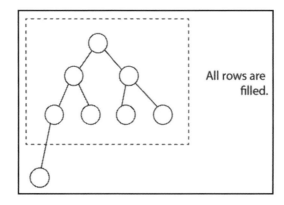

All rows are filled.

To make the math with indexes easier, we are going to leave the first item in the list (index 0) empty. After that, we place the tree nodes into the list, from top to bottom and left to right, as shown in the following diagram:

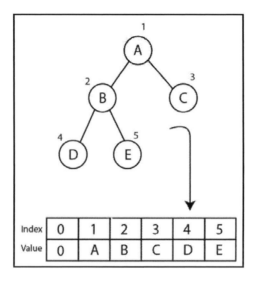

If you observe carefully, you will notice that you can retrieve the children of any node at the n index very easily. The left child is located at 2n, and the right child is located at 2n + 1. This will always hold true. For example, the C node would be at the 3 index, as **C** is a right child of the **A** node, whose index is 1, so it becomes 2n+1 = 2*1 + 1 = 3.

Let's discuss the implementation of the min heap using Python, as implementing the max heap will be more straightforward once we understand the min heap. We start with the heap class, as follows:

```
class Heap:
    def __init__(self):
        self.heap = [0]
        self.size = 0
```

We initialize our heap list with a zero to represent the dummy first element (remember that we are only doing this to make the math simpler). We also create a variable to hold the size of the heap. This would not be necessary as such, since we could check the size of the list, but we would always have to remember to reduce it by one. So, we choose to keep a separate variable instead.

Insert operation

Inserting an item to the min heap works in two steps. First, we add the new element to the end of the list (which we understand to be the bottom of the tree), and we increment the size of the heap by one. Secondly, after each insertion operation, we need to arrange the new element up in the heap tree, to organize all the nodes in such a way that it satisfies the heap property. This is to remind us that the lowest element in the min-heap needs to be the root element.

We first create a helper method, called `arrange`, that takes care of arranging all the nodes after insertion. Let's consider an example of adding an element in the min heap. We provide an example heap in the following diagram, and want to insert the value of 2 in it:

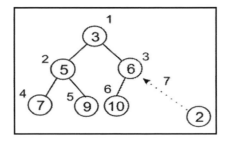

The new element has occupied the last slot in the third row or level. Its index value is **7**. Now we compare that value with its parent. The parent is at index 7/2 = 3 (integer division). That element holds **6**, so we swap the **2**, as follows:

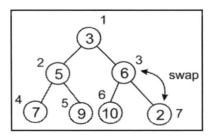

Our new element has been swapped and moved up to the **3** index. We have not reached the top of the heap yet (3/2 > 0), so we continue. The new parent of our element is at index 3/2=1. So we compare and, if necessary, swap again:

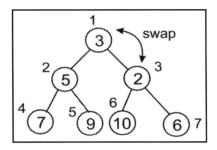

After the final swap, we are left with a heap that looks as follows. Notice that it adheres to the definition of a heap:

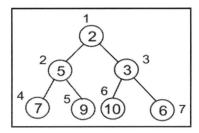

Here is the implementation of `arrange()` method after we insert an element into the min-heap:

```
def arrange(self, k):
```

We are going to loop until we have reached the root node, so that we can keep arranging the element up as high as it needs to go. Since we are using integer division, as soon as we get below 2, the loop will break out:

```
while k // 2 > 0:
```

Compare between the parent and child. If the parent is greater than the child, swap the two values:

```
if self.heap[k] < self.heap[k//2]:
    self.heap[k], self.heap[k//2] = self.heap[k//2],
    self.heap[k]
```

Finally, let's not forget to move up the tree:

```
k //= 2
```

This method ensures that the elements are ordered properly.

Now, we just need to call this from our `insert` method:

```
def insert(self, item):
    self.heap.append(item)
    self.size += 1
    self.arrange(self.size)
```

Notice that the last line in `insert` calls the `arrange()` method to reorganize the heap as necessary.

Pop operation

The `pop` operation removes an element from the heap. The reason for removing an element from the min-heap is, first, to find out the index of the item to be deleted, and then organize the heap so that it satisfies the heap property. However, it is more common to pop off the minimum value from the min-heap, and as per the property of the min-heap, we can get the minimum value by its root value. Therefore, to obtain and remove the minimum value from the min-heap, we remove the root node and re-organize all the nodes of the heap. We also decrement the size of the heap by one.

However, once the root has been popped off, we need a new root node. For this, we just take the last item from the list and make it the new root. That is, we move it to the beginning of the list. However, the selected last node might not be the lowest element of the heap, so we have to reorganize the nodes of the heap. To structure all the nodes according to the min-heap property, we follow a strategy that is opposite to the `arrange()` method that we used while inserting an element into the heap. We make the last node a new root, and then we let it move down (or sink down) as required.

Let's consider an example to help understand this concept in the following heap. First, we pop off the `root` element:

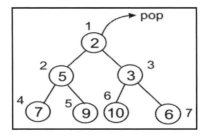

If we choose to move up one of the children of the root, we will have to figure out how to rebalance the entire tree structure, which would have been more complex. So, instead, we do something really interesting. We move up the very last element in the list to fill the position of the `root` element; for example, the last element, **6**, is placed at the root position in the following heap example:

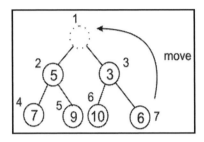

Now, this element is clearly not the lowest in the heap. So, we have to sink it down in the heap. Firstly, we need to determine whether to sink it down toward either the left or right child. We compare the two children, so that the lowest element will be the one to move up as the root sinks down. In the example, we compare the two children of the root, that is, **5** and **3**:

The right child is clearly smaller: its index is **3**, which represents *root index * 2 + 1*. We go ahead and compare our new root node with the value at this index, as follows:

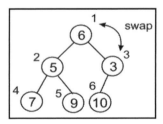

Now our node has moved down to index **3**. We need to compare it to the lesser of its children. However, now we only have one child, so we don't need to worry about which child to compare it against (for a min heap, it is always the lesser child):

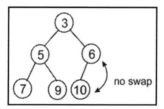

There is no need to swap here. Since there are no more rows, we don't need to do anything else. Notice here that, after the `sink()` operation is completed, the heap adheres to our definition of a heap.

Now we can begin implementing this. But before we implement the `sink()` method, we need to note how we determine which of the children to compare against the parent node. Let's put that selection in its own little method, just to make the code look a little simpler:

```
def minindex(self, k):
```

We may get beyond the end of the list—if we do, then we return the index of the left child:

```
if k * 2 + 1 > self.size:
    return k * 2
```

Otherwise, we simply return the index of the lesser of the two children:

```
elif self.heap[k*2] < self.heap[k*2+1]:
    return k * 2
else:
    return k * 2 + 1
```

Now we can create the `sink` function. As we did before, we are going to loop so that we can sink our element down as far as is needed:

```
def sink(self, k):
    while k*2 <- self.size:
```

Next, we need to know which of the left or the right children to compare against. This is where we make use of the `minindex()` function:

```
mi = self.minindex(k)
```

As we did in the `arrange()` method during the insertion operation, we compare parent and child to see whether we need to make the swap:

```
if self.heap[k] > self.heap[mi]:
    self.heap[k], self.heap[mi] = self.heap[mi],
    self.heap[k]
```

And we need to make sure that we move down the tree, so that we don't get stuck in a loop, as follows:

```
k = mi
```

The only thing remaining now is to implement the main `pop()` method itself. This is very straightforward, as the grunt work is performed by the `sink()` method:

```
def pop(self):
    item = self.heap[1]
    self.heap[1] = self.heap[self.size]
    self.size -= 1
    self.heap.pop()
    self.sink(1)
    return item
```

Testing the heap

Now, let's test the implementation of the heap, and discuss this with an example. We start with the construction of a heap by inserting 10 elements, one by one. Let the elements be {4, 8, 7, 2, 9, 10, 5, 1, 3, 6}. First, we manually create a heap with these elements, and then we will implement it and verify if we are doing it correctly or not:

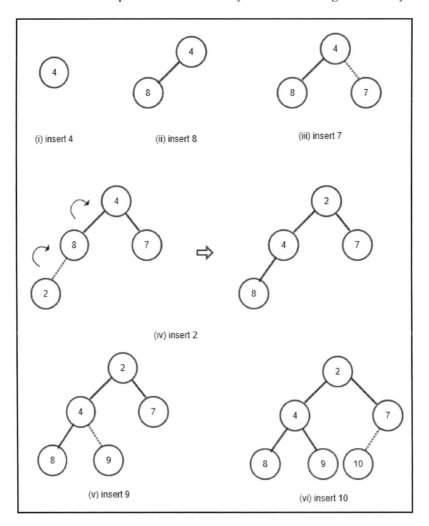

We show, in the preceding diagram, a step-by-step process to insert elements in the heap. Here, we continue adding elements as shown:

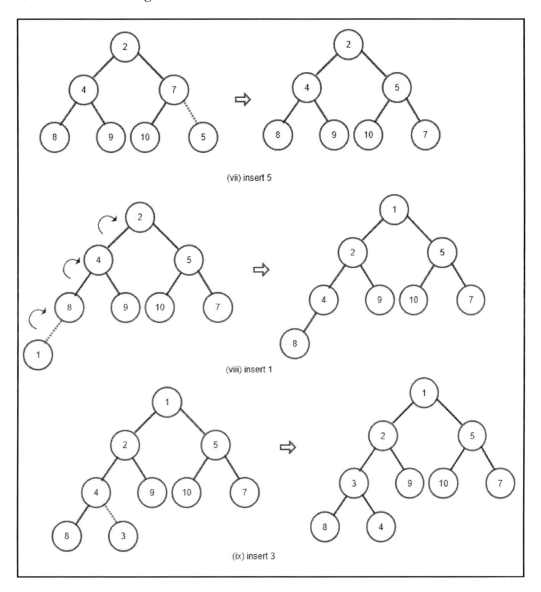

Finally, we insert an element, **6**, to the heap:

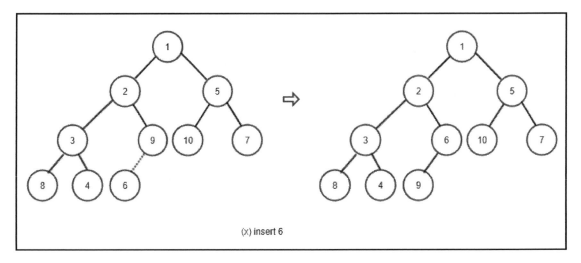

(x) insert 6

Now, let's begin by creating the heap and inserting that data, as shown in the following code:

```
h = Heap()
for i in (4, 8, 7, 2, 9, 10, 5, 1, 3, 6):
    h.insert(i)
```

We can print the heap list, just to inspect how the elements are ordered. If you redraw this as a tree structure, you would notice that it meets the required properties of a heap, similar to what we created manually:

```
print(h.heap)
```

Now we will pop off the items, one at a time. Notice how the items come out in a sorted order, from lowest to highest. Also, notice how the heap list changes after each pop. The sink() method will reorganize all the items in the heap:

```
for i in range(10):
    n = h.pop()
    print(n)
    print(h.heap)
```

We have discussed, in the preceding section, the concepts around using the min-heap, so it should be a simple task to implement a max-heap by simply reversing the logic.

We will use the min-heap that we discussed here again in `Chapter 10`, *Sorting*, on sorting algorithms, and will rewrite the code for sorting the elements in the list. These algorithms are called heap sort algorithms.

Selection algorithms

Selection algorithms fall under a class of algorithms that seek to answer the problem of finding the ith-smallest element in a list. When a list is sorted in ascending order, the first element in the list will be the smallest item in the list. The second element in the list will be the second-smallest element in the list. The last element in the list will be the least-smallest (or, largest) element in the list.

In creating the heap data structure, we have come to understand that a call to the `pop` method will return the smallest element in the min-heap. The first element to pop off a min heap is the smallest element in the list. Similarly, the seventh element to be popped off the min heap will be the seventh-smallest element in the list. Therefore, finding the ith-smallest element in a list will require us to pop the heap i number of times. This is a very simple and efficient way of finding the ith-smallest element in a list.

However, in `Chapter 11`, *Selection Algorithms*, we will study more approaches to find the ith-smallest element in a list.

Selection algorithms have applications in filtering out noisy data, finding the median, smallest, and largest elements in a list, and can even be applied in computer chess programs.

Summary

Graphs and heaps have been discussed in this chapter. The subject of graphs is very important and useful for many real-world applications. We have looked at different ways to represent a graph in Python, using lists and dictionaries. In order to traverse the graph, we used two methods: BFS and DFS.

We then switched our attention to heaps and priority queues, in order to understand their implementation. The chapter ended with a discussion on using the concept of a heap to find the ith-smallest element in a list.

The next chapter will usher us into the arena of searching, and the various methods by which we can efficiently search for items in lists.

9
Searching

One of the most important operations for all data structures is searching for the elements from the stored data. There are various methods to search for an element in the data structures; in this chapter, we shall explore the different strategies that can be used to find elements in a collection of items.

The searching operation is a very important operation for sorting. It is virtually impossible to sort the data without using some variant of a search operation. The sorting algorithm will be fast if the searching algorithm is efficient. In this chapter, we will be discussing different searching algorithms.

The performance of a search operation is heavily influenced by whether the items about to be searched have already been sorted or not, as we will see in the subsequent sections.

By the end of this chapter, you will be able to do the following:

- Understand various searching algorithms
- Understand the implementation of the popular searching algorithm
- Understand the implementation of the binary searching algorithm
- Understand the implementation of interpolation

Technical requirements

The source code used in this chapter is available at the following GitHub link: `https://github.com/PacktPublishing/Hands-On-Data-Structures-and-Algorithms-with-Python-3.7-Second-Edition/tree/master/Chapter09`.

Introduction to searching

Searching algorithms are categorized into two broad types:

- The searching algorithm is applied to the list of items that are already sorted; that is, applied to the ordered set of items
- The searching algorithm is applied to the unordered set of items, which are not sorted

Linear search

The *searching* operation is to find out a given item from the stored data. If the searched item is available in the stored list then it returns the index position where it is located, or else it returns that the item is not found. The simplest approach to search for an item in a list is the linear search method, in which we look for items one by one in the whole list.

Let's take an example of 5 list items {60, 1, 88, 10, 11, 100} to understand the linear search algorithm, as shown in the following diagram:

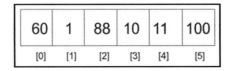

The preceding list has elements that are accessible through the list index. To find an element in the list, we employ the linear searching technique. This technique traverses the list of elements by using the index to move from the beginning of the list to the end. Each element is examined, and if it does not match the search item, the next item is examined. By hopping from one item to the next, the list is traversed sequentially.

We use list items with integer values in this chapter to help you understand the concept, since integers can be compared easily; however, a list item can hold any other data type as well.

Unordered linear search

The linear search approach depends on how the list items are stored—whether they are sorted in order or stored without any order. Let's first see if a list has items that are not sorted.

Consider an example list that contains elements 60, 1, 88, 10, and 100—an unordered list. The items in the list have no order by magnitude. To perform a search operation on such a list, one proceeds from the very first item and compares that with the search item. If the search item is not matched then the next element in the list is examined. This continues till we reach the last element in the list or until a match is found.

Here is the implementation in Python for the linear search on an unordered list of items:

```
def search(unordered_list, term):
    unordered_list_size = len(unordered_list)
    for i in range(unordered_list_size):
        if term == unordered_list[i]:
            return i

    return None
```

The search function takes two parameters; the first is the list that holds our data, and the second parameter is the item that we are looking for, called the **search term**.

The size of the array is obtained and determines the number of times the for loop is executed. The following code depicts this:

```
if term == unordered_list[i]:
    ...
```

On every pass of the for loop, we test if the search term is equal to the indexed item. If this is true, then there is a match, and there is no need to proceed further with the search. We return the index position where the searched item is found in the list.

If the loops run to the end of the list with no match found, then None is returned to signify that there is no such item in the list.

In an unordered list of items, there is no guiding rule for how elements are inserted. Thus, it impacts the way the search is performed. As such, we must visit all the items in the list one after the other. As can be seen in the following diagram, the search for the term **66** starts from the first element and moves to the next element in the list.

Thus, the first **60** is compared with **66**, and if it is not equal, we compare **66** with the next element **1**, then **88**, and so on till we find the search term in the list:

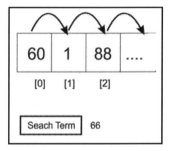

The unordered linear search has a worst-case running time of $O(n)$. All the elements may need to be visited before finding the search term. The worst-case scenario will be when the search term is located at the last position of the list.

Ordered linear search

Another case in a linear search is when the list elements have been sorted; then our search algorithm can be improved. Assuming the elements have been sorted in ascending order, the search operation can take advantage of the ordered nature of the list to make the search more efficient.

The algorithm is reduced to the following steps:

1. Move through the list sequentially
2. If a search item is greater than the object or item currently under inspection in the loop, then quit and return None

In the process of iterating through the list, if the search term is greater than the current item, then there is no need to continue with the search.

Let's consider an example to see how this works. We take a list of items, as shown in the following diagram, and we want to search term 5:

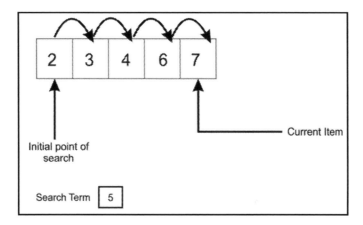

When the search operation starts and the first element is compared with the search term (5), no match is found. However, there are more elements in the list so the search operation moves on to examine the next element. A more compelling reason to move on in the sorted list is that we know the search item may match any of the elements greater than **2**.

After the fourth comparison, we come to the conclusion that the search term cannot be found in any position later in the list where **6** is located. In other words, if the current item is greater than the search term, then it means there is no need to further search the list.

Here is the implementation of the linear search when the list is already sorted:

```
def search(ordered_list, term):
    ordered_list_size = len(ordered_list)
    for i in range(ordered_list_size):
        if term == ordered_list[i]:
            return i
        elif ordered_list[i] > term:
            return None

    return None
```

In the preceding code, the `if` statement now caters for checking if the search item is found in the list or not. `elif` tests the condition where `ordered_list[i] > term`. The method returns `None` if the comparison evaluates to `True`.

The last line in the method returns `None` because the loop may go through the list and still the search item is not matched in the list.

The worst-case time complexity of an ordered linear search is `O(n)`. In general, this kind of search is considered inefficient especially when dealing with large datasets.

Binary search

A binary search is a search strategy used to find elements within a **sorted** array or list; thus, the binary search algorithm finds a given item from the given sorted list of items. It is a very fast and efficient algorithm to search an element, and the only drawback is that we need a sorted list. The worst-case running time complexity of a binary search algorithm is `O(log n)` whereas the linear search has `O(n)`.

A binary search algorithm works as follows. It starts searching the item by dividing the given list by half. If the search item is smaller than the middle value then it will look for the searched item only in the first half of the list, and if the search item is greater than the middle value it will only look at the second half of the list. We repeat the same process every time until we find the search item or we have checked the whole list.

Let's understand the binary search using an example. Suppose we have a book of 1,000 pages, and we want to reach the page number 250. We know that every book has its pages numbered sequentially from 1 upwards. So, according to the binary search analogy, we first check the search item 250 which is less than the 500 (which is the midpoint of the book). Thus, we search the required page only in the first half of the book. We again see the midpoint of the first half of the book, that is, using page 500 as a reference we find the midpoint, that is, 250. That brings us closer to finding the 250th page. And then we find the required page in the book.

Let's consider another example to understand the workings of binary search. We want to search for an item **43** from a list of 12 items, as shown in the following diagram:

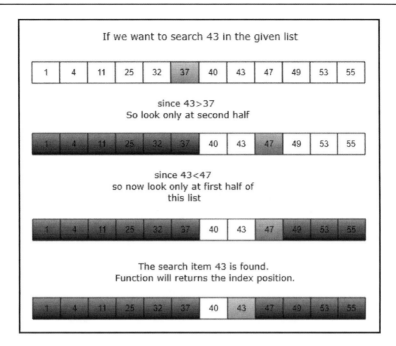

We start searching the item by comparing it to the middle item of the list, which is **37** in the example. If the search item is less than the middle value we only look at the first half of the list; otherwise, we will look in the other half. So we only need to search for the item in the second half. We follow the same concept until we find the search item **43** in the list as shown in the preceding diagram.

The following is the implementation of the binary search algorithm on an ordered list of items:

```
def binary_search(ordered_list, term):

    size_of_list = len(ordered_list) - 1
    index_of_first_element = 0
    index_of_last_element = size_of_list
    while index_of_first_element <= index_of_last_element:
        mid_point = (index_of_first_element + index_of_last_element)//2
        if ordered_list[mid_point] == term:
            return mid_point
        if term > ordered_list[mid_point]:
            index_of_first_element = mid_point + 1
        else:
            index_of_last_element = mid_point - 1
    if index_of_first_element > index_of_last_element:
        return None
```

Let's assume we have to find the position where item **10** is located in the list as follows:

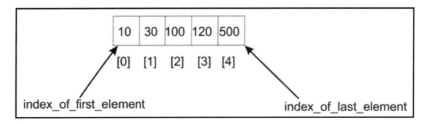

The algorithm uses a `while` loop to iteratively adjust the limits in the list within which we have to find a search item. The terminating condition to stop the `while` loop is that the difference between the starting index, `index_of_first_element`, and the `index_of_last_element` index should be positive.

The algorithm first finds the midpoint of the list by adding the index of the first element (**0**) to that of the last (**4**) and dividing it by **2** to find the middle index, `mid_point`:

```
mid_point = (index_of_first_element + index_of_last_element)//2
```

In this case, the midpoint is `100`, and the value **10** is not found at the middle position in the list. Since we are searching for the item **10**, that is less than the midpoint, so it lies on the first half of the list, thus, we adjust the index range to be `index_of_first_element` to `mid_point-1` as shown in the following diagram, However, if we were searching for **120**, in that case, as 120 is greater than the middle value (100), we would search the item in the second half of the list, and we need to change the list index range to be `mid_point +1` to `index_of_last_element`. It is shown in the following diagram:

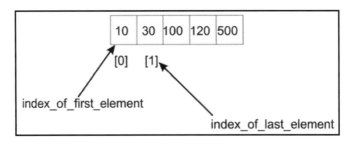

With our new indexes of `index_of_first_element` and `index_of_last_element` now being **0** and **1** respectively, we compute the midpoint `(0 + 1)/2`, which equals 0. The new midpoint is **0**, so we find the middle item and compare it with the search item, `ordered_list[0]`, which yields the value **10**. Now, our search item is found, and the index position is returned.

This reduction of our list size by half, by readjusting the index of
index_of_first_element and index_of_last_element, continues as long as
index_of_first_element is less than index_of_last_element. When this fails to be
the case, it is most likely that our search term is not in the list.

The implementation we discussed is an iterative one. We can also develop a recursive
variant of the algorithm by applying the same principle and shifting the pointers that mark
the beginning and end of the search list. Consider the following code for it:

```
def binary_search(ordered_list, first_element_index, last_element_index,
term):

    if (last_element_index < first_element_index):
        return None
    else:
        mid_point = first_element_index + ((last_element_index -
first_element_index) // 2)

        if ordered_list[mid_point] > term:
            return binary_search(ordered_list, first_element_index,
mid_point-1,term)
        elif ordered_list[mid_point] < term:
            return binary_search(ordered_list, mid_point+1,
last_element_index, term)
        else:
            return mid_point
```

A call to this recursive implementation of the binary search algorithm and its output is as
follows:

```
store = [2, 4, 5, 12, 43, 54, 60, 77]
print(binary_search(store, 0, 7, 2))
```

```
Output:
>> 0
```

Here, the only distinction between the recursive binary search and the iterative binary
search is the function definition and also the way in which mid_point is calculated. The
calculation for mid_point after the ((last_element_index - first_element_index)
// 2) operation must add its result to first_element_index. That way, we define the
portion of the list to attempt the search.

The binary search algorithm has the worst-case time complexity of O(log n). The half of
the list on each iteration follows log(n) of the number of elements and their progression.

It goes without saying that `log x` is assumed to be referring to log base two.

Interpolation search

The interpolation searching algorithm is an improved version of the binary search algorithm. It performs very efficiently when there are uniformly distributed elements in the sorted list. In a binary search, we always start searching from the middle of the list, whereas in the interpolation search we determine the starting position depending on the item to be searched. In the interpolation search algorithm, the starting search position is most likely to be the closest to the start or end of the list depending on the search item. If the search item is near to the first element in the list, then the starting search position is likely to be near the start of the list.

The interpolation search is another variant of the binary search algorithm that is quite similar to how humans perform the search on any list of items. It is based on trying to make a good guess of the index position where a search item is likely to be found in a sorted list of items. It works in a similar way to the binary search algorithm except for the method to determine the splitting criteria to divide the data in order to reduce the number of comparisons. In the case of a binary search, we divide the data into equal halves and in the case of an interpolation search, we divide the data using the following formula:

```
mid_point = lower_bound_index + (( upper_bound_index - lower_bound_index)//
(input_list[upper_bound_index] - input_list[lower_bound_index])) *
(search_value - input_list[lower_bound_index])
```

In the preceding formula, the `lower_bound_index` variable is the lower-bound index, which is the index of the smallest value in the, `upper_bound_index` list, denoting the index position of the highest value in the list. The `input_list[lower_bound_index]` and `input_list[lower_bound_index]` variables are the lowest and highest values respectively in the list. The `search_term` variable contains the value of the item that is to be searched.

Let's consider an example to understand how the interpolation searching algorithm works using the following list of 7 items:

To find **120**, we know that we should look at the right-hand portion of the list. Our initial treatment of binary search would typically examine the middle element first in order to determine if it matches the search term.

A more human-like method would be to pick a middle element in such a way as to not only split the array in half but to get as close as possible to the search term. The middle position was calculated using the following rule:

```
mid_point = (index_of_first_element + index_of_last_element)//2
```

We shall replace this formula with a better one that brings us closer to the search term in the case of the interpolation search algorithm. The `mid_point` will receive the return value of the `nearest_mid` function, which is computed using the following method:

```
def nearest_mid(input_list, lower_bound_index, upper_bound_index,
search_value):

    return lower_bound_index + (( upper_bound_index -lower_bound_index)//
(input_list[upper_bound_index] -input_list[lower_bound_index])) *
(search_value -input_list[lower_bound_index])
```

The `nearest_mid` function takes, as arguments, the lists on which to perform the search. The `lower_bound_index` and `upper_bound_index` parameters represent the bounds in the list within which we are hoping to find the search term. Furthermore, `search_value` represents the value being searched for.

Given our search list, **44, 60, 75, 100, 120, 230,** and **250,** `nearest_mid` will be computed with the following values:

```
lower_bound_index = 0
upper_bound_index = 6
input_list[upper_bound_index] = 250
input_list[lower_bound_index] = 44
search_value = 230
```

Let's compute the `mid_point` value:

```
mid_point= 0 + [(6-0)//(250-44) * (230-44)
         = 5
```

It can now be seen that the `mid_point` value will receive the value 5. So in the case of an interpolation search, the algorithm will start searching from the index position 5, which is the index of the location of our search term. Thus, the item to be searched will be found in the first comparison, whereas in the case of a binary search, we would have chosen **100** as `mid_point`, which would have required another run of the algorithm.

A more visual illustration of how a typical binary search differs from an interpolation is given as follows. In a typical binary search, it finds the **midpoint** that looks like it's in the middle of the list:

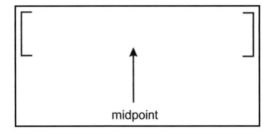

One can see that the **midpoint** is actually standing approximately in the middle of the preceding list. This is as a result of dividing by list two.

In the case of an interpolation search, on the other hand, the **midpoint** is moved to the most likely position where the item can be matched:

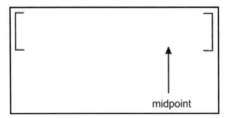

In an interpolation search, the **midpoint** is generally more to the left or right. This is caused by the effect of the multiplier being used when dividing to obtain the **midpoint**. In the preceding diagram, our **midpoint** has been skewed to the right.

The implementation of the interpolation algorithm remains the same as that of the binary search except for the way we compute the **midpoint**.

Here, we provide the implementation of the interpolation search algorithm, as shown in the following code:

```
def interpolation_search(ordered_list, term):

    size_of_list = len(ordered_list) - 1

    index_of_first_element = 0
    index_of_last_element = size_of_list

    while index_of_first_element <= index_of_last_element:
        mid_point = nearest_mid(ordered_list, index_of_first_element,
index_of_last_element, term)

        if mid_point > index_of_last_element or mid_point <
index_of_first_element:
            return None

        if ordered_list[mid_point] == term:
            return mid_point

        if term > ordered_list[mid_point]:
            index_of_first_element = mid_point + 1
        else:
            index_of_last_element = mid_point - 1

    if index_of_first_element > index_of_last_element:
        return None
```

The `nearest_mid` function makes use of a multiplication operation. This can produce values that are greater than `upper_bound_index` or lower than `lower_bound_index`. When this occurs, it means the search term, `term`, is not in the list. `None` is, therefore, returned to represent this.

So what happens when `ordered_list[mid_point]` does not equal the search term? Well, we must now readjust `index_of_first_element` and `index_of_last_element` so that the algorithm will focus on the part of the array that is likely to contain the search term. This is exactly like what we did in the binary search:

```
if term > ordered_list[mid_point]:
    index_of_first_element = mid_point + 1
```

If the search term is greater than the value stored at `ordered_list[mid_point]`, then we only adjust the `index_of_first_element` variable to point to the `mid_point + 1` index.

The following diagram shows how the adjustment occurs. The `index_of_first_element` is adjusted and pointed to the `mid_point+1` index:

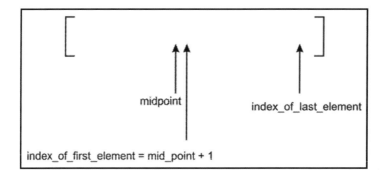

 The diagram only illustrates the adjustment of the midpoint. In interpolation, the midpoint rarely divide the list into two equal halves.

On the other hand, if the search term is less than the value stored at `ordered_list[mid_point]`, then we only adjust the `index_of_last_element` variable to point to the index `mid_point - 1`. This logic is captured in the else part of the if statement `index_of_last_element = mid_point - 1`:

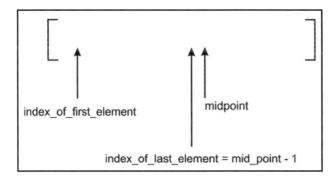

The diagram shows the effect of the recalculation of **index_of_last_element** on the position of the **midpoint**.

Let's use a more practical example to understand the inner workings of both the binary search and interpolation algorithms.

Consider for example the following list of elements:

```
[ 2, 4, 5, 12, 43, 54, 60, 77]
```

At index 0, the value 2 is stored, and at index 7, the value 77 is stored. Now, assume that we want to find the element 2 in the list. How will the two different algorithms go about it?

If we pass this list to the `interpolation search` function, then the `nearest_mid` function will return a value equal to 0 using the formula of `mid_point` computation which is as follows:

```
mid_point= 0 + [(7-0)//(77-2) * (2-2)
        = 0
```

As we get the `mid_point` value 0, we start the interpolation search with the value at index 0. Just with one comparison, we have found the search term.

On the other hand, the binary search algorithm needs three comparisons to arrive at the search term, as illustrated in the following diagram:

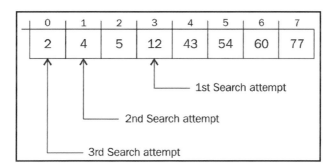

The first `mid_point` value calculated is 3. The second `mid_point` value is 1 and the last `mid_point` value where the search term is found is 0.

Therefore, it is clear that the interpolation search algorithm performs better than binary search in most cases.

Choosing a search algorithm

The binary search and interpolation search algorithms are better in performance compared to both ordered and unordered linear search functions. Because of the sequential probing of elements in the list to find the search term, ordered and unordered linear searches have a time complexity of $O(n)$. This gives a very poor performance when the list is large.

The binary search operation, on the other hand, slices the list in two anytime a search is attempted. On each iteration, we approach the search term much faster than in a linear strategy. The time complexity yields `O(log n)`. Despite the speed gain in using a binary search, the main disadvantage of it is that it cannot be applied on an unsorted list of items, neither is it advised to be used for a list of small size due to an overhead of sorting.

The ability to get to the portion of the list that holds a search term determines, to a large extent, how well a search algorithm will perform. In the interpolation search algorithm, the midpoint is computed in such as way that it gives a higher probability of obtaining our search term faster. The average-case time complexity of the interpolation search is `O( log ( log n))`, whereas the worst-case time complexity of the interpolation search algorithm is `O(n)`. This shows that interpolation search is better than binary search and provides faster searching in most cases.

Summary

In this chapter, we discussed the two important types of search algorithms. The implementation of both linear and binary search algorithms were discussed and their comparisons drawn. The binary search variant, interpolation search, was also discussed in detail in this chapter.

We will be using the concepts of searching for sorting algorithms in the next chapter. We will also use the knowledge that we have gained to perform sorting algorithms on a list of items.

10
Sorting

Sorting means reorganizing the data in such as way that it is in the order of smallest to largest. Sorting is one of the most important issues in data structures and computing. Data is regularly sorted before being sorted, as it can then very efficiently be retrieved, be it a collection of names, telephone numbers, or items on a simple to-do list.

In this chapter, we'll study some of the most important and popular sorting techniques, including the following:

- Bubble sort
- Insertion sort
- Selection sort
- Quick sort
- Heap sort

In this chapter, we compare different sorting algorithms by considering their asymptotic behavior. Some of the algorithms are relatively easy to develop, but may perform poorly, whereas other algorithms are slightly more complex to implement, but show good performance in sorting the list when we have a long lists.

After sorting, it becomes much easier to conduct search operations on a collection of items. We'll start with the simplest of all sorting algorithms; that is, the bubble sort algorithm.

Technical requirements

All source code used to explain the concepts of this chapter is provided in the GitHub repository at the following link: `https://github.com/PacktPublishing/Hands-On-Data-Structures-and-Algorithms-with-Python-Second-Edition/tree/master/Chapter10`.

Sorting algorithms

Sorting means arranging all the items in a list in ascending order of their magnitude. We will be discussing some of the most important sorting algorithms, which each have different performance attributes with respect to runtime complexity. Sorting algorithms are categorized by their memory usage, complexity, recursion, and whether they are comparison-based, among other considerations.

Some of the algorithms use more CPU cycles, and, as such, have bad asymptotic values. Other algorithms chew on more memory and other computing resources as they sort a number of values. Another consideration is how sorting algorithms lend themselves to being expressed recursively, iteratively, or both. There are algorithms that use comparison as the basis for sorting elements. An example of this is the bubble sort algorithm. Examples of a non-comparison sorting algorithm are the bucket sort and pigeonhole sort algorithms.

Bubble sort algorithms

The idea behind the bubble sort algorithm is very simple. Given an unordered list, we compare adjacent elements in the list, and after each comparison, place them in the right order of magnitude. This works by swapping adjacent items if they are not in the correct order. The process is repeated n-1 times for a list of n items. In each such iteration, the largest element is arranged in the end. For example, in the first iteration, the largest element would be placed in the last position of the list, and again, the same process will be followed for the remaining n-1 items. In the second iteration, the second largest element will be placed at the second-to-last position in the list, and the process will then be repeated until the list is sorted.

Let's take a list with only two elements, {5, 2}, to understand the concept of the bubble sort, as shown in the following diagram:

To sort this list, we simply swap the values into the right positions, with **2** occupying index **0** and **5** occupying index **1**. To effectively swap these elements, we need to have a temporary storage area:

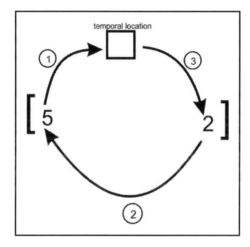

Implementation of the bubble sort algorithm starts with the swap method, illustrated in the preceding diagram. First, element **5** will be copied to a temporary location, `temp`. Then, element **2** will be moved to index **0**. Finally, **5** will be moved from temp to index **1**. At the end of it all, the elements will have been swapped. The list will now contain the elements as [2, 5]. The following code will swap the elements of `unordered_list[j]` with `unordered_list[j+1]` if they are not in the right order:

```
temp = unordered_list[j]
unordered_list[j] = unordered_list[j+1]
unordered_list[j+1] = temp
```

Now that we have been able to swap a two-element array, it should be simple to use this same idea to sort a whole list.

Let's consider another example to understand the working of bubble sort algorithm to sort an unordered list of **6** elements, such as {**45, 23, 87, 12, 32, 4**}. In the first iteration, we start comparing the first two elements, **45** and **23**, and we swap them, as **45** should be placed after **23**. Then, we compare the next adjacent values, **45** and **87**, to see whether they are in the correct order. Swap them if they are not in the correct order. We can see, in the following diagram, that after the first iteration of the bubble sort, the largest element, **87**, is placed in the last position of the list:

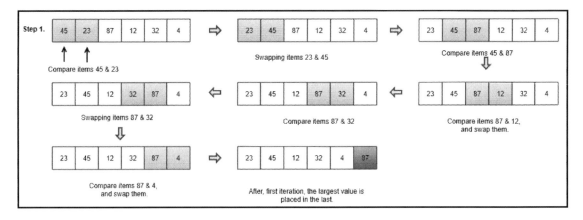

After the first iteration, we just need to arrange the remaining (n−1) elements; we repeat the same process by comparing the adjacent elements for the remaining five elements. After the second iteration, the second largest element, **45**, is placed at the second-to-last position in the list, as shown in the following diagram:

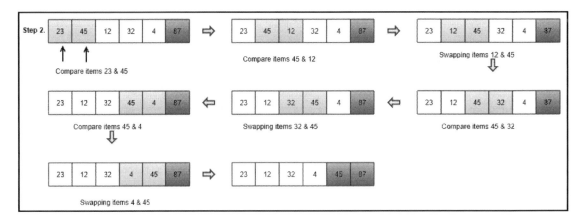

Next, we have to compare the remaining $(n-2)$ elements to arrange them as shown in the following diagram:

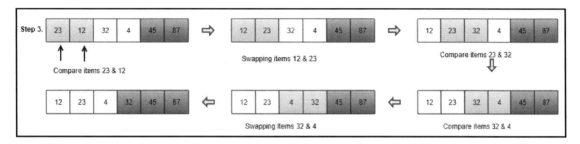

Similarly, we compare the remaining elements to sort them, as well:

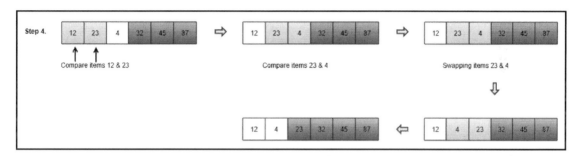

Finally, in the last two remaining elements, we place them in the correct order to obtain the final sorted list, as shown in the following diagram:

The implementation of the bubble sort algorithm would work in a double-nested loop, where the inner loop repeatedly compares and swaps the adjacent elements in each iteration for a given list, and the outer loop keeps track of how many times the inner loop should be repeated. The implementation of the inner loop is as follows:

```
for j in range(iteration_number):
    if unordered_list[j] > unordered_list[j+1]:
        temp = unordered_list[j]
        unordered_list[j] = unordered_list[j+1]
        unordered_list[j+1] = temp
```

It is important to know, when implementing a bubble sort algorithm, how many times the loop will need to run to complete all swaps. To sort a list of three numbers, for example, [3, 2, 1], we need to swap the elements a maximum of two times. This is equal to the length of the list minus 1, and could be written as iteration_number = len(unordered_list)−1. We subtract 1 because it gives us exactly the maximum number of iterations to run. Let's show this with the following example, where, in a list of 3 numbers, by swapping the adjacent elements in exactly two iterations, the largest number ends up at the last position in the list:

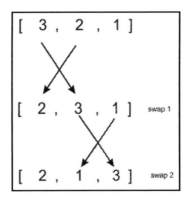

The if statement makes sure that no unnecessary swaps occur if two adjacent elements are already in the right order. The inner for loop only causes the swapping of adjacent elements to occur exactly twice in our list.

How many times does this swapping operation have to occur in order for the entire list to be sorted? We know that, if we repeat the whole process of swapping the adjacent elements a number of times, the list will be sorted. An outer loop is used to make this happen. The swapping of elements in the list results in the following dynamics:

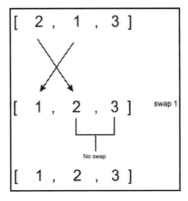

We recognize that a total of four comparisons at most were needed to get our list sorted. Therefore, both inner and outer loops have to run `len(unordered_list)-1` times for all elements to be sorted, as shown:

```
iteration_number = len(unordered_list)-1
    for i in range(iteration_number):
        for j in range(iteration_number):
            if unordered_list[j] > unordered_list[j+1]:
                temp = unordered_list[j]
                unordered_list[j] = unordered_list[j+1]
                unordered_list[j+1] = temp
```

The same principle is used even if the list contains many elements. There are a lot of variations of the bubble sort, too, that minimize the number of iterations and comparisons.

For example, there is a variant of the bubble sort algorithm where, if there is no swapping within the inner loop, we simply quit the entire sorting process, because the absence of any swapping operation in the inner loop suggests that the list has already been sorted. In a way, this can help speed up the algorithm.

The bubble sort is an inefficient sorting algorithm that provides worst-case and average-case runtime complexity of $O(n^2)$, and a best-case complexity of $O(n)$. Generally, the bubble sort algorithm should not be used to sort large lists. However, on relatively small lists, it performs fairly well.

Insertion sort algorithms

The idea of swapping adjacent elements to sort a list of items can also be used to implement the insertion sort. An insertion sorting algorithm maintains a sub-list that is always sorted, while the other portion of the list remains unsorted. We take elements from the unsorted sub-list and insert them in the correct position in the sorted sub-list, in such a way that this sub-list remains sorted.

In insertion sorting, we start with one element, assuming it to be sorted, and then take another element from the unsorted sub-list and place it at the correct position (in relation to the first element) in the sorted sub-list. This means that our sorted sub-list now has two elements. Then, we again take another element from the unsorted sub-list, and place it in the correct position (in relation to the two already sorted elements) in the sorted sub-list. We repeatedly follow this process to insert all the elements one by one from the unsorted sub-list into the sorted sub-list. The shaded elements denote the ordered sub-lists, and in each iteration, an element from the unordered sub-list is inserted at the correct position in the sorted sub-list.

Let's consider an example to understand the working of the insertion sorting algorithm. In our example, we'll be sorting a list of 6 elements: {45, 23, 87, 12, 32, 4}. Firstly, we start with 1 element, assuming it to be sorted, then take the next element, 23, from the unsorted sub-list and insert it at the correct position in the sorted sub-list. In the next iteration, we take the third element, 87, from the unsorted sub-list, and again insert it into the sorted sub-list at the correct position. We follow the same process until all elements are in the sorted sub-list. This whole process is shown in the following diagram:

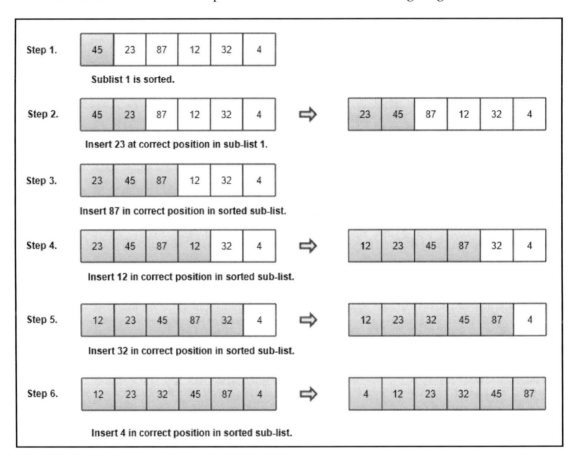

To understand the implementation of the insertion sorting algorithm, let's take another example list of 5 elements, {5, 1, 100, 2, 10}, and examine the process with a detailed explanation.

Let's consider the following array:

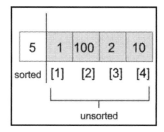

The algorithm starts by using a `for` loop to run between the **1** and **4** indices. We start from index **1** because we assume the sub-array at index **0** to already be in the correctly sorted order:

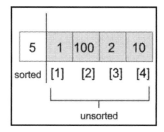

At the start of the execution of the loop, we have the following:

```
for index in range(1, len(unsorted_list)):
    search_index = index
    insert_value = unsorted_list[index]
```

At the beginning of the execution of each run of the `for` loop, the element at `unsorted_list[index]` is stored in the `insert_value` variable. Later, when we find the appropriate position in the sorted portion of the list, `insert_value` will be stored at that index or location:

```
for index in range(1, len(unsorted_list)):
    search_index = index
    insert_value = unsorted_list[index]

    while search_index > 0 and unsorted_list[search_index-1] >
            insert_value :
        unsorted_list[search_index] = unsorted_list[search_index-1]
        search_index -= 1

    unsorted_list[search_index] = insert_value
```

The `search_index` is used to provide information to the `while` loop; that is, exactly where to find the next element that needs to be inserted into the sorted sub-list.

The `while` loop traverses the list backward, guided by two conditions: first, if `search_index` > 0, then it means that there are more elements in the sorted portion of the list; second, for the `while` loop to run, `unsorted_list[search_index-1]` must be greater than the `insert_value` variable. The `unsorted_list[search_index-1]` array will do either of the following things:

- Point to the element, just before the `unsorted_list[search_index]`, before the `while` loop is executed the first time
- Point to one element before `unsorted_list[search_index-1]` after the `while` loop has been run the first time

In our example list, the `while` loop will be executed because *5 > 1*. In the body of the while loop, the element at `unsorted_list[search_index-1]` is stored at `unsorted_list[search_index]`. `search_index -= 1` moves the list traversal backward until it holds a value of `0`.

Our list now looks like the following:

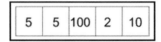

After the `while` loop exits, the last known position of `search_index` (which, in this case, is `0`) now helps us to know where to insert `insert_value`:

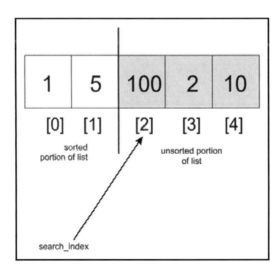

On the second iteration of the `for` loop, `search_index` will have a value of 2, which is the index of the third element in the array. At this point, we start our comparison in the leftward direction (toward index 0). 100 will be compared with 5, but because 100 is greater than 5, the `while` loop will not be executed. 100 will be replaced by itself, because the `search_index` variable never got decremented. As such, `unsorted_list[search_index] = insert_value` will have no effect.

When `search_index` is pointing at index 3, we compare 2 with 100, and move 100 to where 2 is stored. We then compare 2 with 5 and move 5 to where 100 was initially stored. At this point, the `while` loop will break and 2 will be stored in index 1. The array will be partially sorted with the values [1, 2, 5, 100, 10].

The preceding step will occur one last time for the list to be sorted.

The insertion sorting algorithm is considered stable, in the sense that it does not change the relative order of elements that have equal keys. It also only requires no more memory than that consumed by the list, because it does the swapping in-place.

Insertion sorting algorithm gives a worst-case runtime complexity of $O(n^2)$, and a best-case complexity $O(n)$.

Selection sort algorithms

Another popular sorting algorithm is the selection sort. The selection sorting algorithm begins by finding the smallest element in the list, and interchanges it with the data stored at the first position in the list. Thus, it makes the sub-list sorted up to the first element. Next, the second smallest element, which is the smallest element in the remaining list, is identified and interchanged with the second position in the list. This makes the initial two elements sorted. The process is repeated, and the smallest element remaining in the list should be swapped with the element in the third index on the list. This means that the first three elements are now sorted. This process is repeated for $(n-1)$ times to sort n items.

Let's look at an example to understand how the algorithm works. We'll sort the following list of 4 elements using the selection sort algorithm:

5	2	65	10
0	1	2	3

Starting at index **0**, we search for the smallest item in the list that exists between index **1**, and the index of the last element. When this element has been found, it is exchanged with the data found at index **0**. We simply repeat this process until the list is fully sorted.

Searching for the smallest item within the list is an incremental process:

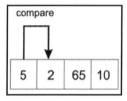

A comparison of elements **2** and **5** selects **2**, as it is the lesser value among these two values, and thus, the two elements are swapped.

After the swap operation, the array looks like this:

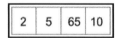

Further, at index **0**, we compare **2** with **65**:

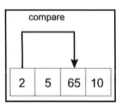

Since **65** is greater than **2**, the two elements are not swapped. A further comparison is made between the element at index **0**, which is **2**, and the element at index **3**, which is **10**. No swap takes place in this case. When we get to the last element in the list, we will have the smallest element occupying index **0**.

In the next iteration, we start comparing elements from position **1** in the index. We repeat the whole process of comparing the element stored at index **1** with all the elements, from index **2** through to the last index.

The second iteration starts by comparing **5** and **65**, which will look like this:

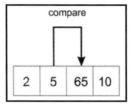

Once we find out that the **5** is the smallest value in the sub-list from indices **1** to **3**, we place it at index **1**. Similarly, the next smallest element from the sub-lists **2** and **3** indices is placed at index **3**.

The following is an implementation of the selection sort algorithm. The argument to the function is the unsorted list of items we want to put in ascending order of magnitude:

```
def selection_sort(unsorted_list):

    size_of_list = len(unsorted_list)

    for i in range(size_of_list):
        for j in range(i+1, size_of_list):

            if unsorted_list[j] < unsorted_list[i]:
                temp = unsorted_list[i]
                unsorted_list[i] = unsorted_list[j]
                unsorted_list[j] = temp
```

The algorithm begins by using the outer `for` loop to go through the list, `size_of_list`, a number of times. Because we pass `size_of_list` to the `range` method, it'll produce a sequence from **0** through to `size_of_list-1`.

 The inner loop is responsible for going through the list and swap elements if we encounter an element less than the element pointed to by `unsorted_list[i]`. Notice that the inner loop begins from `i+1` up to `size_of_list-1`.

The inner loop begins its search for the smallest element from `i+1`, but uses the `j` index:

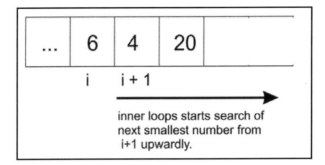

The preceding diagram shows the direction in which the algorithm searches for the next smallest item.

The selection sorting algorithm gives worst-case and best-case runtime complexities of `O(n2)`.

Quick sort algorithms

The quick sort algorithm is very efficient for sorting. The quick sort algorithm falls under the divide and conquer class of algorithms, similar to the merge sort algorithm, where we break (divide) a problem into smaller chunks that are much simpler to solve (conquer).

List partitioning

The concept behind quick sorting is partitioning a given list or array. To partition the list, we first select a pivot. All the elements in the list will be compared with this pivot. At the end of the partitioning process, all elements that are less than the pivot will be to the left of the pivot, while all elements greater than the pivot will lie to the right of the pivot in the array.

Pivot selection

For the sake of simplicity, we'll take the first element in an array as the pivot. This kind of pivot selection degrades in performance, especially when sorting an already sorted list. Randomly picking the middle or last element in the array as the pivot does not improve the performance of the quick sort. We will discuss a better approach to select the pivot and find the smallest element in a list in the next chapter.

An illustration with an example

In this algorithm, we partition an unsorted array into two sub-arrays, in such a way that all the elements on the left side of that partition point (also called a pivot) should be smaller than the pivot, and all the elements on the right side of the pivot should be greater. After the first iteration of the quick sort algorithm, the chosen pivot point is placed in the list at its correct position. After the first iteration, we obtain two unordered sub-lists, and follow the same process again on these two sub-lists. Thus, the quick sort algorithm partitions the list into two parts and recursively applies the quick sort algorithm on these two sub-lists to sort the whole list.

We start by choosing a pivot point with which all the items are to be compared, and at the end of the first iteration, this value will be placed in its correct position in the ordered list. Next, we use two pointers, a left pointer, and a right pointer. The left pointer initially points to the value at index **1**, and the right pointer points to the value at the last index. The main idea behind the quick sort algorithm is to move the items that are on the wrong side of the pivot value. So, we start with the left pointer, moving from in a left-to-right direction, until we reach a position where the item has a greater value than the pivot value. Similarly, we move the right pointer toward the left until we find a value less than a pivot value. Next, we swap these two values indicated by the left and right pointers. We repeat the same process until both pointers cross each other; in other words, when the right pointer index indicates a value less than that of the left pointer index.

Let's take an example of a list of numbers, {**45, 23, 87, 12, 72, 4, 54, 32, 52**}, to understand how the quick sort algorithm works. Let's assume that the pivot point in our list is the first element, **45**. We move the left pointer from index **1** in a rightward direction, and stop when we reach the value **87**, because (**87>45**). Next, we move the right pointer toward the left, and stop when we find the value **32**, because (**32<45**).

Now, we swap these two values, as shown in the following diagram:

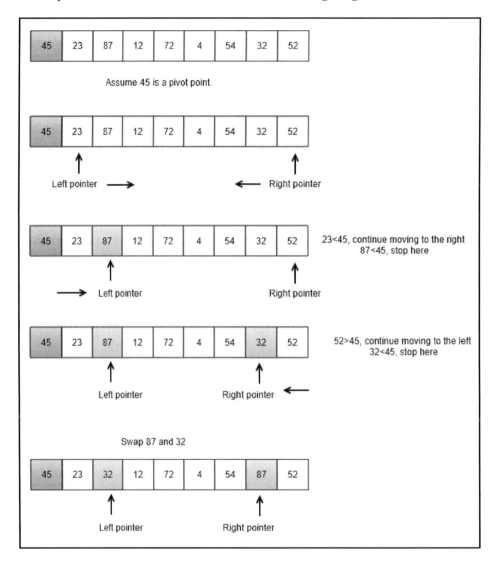

After that, we repeat the same process and move the left pointer toward the right direction, and stop when we find the value **72**, because (**72>45**). Next, we move the right pointer toward the left and stop when we reach the value **4**, because (**4<45**). Now, we swap these two values, because they are in the wrong direction of the pivot value. We repeat the same process and stop once the right pointer index value becomes less than the left pointer index. Here, we find **4** as the splitting point, and swap it with the pivot value. This is shown in the following diagram:

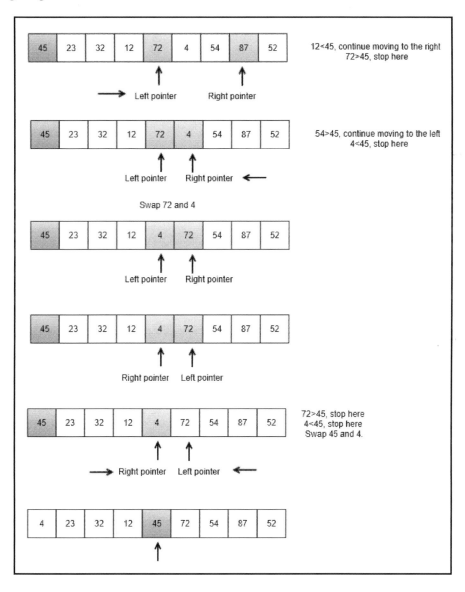

It can be observed that after the first iteration of the quick sort algorithm, the pivot value **45** is placed at its correct position in the list.

Now we have two sub-lists:

1. The sub-list to the left of the pivot value, **45**, has values of less than **45**.
2. Another sub-list to the right of the pivot value contains values greater than 45. We will apply the quick sort algorithm recursively on these two sub-lists, and repeat it until the whole list is sorted.

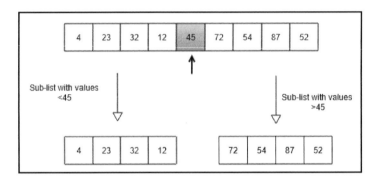

Implementation

The partitioning step is very important in understanding the implementation of the quick sort algorithm, so we will start with an examination of implementing the partitioning first.

Let's look at another example to understand the implementation. Consider the following list of integers. We shall partition this list using the partition function, as follows:

$$[\ 43 \ , \ 3 \ , 20 \ , \ 89 \ , \ 4 \ , 77 \ ]$$

Consider the following code for this:

```python
def partition(unsorted_array, first_index, last_index):

    pivot = unsorted_array[first_index]
    pivot_index = first_index
    index_of_last_element = last_index

    less_than_pivot_index = index_of_last_element
    greater_than_pivot_index = first_index + 1
    ...
```

The partition function receives, as its parameters, the indices of the first and last elements of the array that we need to partition.

The value of the pivot is stored in the `pivot` variable, while its index is stored in `pivot_index`. We are not using `unsorted_array[0]`, because when the unsorted array parameter is called with a segment of an array, index 0 will not necessarily point to the first element in that array. The index of the next element to the pivot, that is, the **left pointer**, `first_index + 1`, marks the position where we begin to look for an element in the array that is greater than the `pivot`, as `greater_than_pivot_index = first_index + 1`. The **right pointer** `less_than_pivot_index` variable points to the position of the last element in the `less_than_pivot_index = index_of_last_element` list, where we begin the search for the element that is less than the pivot:

```
while True:

    while unsorted_array[greater_than_pivot_index] < pivot and
            greater_than_pivot_index < last_index:
        greater_than_pivot_index += 1

    while unsorted_array[less_than_pivot_index] > pivot and
            less_than_pivot_index >= first_index:
        less_than_pivot_index -= 1
```

At the beginning of the execution of the main `while` loop, the array looks like this:

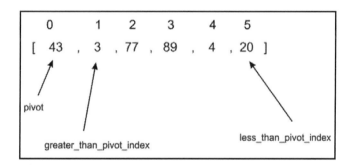

The first inner `while` loop moves one index to the right until it lands on index **2**, because the value at that index is greater than **43**. At this point, the first `while` loop breaks and does not continue. At each test of the condition in the first `while` loop, `greater_than_pivot_index += 1` is evaluated only if the `while` loop's test condition evaluates to `True`. This makes the search for an element, greater than the pivot, progress to the next element on the right.

The second inner `while` loop moves one index at a time to the left, until it lands on index **5**, whose value, **20**, is less than **43**:

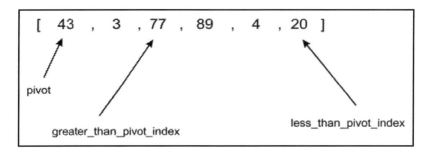

At this point, neither inner `while` loop can be executed any further:

```
if greater_than_pivot_index < less_than_pivot_index:
    temp = unsorted_array[greater_than_pivot_index]
        unsorted_array[greater_than_pivot_index] =
            unsorted_array[less_than_pivot_index]
        unsorted_array[less_than_pivot_index] = temp
else:
    break
```

Since `greater_than_pivot_index` < `less_than_pivot_index`, the body of the `if` statement swaps the element at those indexes. The `else` condition breaks the infinite loop any time that `greater_than_pivot_index` becomes greater than `less_than_pivot_index`. In such a condition, it means that `greater_than_pivot_index` and `less_than_pivot_index` have crossed over each other.

Our array now looks like the following:

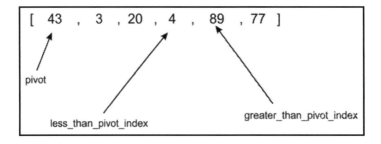

The `break` statement is executed when `less_than_pivot_index` is equal to **3** and `greater_than_pivot_index` is equal to **4**.

As soon as we exit the `while` loop, we interchange the element at
`unsorted_array[less_than_pivot_index]` with that of `less_than_pivot_index`,
which is returned as the index of the pivot:

```
unsorted_array[pivot_index]=unsorted_array[less_than_pivot_index]
unsorted_array[less_than_pivot_index]=pivot
return less_than_pivot_index
```

The following diagram shows how the code interchanges **4** with **43** as the last step in the
partitioning process:

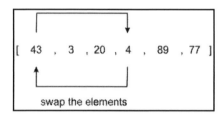

To recap, the first time the `quick_sort` function was called, it was partitioned about the
element at index **0**. After the return of the partitioning function, we obtain the array in the
order of [**4, 3, 20, 43, 89, 77**].

As you can see, all elements to the right of element **43** are greater than **43**, while those to the
left are smaller. Thus, the partitioning is complete.

Using the split point **43** with index **3**, we will recursively sort the two sub-arrays, [**4, 30, 20**]
and [**89, 77**], using the same process we just went through.

The body of the main `quick_sort` function is as follows:

```
def quick_sort(unsorted_array, first, last):
    if last - first <= 0:
        return
else:
    partition_point = partition(unsorted_array, first, last)
    quick_sort(unsorted_array, first, partition_point-1)
    quick_sort(unsorted_array, partition_point+1, last)
```

The `quick_sort` function is a very simple method, taking up no more than six lines of
code. The heavy lifting is done by the `partition` function. When the `partition` method
is called, it returns the partition point. This is the point in the `unsorted_array` array
where all elements to the left are less than the pivot value, and all elements to its right are
greater than it.

When we print the state of `unsorted_array` immediately after the partition progress, we see clearly how the partitioning happens:

```
Output:
[43, 3, 20, 89, 4, 77]
[4, 3, 20, 43, 89, 77]
[3, 4, 20, 43, 89, 77]
[3, 4, 20, 43, 77, 89]
[3, 4, 20, 43, 77, 89]
```

Taking a step back, let's sort the first sub-array after the first partition has happened. The partitioning of the [4, 3, 20] sub-array will stop when `greater_than_pivot_index` is at index 2, and `less_than_pivot_index` is at index 1. At that point, the two markers are said to have crossed. Because `greater_than_pivot_index` is greater than `less_than_pivot_index`, further execution of the `while` loop will cease. Pivot 4 will be exchanged with 3, while index 1 is returned as the partition point.

In the quicksort algorithm, the partition algorithm takes $O(n)$ time. As the quicksort algorithm follows the *divide and conquer* paradigm, it takes $O(\log n)$ time; therefore, the overall average-case runtime complexity of the quicksort algorithm is $O(n) * O(\log n)$ = $O(n \log n)$. The quicksort algorithm gives a worst-case runtime complexity of $O(n^2)$. The worst-case complexity for the quicksort algorithm would be when it selects the worst pivot point every time, and one of the partitions always has a single element. For example, if the list is already sorted, the worst-case complexity would occur if the partition picks the smallest element as a pivot point. When worst-case complexity does occur, the quicksort algorithm can be improved by using the randomized quicksort. The quicksort algorithm is very efficient when sorting large amounts of data compared to the other aforementioned algorithms for sorting.

Heap sort algorithms

In *Chapter 8*, *Graphs and Other Algorithms*, we implemented a binary heap data structure. Our implementation always made sure that, after an element had been removed or added to a heap, the heap order property was maintained, by using the `sink()` and `arrange()` helper methods.

The heap data structure can be used to implement a sorting algorithm called the heap sort. As a recap, let's create a simple heap with the following items:

```
h = Heap()
unsorted_list = [4, 8, 7, 2, 9, 10, 5, 1, 3, 6]
for i in unsorted_list:
    h.insert(i)
print("Unsorted list: {}".format(unsorted_list))
```

The heap, h, is created and the elements in the `unsorted_list` are inserted. After each method call to `insert`, the heap order property is restored by the subsequent call to the `float` method. After the loop is terminated, element 4 will be at the top of our heap.

The number of elements in our heap is 10. If we call the `pop` method on the h heap object 10 times, and store the actual elements being popped, we end up with a sorted list. After each `pop` operation, the heap is readjusted to maintain the heap order property.

The `heap_sort` method is as follows:

```
class Heap:
    ...
    def heap_sort(self):
        sorted_list = []
        for node in range(self.size):
            n = self.pop()
            sorted_list.append(n)

        return sorted_list
```

The `for` loop simply calls the `pop` method `self.size` number of times.
Now, `sorted_list` will contain a sorted list of items after the loop terminates.

The `insert` method is called *n* number of times. Together with the `arrange()` method, the `insert` operation takes a worst-case runtime of `O(n log n)`, as does the `pop` method. As such, this sorting algorithm incurs a worst-case runtime of `O(n log n)`.

A comparison of the complexities of different sorting algorithms is given in the following table:

Algorithm	worst-case	average-case	best-case
Bubble sort	O(n^2)	O(n^2)	O(n)
Insertion sort	O(n^2)	O(n^2)	O(n)
Selection sort	O(n^2)	O(n^2)	O(n^2)
Quicksort	O(n^2)	O(n log n)	O(n log n)
heapsort	O(n log n)	O(n log n)	O(n Log n)

Summary

In this chapter, we explored a number of important and popular sorting algorithms, which are very useful for many real-world applications. We discussed bubble sort, insertion sort, selection sort, quick sort, and heap sort algorithms, along with the explanation of their implementation in Python. Quick sort performs much better than the other sorting algorithms. Of all the algorithms discussed, quick sort preserves the index of the list that it sorts. We'll use this property in the next chapter as we explore the selection algorithms.

In the next chapter, we will be discussing the concepts related to the selection strategy and algorithms.

11
Selection Algorithms

One interesting set of algorithms related to finding elements in an unordered list of items is selection algorithms. Given a list of elements, selection algorithms are used to find the `ith` smallest element from the list. In doing so, we shall be answering questions that have to do with selecting the median of a set of numbers and selecting the ith smallest or largest element in a list.

In this chapter, we will cover the following topics:

- Selection by sorting
- Randomized selection
- Deterministic selection

Technical requirements

All of the source code that's used in this chapter is provided in the given GitHub link: `https://github.com/PacktPublishing/Hands-On-Data-Structures-and-Algorithms-with-Python-Second-Edition/tree/master/Chapter11`.

Selection by sorting

Items in a list may undergo statistical inquiries such as finding the mean, median, and mode values. Finding the mean and mode values does not require the list to be ordered. However, to find the median in a list of numbers, the list must first be ordered. Finding the median requires you to find the element in the middle position of the ordered list. In addition, this can be used when we want to find the last-smallest item in the list or the first-smallest item in the list. In such situations, selection algorithms can be useful.

To find the ith smallest number in an unordered list of items, the index of where that item occurs is important to obtain. Since the elements of the list are not sorted, it is difficult to know whether the element at index 0 in a list is really the first-smallest number.

A pragmatic and obvious thing to do when dealing with unordered lists is to first sort the list. After the list is sorted, you can rest assured that the element at the 0 index will hold the first-smallest element in the list. Likewise, the last element in the list will hold the last-smallest element in the list. However, it is not a good solution to apply a sorting algorithm on a long list of elements to obtain the minimum or maximum value from the list as sorting is quite an expensive operation.

Let's discuss if it's possible to find the ith smallest element without having to sort the list in the first place.

Randomized selection

In the previous chapter, we discussed the quicksort algorithm. The quicksort algorithm allows us to sort an unordered list of items, but has a way of preserving the index of elements as the sorting algorithm runs. Generally speaking, the quicksort algorithm does the following:

1. Selects a pivot
2. Partitions the unsorted list around the pivot
3. Recursively sorts the two halves of the partitioned list using *steps 1* and *2*

One interesting and important fact is that after every partitioning step the index of the pivot will not change, even after the list has become sorted. This means that after each iteration the selected pivot value will be placed at its correct position in the list. It is this property that enables us to be able to work with a not-so-fully sorted list to obtain the ith smallest number. Because randomized selection is based on the quicksort algorithm, it is generally referred to as quick select.

Quick select

The quickselect algorithm is used to obtain the kth smallest element in an unordered list of items, and is based on the quicksort algorithm. In quicksort, we recursively sort the elements of both the sublists from the pivot point. In quicksort, in each iteration, we know that the pivot value reaches its correct position in the list with two sublists (left and right sublists), having all of their elements set to be unordered.

However, in the case of the quickselect algorithm, we recursively call the function exclusively for the sublist that has the kth smallest element. In the quickselect algorithm, we compare the index of the pivot point with the k value to obtain the kth smallest element from the given unordered list. There will be three cases in the quickselect algorithm, and they are as follows:

1. If the index of the pivot point is smaller than k, then we are sure that the kth smallest value will be present in the right sublist from the pivot point. So, we only recursively call the quickselect function for the right sublist.
2. If the index of the pivot point is greater than k, then it is obvious that the kth smallest element will be present in the left side from the pivot point. So, we only recursively look for the ith element in the left sublist.
3. If the index of the pivot point is equal to k, then it means that we have found out the kth smallest value, and we return it.

Let's understand how the quickselect algorithm work by looking at an example. Let's consider a list of elements, {45, 23, 87, 12, 72, 4, 54, 32, 52}, where want to find out the 3rd smallest element from this list—we do this by using the quicksort algorithm.

We start the algorithm by selecting a pivot value, that is, 45. After the first iteration of the algorithm, we place the pivot value to its correct position in the list, that is, at index 4 (the index is starting from 0). Now, we compare the index of the pivot value (that is, 4) with the value of k (that is, 3rd position, or at index 2). Since this is at the k<pivot point (that is, 2<4), we only consider the left sublist, and recursively call the function.

Now, we take the left sublist and select the pivot point (that is, 4). After the run, the **4** is placed at its correct position (that is, the 0th index). As the index of the pivot is less than the value of k, we consider the right sublist. Similarly, we take **23** as the pivot point, which is also placed at its correct position. Now, when we compare the index of the pivot point and the value of k, they are equal, which means we have found the 3rd smallest element, and it will be returned.

This process is also shown in the following diagram:

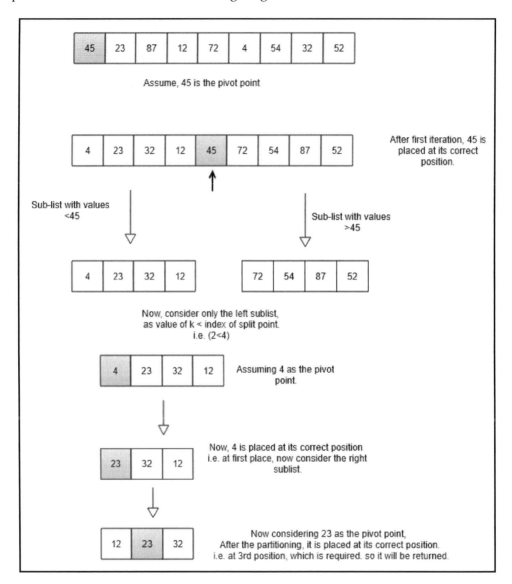

To implement the quickselect algorithm, we first need to understand the main function, where we have three possible conditions. We declare the main method of the algorithm as follows:

```
def quick_select(array_list, left, right, k):

    split = partition(array_list, left, right)

    if split == k:
        return array_list[split]
    elif split < k:
        return quick_select(array_list, split + 1, right, k)
    else:
        return quick_select(array_list, left, split-1, k)
```

The `quick_select` function takes the index of the first element in the list—as well as the last —as parameters. The ith element is specified by the third parameter, k. The value of k should always be positive; the values greater or equal to zero (0) are only allowed in such a way that when k is 0, we know to search for the first-smallest item in the list. Others like to treat the k parameter so that it maps directly with the index that the user is searching for, so that the first-smallest number maps to the 0 index of a sorted list.

A method call to the partition function, `split = partition(array_list, left, right)`, returns the `split` index. This index of the `split` array is the position in the unordered list where all elements between `right` to `split-1` are less than the element contained in the `split` array, while all elements between `split+1` to `left` are greater.

When the `partition` function returns the `split` value, we compare it with k to find out if the `split` corresponds to the kth items.

If `split` is less than `k`, then it means that the kth smallest item should exist or be found between `split+1` and `right`:

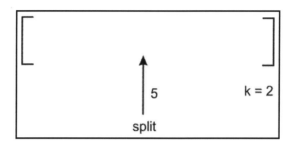

In the preceding example, a split within an imaginary unordered list occurs at index **5**, while we are searching for the second-smallest number. Since 5<2 yields `false`, a recursive call to return `quick_select(array_list, left, split-1, k)` is made so that the other half of the list is searched.

If the `split` index was less than `k`, then we would make a call to `quick_select`, like this:

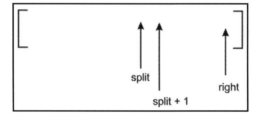

Understanding the partition step

The partition step is similar to what we had in the quicksort algorithm. There are a couple of things that are worth noting:

```
def partition(unsorted_array, first_index, last_index):
    if first_index == last_index:
        return first_index

    pivot = unsorted_array[first_index]
    pivot_index = first_index
    index_of_last_element = last_index

    less_than_pivot_index = index_of_last_element
    greater_than_pivot_index = first_index + 1
```

```
while True:

    while unsorted_array[greater_than_pivot_index] < pivot and
            greater_than_pivot_index < last_index:
        greater_than_pivot_index += 1
    while unsorted_array[less_than_pivot_index] > pivot and
            less_than_pivot_index >= first_index:
        less_than_pivot_index -= 1

    if greater_than_pivot_index < less_than_pivot_index:
        temp = unsorted_array[greater_than_pivot_index]
        unsorted_array[greater_than_pivot_index] =
            unsorted_array[less_than_pivot_index]
        unsorted_array[less_than_pivot_index] = temp
    else:
        break

unsorted_array[pivot_index] =
    unsorted_array[less_than_pivot_index]
unsorted_array[less_than_pivot_index] = pivot

return less_than_pivot_index
```

An `if` statement has been inserted at the beginning of the function definition to cater for situations where `first_index` is equal to `last_index`. In such cases, it means that there is only one element in our sublist. Therefore, we simply return any of the function parameters, in this case, `first_index`.

The first element is always chosen as the pivot. This choice to make the first element the pivot is a random decision. It often does not yield a good split—and subsequently—a good partition. However, the ith element will eventually be found, even though the pivot is chosen at random.

The `partition` function returns the pivot index pointed to by `less_than_pivot_index`, as we saw in the preceding chapter.

Deterministic selection

The worst-case performance of a randomized selection algorithm is $O(n^2)$. It is possible to improve the section of an element of the randomized selection algorithm to obtain a worst-case performance of $O(n)$. We can obtain the performance of $O(n)$ by using an algorithm, that is, **deterministic selection**.

Median of the median is an algorithm that provides us with the approximate median value, that is, a value close to the actual median for a given unsorted list of elements. This approximate median is often used as a pivot point in the quickselect algorithm for selecting the ith smallest element from a list. It is due to the fact that the median of median algorithm finds out the estimated median in a linear time, and when this estimated median is used as a pivot point in the quickselect algorithm, the worst-case running time's complexity drastically improves from $O(n^2)$ to the linear $O(n)$. Therefore, the median of the median algorithm helps the quickselect algorithm to perform significantly better because of the choice of a good pivot value.

The general approach to the deterministic algorithm to select the ith smallest element is listed here:

1. Select a pivot:
    1. Split a list of unordered items into groups of five elements each.
    2. Sort and find the median of all the groups.
    3. Repeat *steps 1* and *2* recursively to obtain the true median of the list.
2. Use the true median to partition the list of unordered items.
3. Recurse into the part of the partitioned list that may contain the ith smallest element.

Let's consider an example list of 15 elements to understand the working of the deterministic approach to determine the third smallest element from the list. First, you need to divide the lists that have 5 elements each, and then we sort the sublists. Once we have sorted the lists, we find out the median of the sublists, that is, items **23**, **52**, and **34** are the medians of these three sublists. We prepare a list of medians of all the sublists, and then we sort the list of medians. Next, we determine the median of this list, that is, the median of the median, which is **34**. This value is the estimated median of the whole list, and is used to select the partition/pivot point for the whole list. Since the index of the pivot value is 7, which is greater than the ith value, we recursively consider the left sublist.

The functionality of the algorithm is shown in the following diagram:

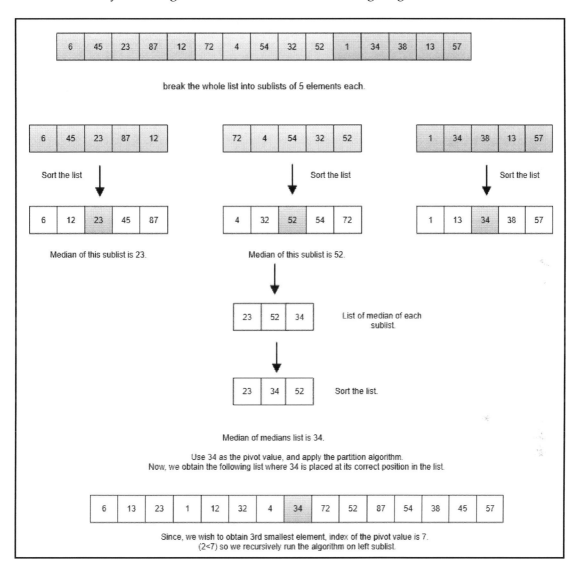

Pivot selection

To implement the deterministic algorithm to efficiently determine the ith smallest value from the list, we start by implementing the pivot selection method. Previously, in the random selection algorithm, we selected the first element as the pivot. We shall replace that step with a sequence of steps that enables us to obtain the approximate median. This will improve the partitioning of the list regarding the pivot:

```
def partition(unsorted_array, first_index, last_index):

    if first_index == last_index:
        return first_index
    else:
        nearest_median =
        median_of_medians(unsorted_array[first_index:last_index])

    index_of_nearest_median =
        get_index_of_nearest_median(unsorted_array, first_index,
                                    last_index, nearest_median)

    swap(unsorted_array, first_index, index_of_nearest_median)

    pivot = unsorted_array[first_index]
    pivot_index = first_index
    index_of_last_element = last_index

    less_than_pivot_index = index_of_last_element
    greater_than_pivot_index = first_index + 1
```

Let's now understand the code for the `partition` function. The `nearest_median` variable stores the true or approximate median of a given list:

```
def partition(unsorted_array, first_index, last_index):

    if first_index == last_index:
        return first_index
    else:
        nearest_median =
        median_of_medians(unsorted_array[first_index:last_index])
    ....
```

If the `unsorted_array` parameter has only one element, `first_index` and `last_index` will be equal. Therefore, `first_index` is, returned anyway.

However, if the list size is greater than one, we call the `median_of_medians` function with the section of the array, demarcated by `first_index` and `last_index`. The return value is yet again stored in `nearest_median`.

Median of medians

The `median_of_medians` function is responsible for finding the approximate median of any given list of items. The function uses recursion to return the true median:

```
def median_of_medians(elems):

    sublists = [elems[j:j+5] for j in range(0, len(elems), 5)]

    medians = []
    for sublist in sublists:
        medians.append(sorted(sublist)[len(sublist)//2])

    if len(medians) <= 5:
        return sorted(medians)[len(medians)//2]
    else:
        return median_of_medians(medians)
```

The function begins by splitting the list, `elems`, into groups of five elements each. This means that if `elems` contains 100 items, there will be 20 groups that are created by the `sublists = [elems[j:j+5] for j in range(0, len(elems), 5)]` statement, with each containing exactly five elements or fewer:

```
    medians = []
        for sublist in sublists:
            medians.append(sorted(sublist)[len(sublist)/2])
```

An empty array is created and assigned to `medians`, which stores the medians in each of the five element arrays assigned to `sublists`.

The for loop iterates over the list of lists inside `sublists`. Each sublist is sorted, the median is found, and is stored in the `medians` list.

The `medians.append(sorted(sublist)[len(sublist)//2])` statement will sort the list and obtain the element stored in its middle index. This becomes the median of the five-element list. The use of an existing sorting function will not impact the performance of the algorithm due to the list's small size.

We understood from the outset that we would not sort the list in order to find the ith smallest element, so why employ Python's sorted method? Well, since we are sorting a very small list of five elements or fewer, the impact of that operation on the overall performance of the algorithm is considered negligible.

Thereafter, if the list now contains five or fewer elements, we shall sort the `medians` list and return the element located in its middle index:

```
if len(medians) <= 5:
        return sorted(medians)[len(medians)/2]
```

If, on the other hand, the size of the list is greater than five, we recursively call the `median_of_medians` function again, supplying it with the list of the medians stored in `medians`.

Take, for instance, another example to better understand the concept of the median of median algorithm, with the following list of numbers:

[2, 3, 5, 4, 1, 12, 11, 13, 16, 7, 8, 6, 10, 9, 17, 15, 19, 20, 18, 23, 21, 22, 25, 24, 14]

We can break this list into groups of five elements each with the `sublists = [elems[j:j+5] for j in range(0, len(elems), 5)]` code statement in order to obtain the following list:

[[2, 3, 5, 4, 1], [12, 11, 13, 16, 7], [8, 6, 10, 9, 17], [15, 19, 20, 18, 23], [21, 22, 25, 24, 14]]

Sorting each of the five-element lists and obtaining their medians produces the following list:

[3, 12, 9, 19, 22]

Since the list is five elements in size, we only return the median of the sorted list; otherwise, we would have made another call to the `median_of_median` function.

The median of medians algorithm can also be used to choose a pivot point in the quicksort algorithm for sorting a list of elements. This significantly improves the worst-case performance of the quicksort algorithm from $O(n^2)$ to a complexity of $O(n \log n)$.

Partitioning step

Now that we have obtained the approximate median, the
`get_index_of_nearest_median` function takes the bounds of the list indicated by the
`first` and `last` parameters:

```
def get_index_of_nearest_median(array_list, first, second, median):
    if first == second:
        return first
    else:
        return first + array_list[first:second].index(median)
```

Once again, we only return the first index if there is only one element in the list.
However, `arraylist[first:second]` returns an array with an index of `0` up to the size
of the `list` `-1`. When we find the index of the median, we lose the portion in the list where
it occurs because of the new range indexing that the `[first:second]` code returns.
Therefore, we must add whatever index is returned by `arraylist[first:second]` to
`first` to obtain the true index where the median was found:

```
swap(unsorted_array, first_index, index_of_nearest_median)
```

We then swap the first element in `unsorted_array` with `index_of_nearest_median`,
using the `swap` function.

The `utility` function to swap two array elements is shown here:

```
def swap(array_list, first, second):
    temp = array_list[first]
    array_list[first] = array_list[second]
    array_list[second] = temp
```

Our approximate median is now stored at `first_index` of the unsorted list.

The partition function continues as it would in the code of the quickselect algorithm. After
the partitioning step, the array looks like this:

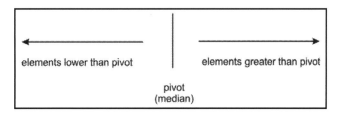

```
def deterministic_select(array_list, left, right, k):

        split = partition(array_list, left, right)
        if split == k:
            return array_list[split]
        elif split < k :
            return deterministic_select(array_list, split + 1, right, k)
        else:
                return deterministic_select(array_list, left, split-1, k)
```

As you will have already observed, the main function of the deterministic selection algorithm looks exactly the same as its random selection counterpart. After the initial `array_list` has been partitioned for the approximate median, a comparison with the kth element is made.

If `split` is less than k, then a recursive call to `deterministic_select(array_list, split + 1, right, k)` is made. This will look for the kth element in that half of the array. Otherwise, the function call to `deterministic_select(array_list, left, split-1, k)` is made.

Summary

In this chapter, we discussed various ways to answer the question of how to find the ith smallest element in a list. The trivial solution of simply sorting a list to perform the operation of finding the ith smallest element was explored.

There is also the possibility of not necessarily sorting the list before we can determine the ith smallest element. The random selection algorithm allows us to modify the quicksort algorithm to determine the ith smallest element.

To further improve upon the random selection algorithm so that we can obtain a time complexity of $O(n)$, we embarked on finding the median of medians to enable us to find a good split during partitioning.

In the next chapter, we will explore the world of strings. We will learn how to efficiently store and manipulate large amounts of text. Data structures and common string operations will be covered too.

12
String Algorithms and Techniques

There are many popular string processing algorithms available, depending upon the problem being solved. However, one of the most important, popular, and useful string processing problems is to find a given substring or pattern from some given text. It has various application uses, such as searching an element from a text document, plagiarism detection, and so on.

In this chapter, we will study the standard string processing or pattern matching algorithms that find out the locations of the given pattern or substring in some given text. We will also be discussing the brute-force algorithm, as well as the Rabin-Karp, **Knuth-Morris-Pratt** (**KMP**), and Boyer-Moore pattern matching algorithms. We will also discuss some basic concepts related to strings. We will be discussing all of the algorithms with an easy explanation, including examples and implementation.

This chapter is aimed at discussing algorithms that are focused on being related to strings. The following topics will be covered in this chapter:

- Learning the basic concepts of strings in Python
- Learning pattern matching algorithms and their implementation
- Understanding and implementing the Rabin-Karp pattern matching algorithm
- Understanding and implementing the Knuth-Morris-Pratt (KMP) algorithm
- Understanding and implementing the Boyer-Moore pattern matching algorithm

Technical requirements

All of the programs based on the concepts and algorithms discussed in this chapter are provided in the book as well as in the GitHub repository at the following link: `https://github.com/PacktPublishing/Hands-On-Data-Structures-and-Algorithms-with-Python-Second-Edition/tree/master/Chapter12`.

String notations and concepts

Strings are basically a sequence of objects, mainly a sequence of characters. As with any other data type, such as an int or float, we need to store the data and operations that have to be applied to them. String data types allow us to store the data, and Python provides a rich set of operations and functions that can be applied to the data of the string data type. Most of the operations and functions provided by Python 3.7 that can be applied to the strings were described in detail in `Chapter 1`, *Python Objects, Types, and Expressions*.

Strings are mainly textual data that is generally handled very efficiently. The following is an example of a string (S)—`"packt publishing"`.

A substring is also a sequence of characters that's part of the given string. For example, `"packt"` is the substring for the string `"packt publishing"`.

A subsequence is a sequence of characters that can be obtained from the given string by removing some of the characters from the string but by keeping the order of occurrence of the characters. For example, `"pct pblishing"` is a valid subsequence for the string `"packt publishing"` that is obtained by removing the characters a, k, and u. However, this is not a substring. A subsequence is different from a substring, since it can be considered as a generalization of substrings.

The prefix of a string, `s`, is the substring of `s` in that it is present in the starting of the string. There is also another string, `u`, that exists in the string s after the prefix. For example, the substring `"pack"` is a prefix for the string `(s) = "packt publishing"` as it is starting the substring and there is another substring after it.

The suffix `(d)` is a substring that is present at the end of the string (s) so that there is another nonempty substring existing before substring d. For example, the substring `"shing"` is the suffix for the string `"packt publishing"`. Python has built-in functions to check whether a string has a given prefix or suffix, as shown in the following code snippet:

```
string = "this is data structures book by packt publisher";
suffix = "publisher";
```

```
prefix = "this";

print(string.endswith(suffix))  #Check if string contains given suffix.
print(string.startswith(prefix)) #Check if string starts with given prefix.

#Outputs
>>True
>>True
```

Pattern matching algorithms are the most important string processing algorithms, and we will be discussing them in subsequent sections.

Pattern matching algorithms

A pattern matching algorithm is used to determine the index positions where a given pattern string (P) is matched in a text string (T). It returns `"pattern not found"` if the pattern does not match in the text string. For example, for the given string (s) = `"packt publisher"`, and the pattern (p)= `"publisher"`, the pattern matching algorithm returns the index position where the pattern is matched in the text string.

In this section, we will discuss four pattern matching algorithms, that is, the brute-force method, as well as the Rabin-Karp algorithm, Knuth-Morris-Pratt (KMP), and Boyer Moore pattern matching algorithms.

The brute-force algorithm

The brute-force algorithm, or naive approach for the pattern matching algorithm, is very basic. Using this, we simply test all the possible combinations of the input pattern in the given string to find the position of the occurrence of the pattern. This algorithm is very naive and is not suitable if the text is very long.

Here, we start by comparing the characters of the pattern and the text string one by one, and if all the characters of the pattern are matched with the text, we return the index position of the text where the first character of the pattern is placed. If any character of the pattern is mismatched with the text string, we shift the pattern by one place. We continue comparing the pattern and text string by shifting the pattern by one index position.

To better understand how the brute-force algorithm works, let's look at an example. Suppose we have a text string (T)= **acbcabccababcaacbcac**, and the pattern string (P) is **acbcac**. Now, the objective of the pattern matching algorithm is to determine the index position of the pattern string in the given text, T, as shown in the following figure:

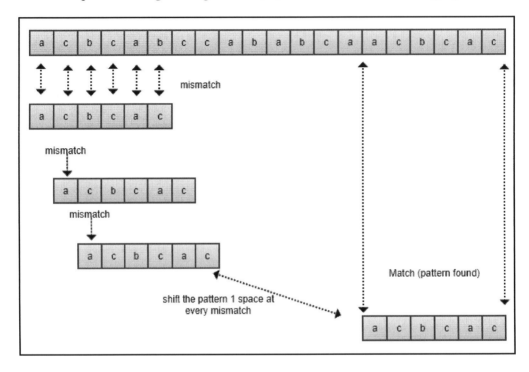

We start by comparing the first character of the text, that is, **a**, and the characters of the pattern. Here, the initial five characters of the pattern are matched, and there is a mismatch in the last character of the pattern. Since there is a mismatch, we further shift the pattern by one place. We again start comparing the first character of the pattern and the second character of the text string one by one. Here, character **c** of the text string does not match with the character **a** of the pattern. Since it is a mismatch, we shift the pattern by one space, as shown in the preceding diagram. We continue comparing the characters of the pattern and the text string until we traverse the whole text string. In the preceding example, we find a match at index position **14**, which is shown with the arrows to **aa**.

Here, let's consider the Python implementation of the brute-force algorithm for pattern matching:

```python
def brute_force(text, pattern):
    l1 = len(text)        # The length of the text string
    l2 = len(pattern)     # The length of the pattern
    i = 0
    j = 0                 # looping variables are set to 0
    flag = False          # If the pattern doesn't appear at all, then set
this to false and execute the last if statement

    while i < l1:            # iterating from the 0th index of text
        j = 0
        count = 0
        # Count stores the length upto which the pattern and the text have
matched

        while j < l2:
            if i+j < l1 and text[i+j] == pattern[j]:
            # statement to check if a match has occoured or not
            count += 1     # Count is incremented if a character is matched
                j += 1
            if count == l2:  # it shows a matching of pattern in the text
                print("\nPattern occours at index", i)
                    # print the starting index of the successful match
                flag = True
        # flag is True as we wish to continue looking for more matching of
        pattern in the text.
            i += 1
    if not flag:
        # If the pattern doesn't occours at all, means no match of
        pattern in the text string
        print('\nPattern is not at all present in the array')


brute_force('acbcabccababcaacbcac','acbcac')        # function call

#outputs
#Pattern occours at index 14
```

In the preceding code for the brute-force approach, we start by computing the length of the given text strings and pattern. We also initialize the looping variables with 0 and set the flag to `False`. This variable is used to continue searching for a match of the pattern in the string. If the flag is `False` by the end of the text string, it means that there is no match of the pattern at all in the text string.

Next, we start the searching loop from the `0th` index to the end of the text string. In this loop, we have a count variable that is used to keep track of the length up to which the pattern and the text have been matched. Next, we have another nested loop that runs from the `0th` index to the length of the pattern. Here, the variable `i` keeps track of the index position in the text string and the variable `j` keeps track of the characters in the pattern. Next, we compare the characters of the patterns and the text string using the following code fragment:

```
if i+j<l1 and text[i+j] == pattern[j]:
```

Furthermore, we increment the count variable after every match of the character of the pattern in the text string. Then, we continue matching the characters of the pattern and text string. If the length of the pattern becomes equal to the count variable, it means there is a match.

We print the index position of the text string if there is a match of the pattern in the text string, and keep the flag variable to `True` as we wish to continue searching for more matches of the patterns in the text string. Finally, if the value of the variable flag is `False`, it means that there was not a match of the pattern in the text string at all.

The best-case and worst-case time complexity for the naive string matching algorithms are $O(n)$ and $O(m*(n-m+1))$, respectively. The best-case occurs when the pattern is not found in the text and the first character of the pattern is not present in the text at all, for example, if the text string is ABAACEBCCDAAEE, and the pattern is FAA. Here, as the first character of the pattern will not match in the text, it will have the comparisons equal to the length of the text (n).

The worst-case occurs when all characters of the text string and the pattern are the same, for example, if the text string is AAAAAAAAAAAAAAAA, and the pattern is AAAA. Another worst-case scenario occurs when only the last character is different, for example, if the text string is AAAAAAAAAAAAAAAF and the pattern is AAAAF. Thus, worst-case time complexity would be $O(m*(n-m+1))$.

The Rabin-Karp algorithm

The Rabin-Karp pattern matching algorithm is an improved version of the brute-force approach for finding the location of the given pattern in the text string. The performance of the Rabin-Karp algorithm is improved by reducing the number of comparisons with the help of hashing. We described hashing in detail in Chapter 7, *Hashing and Symbol Tables*. The hashing function returns a unique numeric value for a given string.

This algorithm is faster than the brute-force approach as it avoids unnecessary comparisons, character by character. Instead, the hash value of the pattern is compared with the hash of the substring of the text string all at once. If the hash values are not matched, the pattern is moved one position, and so there is no need to compare all the characters of the pattern one by one.

This algorithm is based on the concept that if the hash values of the two strings are equal, then it is assumed that both of these strings are also equal. The main problem with this algorithm is that there can be two different strings whose hash values are equal. In that case, the algorithm may not work; this situation is known as a spurious hit. To avoid this problem, after matching the hash values of the pattern and the substring, we ensure that the pattern is actually matched by comparing them character by character.

The Rabin-Karp pattern matching algorithm works as follows:

1. First, we preprocess the pattern before starting the search, that is, we compute the hash value of the pattern of length m and the hash values of all the possible substrings of the text of length m. So, the total number of possible substrings would be (n−m+1). Here, n is the length of the text.
2. We compare the hash value of the pattern and compare it with the hash value of the substrings of the text one by one.
3. If the hash values are not matched, then we move the pattern by one position.
4. If the hash value of the pattern and the hash value of the substring of the text matches, then we compare the pattern and substring character by character to ensure that the pattern is actually found in the text.
5. We continue the process of steps 2-4 until we reach the end of the given text string.

In this algorithm, we can compute the numerical hash values using Horner's rule or any other hashing function that returns a unique value for the given string. We can also compute the hashing value using the sum of the ordinal values of all the characters of the string.

Let's consider an example to understand the Rabin-Karp algorithm. Let's say we have a text string (T)= "publisher paakt packt", and the pattern (P)= "packt". First, we compute the hash value of the pattern (length m) and all the substrings (of length m) of the text string.

We start comparing the hash of the pattern "packt" with the first substring, "publi". Since the hash values do not match, we move the pattern by one location, and once again we compare the hash value of pattern with the hash value of the next substring of the text, "ublis". As these hash values also do not match, we again move the pattern by one location. We always move the pattern by one location if the hash values do not match.

Furthermore, if the hash value of the pattern and the hash value of the substring match, we compare the pattern and substring character by character and we return the location of the text string. In this example, these values are matched at location 17. It is important to note that there can be a different string whose hash value can match with the hash of the pattern. This situation is called a spurious hit, and is due to a collision in hashing. The functionality of the Rabin-Karp algorithm is shown here:

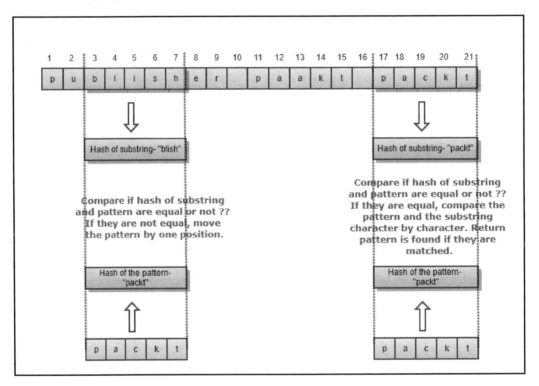

Implementing the Rabin-Karp algorithm

The first step to implementing the Rabin-Karp algorithm is to choose the hash function. We use the sum of all the ordinal values of the characters of the string as the hashing function.

We start by storing the ordinal values of all the characters of the text and the pattern. Next, we store the length of the text and the pattern in the `len_text` and `len_pattern` variables. Next, we compute the hash value for the pattern by summing up the ordinal values of all the characters in the pattern.

Next, we create a variable called `len_hash_array` that stores the total number of possible substrings of length (equal to the length of the pattern) using `len_text - len_pattern + 1`, and we create an array called `hash_text` that stores the hash value for all the possible substrings.

Next, we start a loop that will run for all the possible substrings of the text. Initially, we compute the hash value for the first substring by summing the ordinal values of all of its characters using `sum(ord_text[:len_pattern])`. Furthermore, the hash values for all of the substrings are computed using the hash value of its previous substrings as `((hash_text[i-1] - ord_text[i-1]) + ord_text[i+len_pattern-1])`.

The complete Python implementation to compute the hashing values is shown here:

```python
def generate_hash(text, pattern):
    ord_text = [ord(i) for i in text]
                        # stores unicode value of each character in text
    ord_pattern = [ord(j) for j in pattern]
                    # stores unicode value of each character in pattern
    len_text = len(text)          # stores length of the text
    len_pattern = len(pattern)     # stores length of the pattern
    hash_pattern = sum(ord_pattern)
    len_hash_array = len_text - len_pattern + 1
     #stores the length of new array that will contain the hash
     values of text
    hash_text = [0]*(len_hash_array)
                        # Initialize all the values in the array to 0.
    for i in range(0, len_hash_array):
        if i == 0:
            hash_text[i] = sum(ord_text[:len_pattern])
                                # initial value of hash function
        else:
            hash_text[i] = ((hash_text[i-1] - ord_text[i-1]) +
            ord_text[i+len_pattern-1])
                # calculating next hash value using previous value

    return [hash_text, hash_pattern]        # return the hash values
```

After preprocessing the pattern and text, we have precomputed hash values that we will use for comparing the pattern and the text.

The implementation of the main Rabin-Karp algorithm works as follows. First, we convert the given text and pattern in string format as the ordinal values can only be computed for the strings.

Next, we call the `generate_hash` function to compute the hash values. We also store the length of the text and patterns in the `len_text` and `len_pattern` variables. We also initialize the `flag` variable to `False` so that it keeps track of whether the pattern is present in the text at least once.

Next, we start a loop that implements the main concept of the algorithm. This loop will run for the length of the `hash_text`, which is the total number of possible substrings. Initially, we compare the first hash value of the substring with the hash of the pattern by using `if hash_text[i] == hash_pattern`. They do not match; we do nothing and look for another substring. If they match, we compare the substring and the pattern character by character through a loop by using `if pattern[j] == text[i+j]`.

We then create a `count` variable to keep track of how many characters match in the pattern and the substring. If the length of the count and length of the pattern become equal, this means that all of the characters match, and the index location is returned where the pattern was found. Finally, if the `flag` variable remains `False`, this means that the pattern does not match at all in the text.

The complete Python implementation of the Rabin-Karp algorithm is shown as follows:

```python
def Rabin_Karp_Matcher(text, pattern):
    text = str(text)                    # convert text into string format
    pattern = str(pattern)              # convert pattern into string format
    hash_text, hash_pattern = generate_hash(text, pattern)
                    # generate hash values using generate_hash function
    len_text = len(text)                # length of text
    len_pattern = len(pattern)          # length of pattern
    flag = False # checks if pattern is present atleast once or not at all
    for i in range(len(hash_text)):
        if hash_text[i] == hash_pattern:    # if the hash value matches
            count = 0
            for j in range(len_pattern):
                if pattern[j] == text[i+j]:
                        # comparing patten and substring character by
character
                    count += 1
                else:
                    break
            if count == len_pattern:        # Pattern is found in the
text
                    flag = True                 # update flag accordingly
```

```
                    print("Pattern occours at index", i)
            if not flag:                    # Pattern doesn't match even
    once.
                    print("Pattern is not at all present in the text")
```

The Rabin-Karp pattern matching algorithm preprocesses the pattern before the searching, that is, it computes the hash value for the pattern that has the complexity of $O(m)$. Also, the worst-case running time complexity of the Rabin-Karp algorithm is $O(m * (n-m+1))$.

The worse-case would be when the pattern does not occur in the text at all.

The average-case would occur when the pattern occurs at least once.

The Knuth-Morris-Pratt algorithm

The **Knuth-Morris-Pratt (KMP)** algorithm is a pattern matching algorithm that is based on a precomputed prefix function that stores the information of an overlapping text portion in the pattern. The KMP algorithm preprocesses this pattern to avoid unnecessary comparisons when using the prefix function. The algorithm utilizes the prefix function to estimate how much the pattern should be shifted to search the pattern in the text string whenever we get a mismatch. The KMP algorithm is efficient as it minimizes the comparisons of the given patterns with respect to the text string.

The motivation behind the KMP algorithm can be seen in the following explanatory diagram:

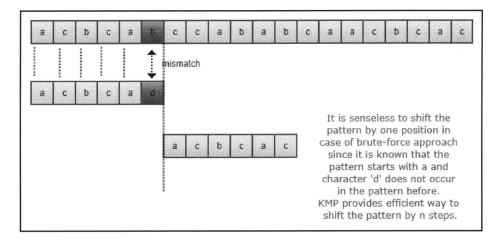

The prefix function

The `prefix` function (also known as the failure function) finds the pattern in the pattern itself. It tries to find how much the previous comparisons can be reused due to repetition in the pattern itself when there is a mismatch. It has a value that is mainly the longest prefix, which is also a suffix.

For example, if we have a `prefix` function for a pattern where all of the characters are different, the `prefix` function would have a value of `0`, meaning that if we find any mismatch, the pattern would be shifted by the number of characters in the pattern. It also means that there is no overlap in the pattern, and no previous comparisons would be reused. We start by comparing from the first character of the pattern with the text string if it contains only different characters. Consider the following example: the pattern **abcde** contains all different characters, so it would be shifted to the number of characters in the pattern, and we would start comparing the first character of the pattern with the next character of the text string, as shown in the following diagram:

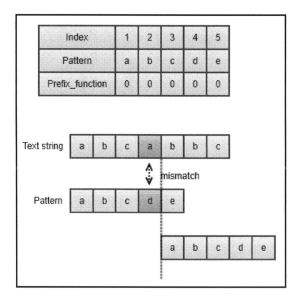

Let's consider another example to better understand how the `prefix` function works for the pattern (P) **abcabbcab** as shown in the following diagram:

Index	1	2	3	4	5	6	7	8	9
Pattern	a	b	c	a	b	b	c	a	b
Prefix_function	0	0	0						

In the preceding diagram, we start calculating the values of the `prefix` function starting from index **1**. We assign value **0** if there is no repetition of the characters. In the preceding example, we assign **0** to the `prefix` function for the index positions **1** to **3**. Next, at index position **4**, we can see that there is a character, **a**, which is the repetition of the first character of the pattern in itself, so we assign value **1** here, shown as follows:

Index	1	2	3	4	5	6	7	8	9
Pattern	a	b	c	a	b	b	c	a	b
Prefix_function	0	0	0	1					

Next, we look at the next character at position **5**. It has the longest suffix pattern, **ab**, and so it would have a value of **2**, as shown in the following diagram:

Index	1	2	3	4	5	6	7	8	9
Pattern	a	b	c	a	b	b	c	a	b
Prefix_function	0	0	0	1	2				

Similarly, we look at the next index position of 6. Here, the character is **b**. This character does not have the longest suffix in the pattern, so it has the value **0**. Next, we assign value **0** at index position 7. Then, we look at the index position 8, and we assign the value **1** as it has the longest suffix of length **1**. Finally, at the index position of **9**, we have the longest suffix of **2**:

Index	1	2	3	4	5	6	7	8	9
Pattern	a	b	c	a	b	b	c	a	b
Prefix_function	0	0	0	1	2	0	0	1	2

The value of the `prefix` function shows how much of the start of the string can be reused if there is a mismatch. For example, if the comparison fails at the index position of 5, the `prefix` function value is **2**, which means that the two starting characters don't need to be compared.

Understanding KMP algorithms

The KMP pattern matching algorithm uses a pattern that has overlap in the pattern itself so that it avoids unnecessary comparisons. The main idea behind the KMP algorithm is to detect how much the pattern should be shifted, based on the overlaps in the patterns. The algorithm works as follows:

1. First, we precompute the `prefix` function for the given pattern and initialize a counter, q, that represents the number of characters that matched.
2. We start by comparing the first character of the pattern with the first character of the text string, and if this matches, then we increment the counter, **q**, for the pattern and the counter for the text string, and we compare the next character.
3. If there is a mismatch, then we assign the value of the precomputed `prefix` function for **q** to the index value of **q**.
4. We continue searching the pattern in the text string until we reach the end of the text, that is, if we do not find any matches. If all of the characters in the pattern are matched in the text string, we return the position where the pattern is matched in the text and continue to search for another match.

Let's consider the following example to understand this:

The `prefix` function for the given pattern would be as follows:

Index	1	2	3	4	5	6
Pattern	a	c	a	c	a	c
Prefix_function	0	0	1	2	1	2

Now, we start comparing the first character of the pattern with the first character of the text string and continue comparing it until we find a match. For example, in the following diagram, we start by comparing character **a** of the text string with the character **a** of the pattern. As it is matched, we continue comparing until we find a mismatch or we have compared the whole pattern. Here, we find a mismatch at index position **6**, so now we have to shift the pattern.

We find the number of shifts the pattern should take by using the help of the `prefix` function. This is because the `prefix` function has the value of **2** at the mismatch position (that is, `prefix_function(6)` is **2**), and so we start comparing the pattern from index position 2 of the pattern. Due to the efficiency of the KMP algorithm, we do not need to compare the character at **1** index position, and we compare the characters **c** of the pattern, and character **b** of the text. Since these do not match, we shift the pattern by **1** position, as follows:

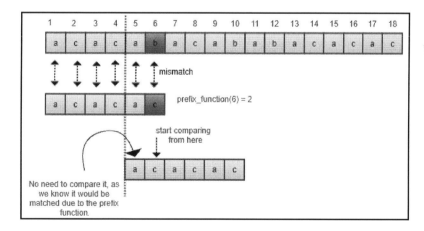

Next, the compared characters are **b** and **a**—these do not match, so we shift the pattern by **1** distance. Next, we compare the pattern and text string and find a mismatch at index position 10 in the text between characters **b** and **c**. Here, we use the precomputed `prefix` function to shift the pattern, as the `prefix_function(4)` is **2**, so we shift the at its index position of **2**, as shown in the following diagram:

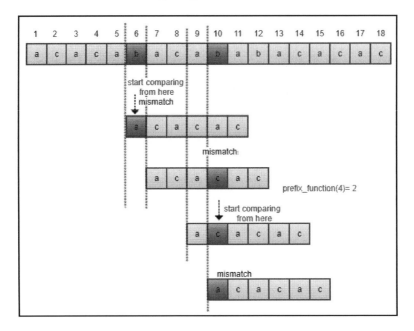

After that, we shift the pattern by 1 location as there is a mismatch between characters **b** and **c**. Next, we compare the characters at index **11** in the text, and continue until a mismatch is found. We find a mismatch between characters **b** and **c**, as shown in the following diagram. We shift the pattern and move it to the index of 0 of the pattern as the `prefix_function(2)` is 0. We repeat the same process until we reach the end of the string. We find a match of the pattern in the text string at the index location of **13** in the text string, as follows:

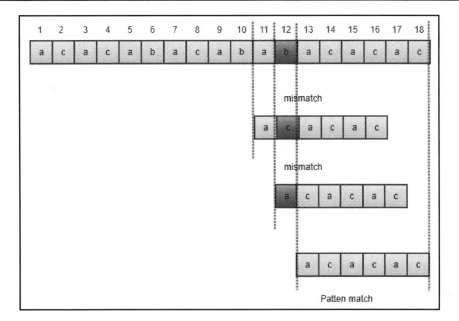

The KMP algorithm has two phases, the preprocessing phase, which is where we compute the `prefix` function, It takes the space and time complexity of `O(m)` and further, in the second phase, that searching, the KMP algorithm takes time complexity of `O(n)`.

Now, we will discuss the implementation of the KMP algorithm by using Python.

Implementing the KMP algorithm

The Python implementation of the KMP algorithm is explained here. We start by implementing the `prefix` function for the given pattern. For this, first, we compute the length of the pattern by using the `len()` function, and then we initialize a list to store the computed values by the `prefix` function.

Next, we start the loop that executes from 2 to the length of the pattern. Then, we have a nested loop that is executed until we have processed the whole pattern. The variable k is initialized to 0, which is the `prefix` function for the first element of the pattern. If the kth element of the pattern is equal to the qth element, then we increment the value of k by 1.

The value of k is the computed value by the `prefix` function, and so we assign it at the index position of the q of the pattern. Finally, we return the list of the `prefix` function that has the computed value for each character of the pattern. The code for the `prefix` function is shown as follows:

```
def pfun(pattern): # function to generate prefix function for the given
pattern
    n = len(pattern) # length of the pattern
    prefix_fun = [0]*(n) # initialize all elements of the list to 0
    k = 0
    for q in range(2,n):
        while k>0 and pattern[k+1] != pattern[q]:
            k = prefix_fun[k]
            if pattern[k+1] == pattern[q]: # If the kth element of the pattern
is equal to the qth element
                k += 1           # update k accordingly
            prefix_fun[q] = k
    return prefix_fun            # return the prefix function
```

Once we have created the `prefix` function, we implement the main KMP matching algorithm. We start by computing the length of the text string and the pattern, which are stored in the variables m and n, respectively. The following code shows this in detail:

```
def KMP_Matcher(text,pattern):
    m = len(text)
    n = len(pattern)
    flag = False
    text = '-' + text       # append dummy character to make it 1-based
indexing
    pattern = '-' + pattern       # append dummy character to the pattern
also
    prefix_fun = pfun(pattern) # generate prefix function for the pattern
    q = 0
    for i in range(1,m+1):
        while q>0 and pattern[q+1] != text[i]:
        # while pattern and text are not equal, decrement the value of q if
it is > 0
            q = prefix_fun[q]
        if pattern[q+1] == text[i]: # if pattern and text are equal, update
value of q
            q += 1
        if q == n: # if q is equal to the length of the pattern, it means
that the pattern has been found.
            print("Pattern occours with shift",i-n) # print the index,
```

```
where first match occours.
            flag = True
            q = prefix_fun[q]
    if not flag:
            print('\nNo match found')


KMP_Matcher('aabaacaadaabaaba','abaac')          #function call
```

The Boyer-Moore algorithm

As we have already discussed, the main objective of the string pattern matching algorithm is to find ways of skipping comparisons as much as possible by avoiding unnecessary comparisons.

The Boyer-Moore pattern matching algorithm is another such algorithm (apart from the KMP algorithm) that further improves the performance of pattern matching by skipping some comparisons using some methods. You need to understand the following concepts to be able to use the Boyer-Moore algorithm:

1. In this algorithm, we shift the pattern in the direction from left to right, similar to the KMP algorithm
2. We compare the characters of the pattern and the text string from the right to the left direction, which is the opposite of the KMP algorithm
3. The algorithm skips the unnecessary comparisons by using the good-suffix and bad-character shifts concept

Understanding the Boyer-Moore algorithm

The Boyer-Moore algorithm compares the pattern over the text from right to left. It uses the information of the various possible alignments in the pattern by preprocessing it. The main idea of this algorithm is that we compare the end characters of the pattern with the text. If they do not match, then the pattern can be moved on further. If the characters do not match in the end, there is no need to do further comparisons. In addition, in this algorithm, we can also see what portion of the pattern has matched (with the matched suffix), so we utilize this information and align the text and pattern by skipping any unnecessary comparisons.

The Boyer-Moore algorithm has two heuristics to determine the maximum shift possible for the pattern when we find a mismatch:

- Bad character heuristic
- Good suffix heuristic

At the time of a mismatch, each of these heuristics suggests possible shifts, and the Boyer-Moore algorithm shifts the pattern by considering the maximum shift possible due to bad character and good suffix heuristics. The details of the bad character and good suffix heuristics are explained in detail with examples in the following subsections.

Bad character heuristic

The Boyer-Moore algorithm compares the pattern and the text string in the direction from right to left. It uses the bad character heuristic to shift the pattern. According to the bad character shift concept, if there is a mismatch between the character of the pattern and the text, then we check if the mismatched character of the text occurs in the pattern or not. If this mismatched character (also known as a bad character) does not appear in the pattern, then the pattern will be shifted next to this character, and if that character appears somewhere in the pattern, we shift the pattern to align with the occurrence of that character with the bad character of the text string.

Let's understand this concept by using an example. Consider a text string (T) and the pattern = {**acacac**}. We start by comparing the characters from right to left, that is, character **b** of the text string and character **c** of the pattern. They do not match, so we look for the mismatched character of the text string, that is, **b**, in the pattern. Since it does not occur in the pattern, we shift the pattern next to the mismatched character, as shown in the following diagram:

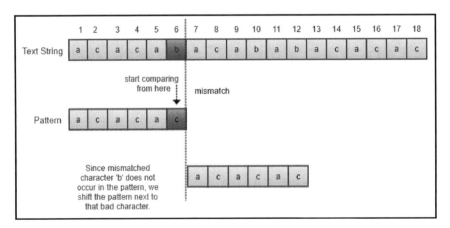

Let's look at another example. We start by comparing characters of the text string and the pattern from right to the left, and we get a mismatch for the character **d** of the text. Here, the suffix **ac** is matched, but the characters **d** and **c** do not match, and the mismatched character **d** does not occur in the pattern. Therefore, we shift the pattern to the mismatched character, as shown in the following diagram:

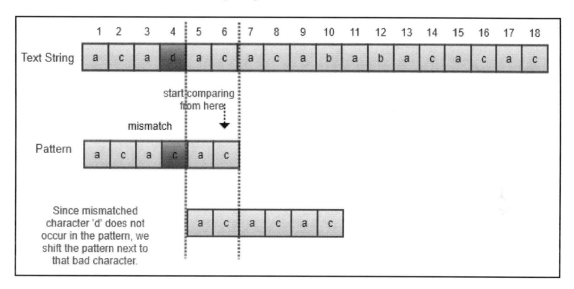

Let's consider another example case for the bad character heuristic. Here, the suffix **ac** is matched, but the next characters, **a** and **c**, do not match, so we search for the occurrences of the mismatched character **a** in the pattern. Since it has two occurrences in the pattern, we have two options so that we can align the mismatched character, as shown in the following diagram. In such a situation, where we have more than one option to shift the pattern, we move the pattern with the minimum amount of shifts to avoid any possible match. (In other words, it would be the rightmost occurrence of that character in the pattern.) If we would have only one occurrence of the mismatched character in the pattern, we can easily shift the pattern in such a way that the mismatched character is aligned.

In the following example, we would prefer option **1** to shift the pattern:

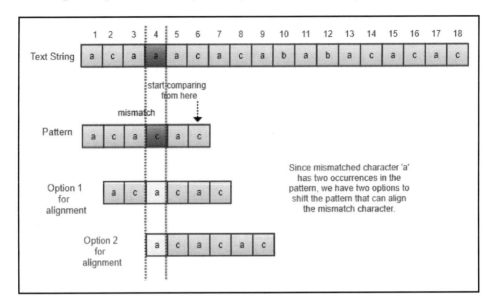

Good suffix heuristic

The bad character heuristic does not always provide good suggestions. The Boyer-Moore algorithm also uses good suffix heuristic as well to shift the pattern over the text string to find out the location of the matched patterns.

Good suffix heuristic is based on the matched suffix. Here, we shift the pattern to the right in such a way that the matched suffix subpattern is aligned with another occurrence of the same suffix in the pattern. It works like this: we start by comparing the pattern and the text string from right to left. If we find any mismatch, then we check the occurrence of the suffix that we have matched so far. This is known as the good suffix. We shift the pattern in such a way that we align another occurrence of the good suffix to the text. Good suffix heuristic has mainly two cases:

1. The matching suffix has one or more occurrences in the pattern.
2. Some part of the matching suffix is present in the start of the pattern (this means that the suffix of the matched suffix exists as the prefix of the pattern).

Let's understand these cases with the following examples. Suppose we have a pattern, **acabac**. We get a mismatch for the characters **a** and **b**, but at this moment in time, we have already matched the suffix, that is, **ac**. Now, we search for another occurrence of the good suffix **ac** in the pattern and we shift the pattern by aligning that suffix, as follows:

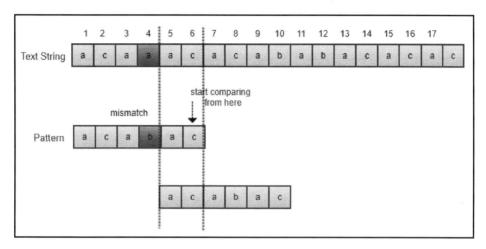

Let's consider another example, where we have two options to align the shift of the pattern so that we get two good suffix strings. Here, we will take the option **1** to align the good suffix by considering the option that has the minimum shifts, as follows:

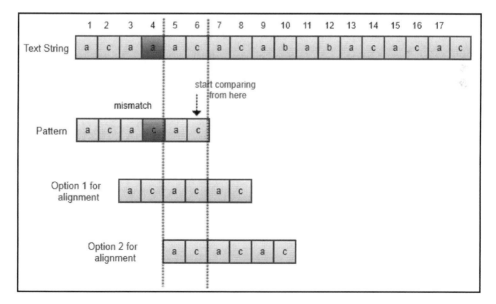

Let's take a look at another example. Here, we get a suffix match of **aac**, but we get a mismatch for the characters **b** and **a**. We search for the good suffix **aac**, but we do not find another occurrence in the pattern. However, we find that the prefix, **ac**, at the start of the pattern does not match with the whole suffix, but it does match with the suffix **ac** of the matched suffix **aac**. In such a situation, we shift the pattern by aligning with the suffix of **aac** that is also a prefix of the pattern and align that prefix with the suffix, as follows:

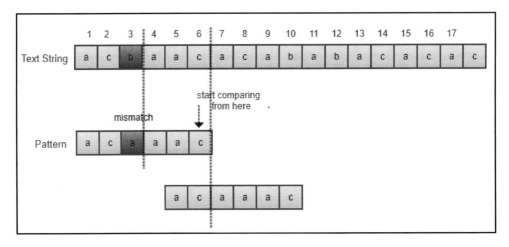

Another case for the good suffix heuristic is as follows. In this case, we match the suffix **aac**, but we mismatch it at characters **b** and **a**. We try to search for the matched suffix in the pattern, but there is no occurrence of the suffix in the pattern, so in this situation, we shift the pattern after the matched suffix, as follows:

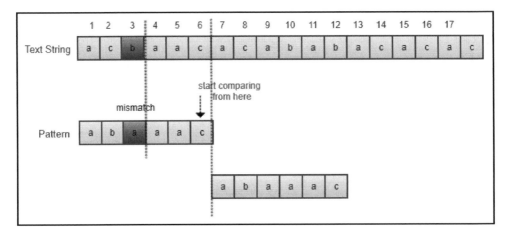

We shift the pattern by the longer distance that is given by the bad character heuristics and the good suffix heuristics.

The Boyer-Moore algorithm takes the time of `O(m)` for the preprocessing of the pattern, and further searching takes the time complexity of `O(mn)`.

Implementing the Boyer-Moore algorithm

Let's understand the implementation of the Boyer-Moore algorithm. Initially, we have the text string and the pattern. After initializing the variables, we start with a while loop that starts by comparing the last character of the pattern to the corresponding character of the text.

Then, the characters are compared from right to left by the use of the nested loop from the last index of the pattern to the first character of the pattern. This uses `range(len(pattern)-1, -1, -1)`.

The outer while loop keeps tracks of the index in the text string while the inner for loop keeps track of the index position in the pattern.

Next, we start comparing the characters by using `pattern[j] != text[i+j]`. If they are mismatched, we make the flag variable `False`, denoting that there is a mismatch.

Now, we check if the good suffix is present or not by using the condition `j == len(pattern)-1`. If this condition is true, it means that there is no good suffix possible, so we check for the bad character heuristics, that is, if a mismatched character is present in the pattern or isn't using the condition `text[i+j] in pattern[0:j]`, and if the condition is true, then it means that the bad character is present in the pattern. In this case, we move the pattern to align this bad character to the other occurrence of this character in the pattern by using `i=i+j-pattern[0:j].rfind(text[i+j])`. Here, `(i+j)` is the index of the bad character.

If the bad character is not present in the pattern (it isn't in the `else` part of it), we move the whole pattern next to the mismatched character by using the index `i=i+j+1`.

Next, we go into the `else` part of the condition to check the good suffix. When we find the mismatch, we further test to see whether we have any subpart of a good suffix present in the prefix of the pattern. We do this by using the following condition:

```
text[i+j+k:i+len(pattern)] not in pattern[0:len(pattern)-1]
```

Furthermore, we check whether the length of the good suffix is 1 or not. If the length of the good suffix is 1, we do not consider this shift. If the good suffix is more than 1, we find out the number of shifts by using the good suffix heuristics and store this in the `gsshift` variable. This is the pattern to a position where the good suffix of a pattern matches with the good suffix of text using the instruction `gsshift=i+j+k-pattern[0:len(pattern)-1].rfind(text[i+j+k:i+len(pattern)])`. Furthermore, we computed the number of shifts possible due to the bad character heuristic and stored this in the `bcshift` variable. The number of shifts possible is `i+j-pattern[0:j].rfind(text[i+j])` when the bad character is present in the pattern, and the number of shifts possible would be `i+j+1` in the case of the bad character not being present in the pattern.

Next, we shift the pattern on the text string by the maximum number of moves given by a bad character and good suffix heuristics by using the instruction `i=max((bcshift, gsshift))`. Finally, we check whether the flag variable is `True` or not. If it is `True`, this means that the pattern has been found and that the matched index has been stored in the `matched_indexes` variable.

The complete implementation of the Boyer-Moore algorithm is shown as follows:

```
text= "acbaacacababacacac"
pattern = "acacac"

matched_indexes = []
i=0
flag = True
while i<=len(text)-len(pattern):
    for j in range(len(pattern)-1, -1, -1): #reverse searching
        if pattern[j] != text[i+j]:
            flag = False #indicates there is a mismatch
            if j == len(pattern)-1: #if good-suffix is not present, we test
bad character
                if text[i+j] in pattern[0:j]:
                    i=i+j-pattern[0:j].rfind(text[i+j]) #i+j is index of
bad character, this line is used for jumping pattern to match bad character
of text with same character in pattern
                else:
                    i=i+j+1 #if bad character is not present, jump pattern
next to it
            else:
                k=1
                while text[i+j+k:i+len(pattern)] not in
pattern[0:len(pattern)-1]: #used for finding sub part of a good-suffix
                    k=k+1
                if len(text[i+j+k:i+len(pattern)]) != 1: #good-suffix
```

```
should not be of one character
                        gsshift=i+j+k-
pattern[0:len(pattern)-1].rfind(text[i+j+k:i+len(pattern)]) #jumps pattern
to a position where good-suffix of pattern matches with good-suffix of text
                else:
                        #gsshift=i+len(pattern)
                        gsshift=0 #when good-suffix heuristic is not
applicable, we prefer bad character heuristic
                if text[i+j] in pattern[0:j]:
                        bcshift=i+j-pattern[0:j].rfind(text[i+j]) #i+j is index
of bad character, this line is used for jumping pattern to match bad
character of text with same character in pattern
                else:
                        bcshift=i+j+1
                i=max((bcshift, gsshift))
        break
    if flag: #if pattern is found then normal iteration
        matched_indexes.append(i)
        i = i+1
    else: #again set flag to True so new string in text can be examined
        flag = True
print ("Pattern found at", matched_indexes)
```

Summary

In this chapter, we have discussed the most popular and important string processing algorithms that have wide applications in real-time scenarios. We started this chapter by looking at the basic concepts and definitions related to strings. Next, we described the brute-force, Rabin-Karp, KMP, and Boyer-Moore pattern matching algorithms in detail for pattern matching problems. We have seen that the brute-force pattern matching algorithm is quite slow as it compared the characters of the pattern and the text string character by character.

In pattern matching algorithms, we try to find out ways to skip unnecessary comparisons and move the pattern over the text as fast as possible to quickly find out the positions of the matched patterns. The KMP algorithm finds out the unnecessary comparisons by looking at the overlapping substrings in the pattern itself to avoid unimportant comparisons. Furthermore, we discussed the Boyer-Moore algorithm, which is very efficient when the text and pattern are long. It is the most popular algorithm that is being used in practice for pattern matching.

In the next chapter, we will be discussing data structure design strategies and techniques in more detail.

13
Design Techniques and Strategies

In this chapter, we take a step back and look at broader topics in computer algorithm design. As your experience with programming grows, certain patterns start to become apparent. The world of algorithms contains a plethora of techniques and design principles. A mastery of these techniques is required to tackle harder problems in the field.

In this chapter, we will discuss the ways in which different kinds of algorithms can be categorized. Design techniques will be described and illustrated. We will also further discuss the analysis of algorithms. Finally, we will provide detailed implementations for a few very important algorithms.

This chapter will cover the following topics:

- The classification of algorithms
- Various algorithm design methodologies
- The implementation and explanation of various important algorithms

Technical requirements

The source code used in this chapter is available at the following GitHub link:

```
https://github.com/PacktPublishing/Hands-On-Data-Structures-and-Algorithms-
with-Python-3.7-Second-Edition/tree/master/Chapter13.
```

Classification of algorithms

There are a number of classification schemes, based on what the algorithm is designed to achieve. In previous chapters, we implemented various algorithms. The question to ask is: do these algorithms share the same form or any similarities? If the answer is yes, then ask: what are the similarities and characteristics being used as the basis for comparison? If the answer is no, then can the algorithms be grouped into classes?

These are the questions that we will discuss in the subsequent subsections. Here we present the major methods for classifying algorithms.

Classification by implementation

When translating a series of steps or processes into a working algorithm, there are a number of forms that it may take. The heart of the algorithm may employ one or more of the following assets.

Recursion

Recursive algorithms are the ones that call themselves to repeatedly execute code until a certain condition is satisfied. Some problems are more easily expressed by implementing their solution through recursion. One classic example is the Towers of Hanoi.

In simple terms, an iterative function is one that loops to repeat some part of the code, and a recursive function is one that calls itself to repeat the code. An iterative algorithm, on the other hand, uses a series of steps or a repetitive construct to formulate a solution; it iteratively executes a part of the code.

This repetitive construct could be a simple `while` loop, or any other kind of loop. Iterative solutions also come to mind more easily than their recursive implementations.

Logic

One implementation of an algorithm is expressing it as a controlled logical deduction. This logic component is comprised of the axioms that will be used in the computation. The control component determines the manner in which deduction is applied to the axioms. This is expressed in the form a*lgorithm = logic + control*. This forms the basis of the logic programming paradigm.

The logic component determines the meaning of the algorithm. The control component only affects its efficiency. Without modifying the logic, the efficiency can be improved by improving the control component.

Serial or parallel algorithms

The RAM model of most computers allows for the assumption that computing is carried out one instruction at a time.

Serial algorithms, also known as **sequential algorithms**, are algorithms that are executed sequentially. Execution commences from start to finish without any other execution procedure.

To be able to process several instructions at once, a different model or computing technique is required. Parallel algorithms perform more than one operation at a time. In the PRAM model, there are serial processors that share a global memory. The processors can also perform various arithmetic and logical operations in parallel. This enables the execution of several instructions at one time.

Parallel/distributed algorithms divide a problem into subproblems among its processors to collect the results. Some sorting algorithms can be efficiently parallelized, while iterative algorithms are generally parallelizable.

Deterministic versus nondeterministic algorithms

Deterministic algorithms produce the same output without fail every time the algorithm is run with the same input. There are some sets of problems that are so complex in the design of their solutions that expressing their solution in a deterministic way can be a challenge.

Nondeterministic algorithms can change the order of execution or some internal subprocess, leading to a change in the final result each time the algorithm is run.

As such, with every run of a nondeterministic algorithm, the output of the algorithm will be different. For instance, an algorithm that makes use of a probabilistic value will yield different outputs on successive executions, depending on the value of the random number generated.

Classification by complexity

To determine the complexity of an algorithm is to estimate how much space (memory) and time is needed during computation or program execution. Generally, the performance of the two algorithms is compared with their complexity. The lower complexity algorithm—that is, the one requiring less space and time to perform a given task—is preferred.

Chapter 3, *Principles of Algorithm Design*, presents more comprehensive coverage of complexity. We will summarize what we have learned here.

Complexity curves

Let's consider a problem of magnitude n. To determine the time complexity of an algorithm, we denote it with $T(n)$. The value may fall under $O(1)$, $O(log\ n)$, $O(n)$, $O(n\ log(n))$, $O(n^2)$, $O(n^3)$, or $O(2^n)$. Depending on the steps an algorithm performs, the time complexity may or may not be affected. The notation $O(n)$ captures the growth rate of an algorithm.

Let's now examine a practical scenario, to determine which algorithm is better for solving a given problem. How do we come to the conclusion that the bubble sort algorithm is slower than the quick sort algorithm? Or, in general, how do we measure the efficiency of one algorithm against the other?

Well, we can compare the Big O of any number of algorithms to determine their efficiency. This approach gives us a time measure or growth rate, which charts the behavior of the algorithm as n gets bigger.

Here is a graph of the different runtimes that an algorithm's performance may fall under:

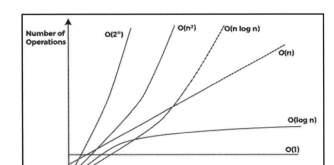

In ascending order, the list of runtimes from best to worst is **O(1)**, **O(log n)**, **O(n)**, **O(n log n)**, **O(n^2)**, **O(n^3)**, and **O(2^n)**. Therefore, if an algorithm has a time complexity of **O(1)**, and another algorithm for the same task has the complexity **O(log n)**, the first algorithm should be preferred.

Classification by design

In this section, we present categories of algorithms based on their design.

A given problem may have a number of solutions. When these solutions are analyzed, it is observed that each one follows a certain pattern or technique. We can categorize the algorithms based on how they solve the problem, as in the following subsections.

Divide and conquer

This approach to problem-solving is just as its name suggests. To solve (conquer) a certain problem, the algorithm divides it into subproblems that can easily be solved. Further, the solutions to each of these subproblems are combined in such a way that the final solution is the solution of the original problem.

The way in which the problems are broken down into smaller subproblems is mostly done by recursion. We will examine this technique in detail in the subsequent subsections. Some algorithms that use this technique include merge sort, quick sort, and binary search.

Dynamic programming

This technique is similar to divide and conquer, in that a problem is broken down into smaller problems. However, in divide and conquer, each subproblem has to be solved before its results can be used to solve bigger problems.

By contrast, dynamic programming does not compute the solution to an already encountered subproblem. Rather, it uses a remembering technique to avoid the recomputation.

Dynamic programming problems have two characteristics—**optimal substructure**, and **overlapping subproblem**. We will discuss this further in the next section.

Greedy algorithms

It may be quite difficult to determine the best solution for a certain problem. To overcome this, we resort to an approach where we select the most promising choice from multiple available options or choices.

With greedy algorithms, the guiding rule is to always select the option that yields the most beneficial results and to continue doing that, hoping to reach a perfect solution. This technique aims to find a global optimal final solution by making a series of local optimal choices. The local optimal choice seems to lead to the solution.

Technical implementation

Let's dig into the implementation of some of the theoretical programming techniques we have discussed. We start with dynamic programming.

Implementation using dynamic programming

As we have already described, in this approach, we divide a given problem into smaller subproblems. In finding the solution, care is taken not to recompute any of the previously encountered subproblems.

This sounds a bit like recursion, but things are a little different here. A problem may lend itself to being solved by using dynamic programming, but will not necessarily take the form of making recursive calls.

One property that makes a problem an ideal candidate for being solved with dynamic programming is that it has an **overlapping set of subproblems**.

Once we realize that the form of subproblems has repeated itself during computation, we need not compute it again. Instead, we return a pre-computed result for that previously encountered subproblem.

To ensure that we never have to re-evaluate a subproblem, we need an efficient way to store the results of each subproblem. The following two techniques are readily available.

Memoization

This technique starts from the initial problem set, and divides it into small subproblems. After the solution to a subprogram has been determined, we store the result to that particular subproblem. In the future, when this subproblem is encountered, we only return its pre-computed result.

Tabulation

In tabulation, we fill a table with solutions to subproblems, and then combine them to solve bigger problems.

The Fibonacci series

Let's consider an example to understand how dynamic programming works. We use the Fibonacci series to illustrate both the memoization and tabulation techniques.

The Fibonacci series can be demonstrated using a recurrence relation. Recurrence relations are recursive functions that are used to define mathematical functions or sequences. For example, the following recurrence relation defines the Fibonacci sequence [1, 1, 2, 3, 5, 8 ...]:

```
func(1) = 1
func(0) = 1
func(n) = func(n-1) + func(n-2)
```

Note that the Fibonacci sequence can be generated by putting the values of *n* in sequence [1, 2, 3, 4, ...].

The memoization technique

Let's generate the Fibonacci series to the fifth term:

```
1 1 2 3 5
```

A recursive-style program to generate the sequence would be as follows:

```
def fib(n):
    if n <= 2:
        return 1
    else:
        return fib(n-1) + fib(n-2)
```

The code is very simple, but a little tricky to read because of the recursive calls being made that end up solving the problem.

When the base case is met, the `fib()` function returns 1. If *n* is equal to or less than 2, the base case is met.

If the base case is not met, we will call the `fib()` function again, and this time supply the first call with `n-1`, and the second with `n-2`:

```
return fib(n-1) + fib(n-2)
```

The layout of the strategy to solve the ith term in the Fibonacci sequence is as follows:

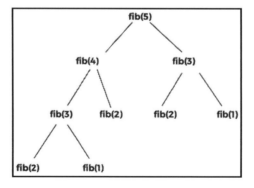

Careful observation of the tree diagram shows some interesting patterns. The call to **fib(1)** happens twice. The call to **fib(2)** happens thrice. Also, the call to **fib(3)** happens twice.

The return values of the same function call never change; for example, the return value for **fib(2)** will always be the same whenever we call it. It will also be the same for **fib(1)** and **fib(3)**. Thus, computational time will be wasted if we compute again whenever we encounter the same function, since the same result is returned.

These repeated calls to a function with the same parameters and output suggest that there is an overlap. Certain computations reoccur down in the smaller subproblems.

A better approach is to store the results of the computation of **fib(1)** the first time it is encountered. Similarly, we should store return values for **fib(2)** and **fib(3)**. Later, anytime we encounter a call to **fib(1)**, **fib(2)**, or **fib(3)**, we simply return their respective results.

The diagram of our fib calls will now look like this:

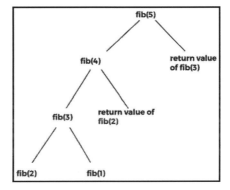

We have eliminated the need to compute **fib(3)**, fib(2), and **fib(1)** if they are encountered multiple times. This typifies the memoization technique, wherein there is no recomputation of overlapping calls to functions when breaking a problem into its subproblems.

The overlapping function calls in our Fibonacci example are **fib(1)**, **fib(2)**, and **fib(3)**:

```
def dyna_fib(n, lookup):
    if n <= 2:
        lookup[n] = 1

    if lookup[n] is None:
        lookup[n] = dyna_fib(n-1, lookup) + dyna_fib(n-2, lookup)

    return lookup[n]
```

To create a list of 1,000 elements, we do the following and pass it to the lookup parameter of the dyna_fib function:

```
map_set = [None]*(1000)
```

This list will store the value of the computation of the various calls to the `dyna_fib()` function:

```
if n <= 2:
    lookup[n] = 1
```

Any call to the `dyna_fib()` function with *n* being less than or equal to 2 will return 1. When `dyna_fib(1)` is evaluated, we store the value at index 1 of `map_set`.

Write the condition for `lookup[n]` as the following:

```
if lookup[n] is None:
    lookup[n] = dyna_fib(n-1, lookup) + dyna_fib(n-2, lookup)
```

We pass lookup so that it can be referenced when evaluating the subproblems. The calls to `dyna_fib(n-1, lookup)` and `dyna_fib(n-2, lookup)` are stored in `lookup[n]`.

When we run our updated implementation of the function to find the ith term of the Fibonacci series, we can see a considerable improvement. This implementation runs much faster than our initial implementation. Supply the value 20 to both implementations, and witness the difference in the execution speed.

However, the updated algorithm has sacrificed space complexity to achieve this, because of the use of additional memory in storing the results of the function calls.

The tabulation technique

A second technique in dynamic programming involves the use of a table of results, or matrix in some cases, to store the results of computations for later use.

This approach solves the bigger problem by first working out a route to the final solution. In the case of the `fib()` function, we develop a table with the values of `fib(1)` and `fib(2)` predetermined. Based on these two values, we will work our way up to `fib(n)`:

```
def fib(n):

    results = [1, 1]

    for i in range(2, n):
        results.append(results[i-1] + results[i-2])

    return results[-1]
```

The `results` variable stores the values 1 and 1 at indices 0 and 1. This represents the return values of `fib(1)` and `fib(2)`. To calculate the values of the `fib()` function for values higher than 2, we simply call the `for` loop, which appends the sum of the `results[i-1]` + `results[i-2]` to the list of results.

Implementation using divide and conquer

This programming approach to problem-solving emphasizes the need to break down a problem into smaller subproblems of the same type or form of the original problem. These subproblems are solved and combined to obtain the solution of the original problem.

The following three steps are associated with this kind of programming.

Divide

To divide means to break down an entity or problem. Here, we devise the means to break down the original problem into subproblems. We can achieve this through iterative or recursive calls.

Conquer

It is impossible to continue breaking the problems into subproblems indefinitely. At some point, the smallest indivisible problem will return a solution. Once this happens, we can reverse our thought process and say that if we know the solution to the smallest subproblem, we can obtain the final solution to the original problem.

Merge

To obtain the final solution, we need to combine the solutions to the smaller problems in order to solve the bigger problem.

There are other variants to the divide and conquer algorithms, such as merge and combine, and conquer and solve. Many algorithms make use of the divide and conquer principle, such as merge sorting, quick sort, and Strassen's matrix multiplication.

We will now describe implementation of a merge sort algorithm, as we saw earlier in `Chapter 3`, *Principles of Algorithm Design*.

Merge sort

Merge sort algorithms are based on the divide and conquer rule. Given a list of unsorted elements, we split the list into two approximate halves. We continue to divide the list into two halves recursively.

After a while, the sublists created as a result of the recursive call will contain only one element. At that point, we begin to merge the solutions in the conquer or merge step:

```python
def merge_sort(unsorted_list):
    if len(unsorted_list) == 1:
        return unsorted_list

    mid_point = int((len(unsorted_list))//2)

    first_half = unsorted_list[:mid_point]
    second_half = unsorted_list[mid_point:]

    half_a = merge_sort(first_half)
    half_b = merge_sort(second_half)

    return merge(half_a, half_b)
```

Our implementation starts by accepting the list of unsorted elements into the `merge_sort` function. The `if` statement is used to establish the base case, where, if there is only one element in the `unsorted_list`, we simply return that list again. If there is more than one element in the list, we find the approximate middle using `mid_point = int((len(unsorted_list)) // 2)`.

Using this `mid_point`, we divide the list into two sublists, namely, `first_half` and `second_half`:

```python
    first_half = unsorted_list[:mid_point]
    second_half = unsorted_list[mid_point:]
```

A recursive call is made by passing the two sublists to the `merge_sort` function again:

```python
    half_a = merge_sort(first_half)
    half_b = merge_sort(second_half)
```

Now for the merge step. When `half_a` and `half_b` have been passed their values, we call the `merge` function, which will merge or combine the two solutions stored in `half_a` and `half_b`, which are lists:

```python
def merge(first_sublist, second_sublist):
    i = j = 0
    merged_list = []

    while i < len(first_sublist) and j < len(second_sublist):
        if first_sublist[i] < second_sublist[j]:
            merged_list.append(first_sublist[i])
            i += 1
        else:
            merged_list.append(second_sublist[j])
            j += 1

    while i < len(first_sublist):
        merged_list.append(first_sublist[i])
        i += 1

    while j < len(second_sublist):
        merged_list.append(second_sublist[j])
        j += 1

    return merged_list
```

The `merge` function takes the two lists we want to merge together, `first_sublist` and `second_sublist`. The `i` and `j` variables are initialized to 0, and are used as pointers to tell us where we are in the two lists with respect to the merging process.

The final `merged_list` will contain the merged list:

```python
while i < len(first_sublist) and j < len(second_sublist):
    if first_sublist[i] < second_sublist[j]:
        merged_list.append(first_sublist[i])
        i += 1
    else:
        merged_list.append(second_sublist[j])
        j += 1
```

The `while` loop starts comparing the elements in `first_sublist` and `second_sublist`. The `if` statement selects the smaller of the two, `first_sublist[i]` or `second_sublist[j]`, and appends it to `merged_list`. The `i` or `j` index is incremented to reflect where we are with the merging step. The `while` loop stops when either sublist is empty.

There may be elements left behind in either `first_sublist` or `second_sublist`. The last two `while` loops make sure that those elements are added to `merged_list` before it is returned.

The last call to `merge(half_a, half_b)` will return the sorted list.

Let's give the algorithm a dry run by merging the two sublists `[4, 6, 8]` and `[5, 7, 11, 40]`:

Step	first_sublist	second_sublist	merged_list
Step 0	[4 6 8]	[5 7 11 40]	[]
Step 1	[6 8]	[5 7 11 40]	[4]
Step 2	[6 8]	[7 11 40]	[4 5]
Step 3	[8]	[7 11 40]	[4 5 6]
Step 4	[8]	[11 40]	[4 5 6 7]
Step 5	[ ]	[11 40]	[4 5 6 7 8]
Step 6	[]	[ ]	[4 5 6 7 8 11 40]

Note that the text in bold represents the current item referenced in the loops `first_sublist` (which uses the i *index*) and `second_sublist` (which uses the j index).

At this point in the execution, the third `while` loop in the merge function kicks in to move 11 and 40 into `merged_list`. The returned `merged_list` will contain the fully sorted list.

Note that while the merge algorithm takes `O(n)` time, the merge sort algorithm has a running time complexity of `O(log n) T(n) = O(n)*O(log n) = O(n log n)`.

Implementation using greedy algorithms

As we discussed earlier, greedy algorithms make decisions to yield the best possible local solution, which in turn provides the optimal solution. It is the hope of this technique that by making the best possible choices at each step, the total path will lead to an overall optimal solution or end.

Examples of greedy algorithms include **Prim's algorithm** for finding a minimum spanning tree, the **Knapsack problem**, and the **Traveling Salesman problem**, to mention just a few.

Coin-counting problem

To demonstrate how the greedy technique works, let's look at an example. Consider a problem in which we wish to compute the minimum number of coin required to make a given amount A, where we have an infinite supply of the given coins' values.

For example, in some arbitrary country, we have the following coin denominations: 1, 5, and 8 GHC. Given an amount (for example, 12 GHC), we want to find the smallest possible number of coins needed to provide this amount.

The algorithm to obtain the minimum number of coins to provide a given amount A using denominations $\{a_1, a_2, a_3 \ldots a_n\}$ is as follows:

1. We sort the list of denominations $\{a_1, a_2, a_3 \ldots a_n\}$.
2. We get the largest denomination in $\{a_1, a_2, a_3 \ldots a_n\}$ which is smaller than A.
3. We obtain the division by dividing A by the largest denomination.
4. We get the remaining amount A by getting the remainder using (A % largest denominator).
5. If the value of A becomes 0, then we return the result.
6. Else If the value of A is greater than 0, we append the largest denominator and division variable in the result variable. And repeat the steps 2-5.

Using the greedy approach, we first pick the largest value from the available denominations—which is 8—to divide into 12. The remainder, 4, cannot be divided by either 8 or the next lowest denomination, 5. So, we try the 1 GHC denomination coin, of which we need four. In the end, using this greedy algorithm, we return an answer of one 8 GHC coin and four 1 GHC coins.

So far, our greedy algorithm seems to be doing pretty well. A function that returns the respective denominations is as follows:

```
def basic_small_change(denom, total_amount):
    sorted_denominations = sorted(denom, reverse=True)

    number_of_denoms = []

    for i in sorted_denominations:
        div = total_amount // i
        total_amount = total_amount % i
        if div > 0:
            number_of_denoms.append((i, div))

    return number_of_denoms
```

This greedy algorithm always starts by using the largest denomination possible. Note that denom is a list of denominations, and that sorted(denom, reverse=True) will sort the list in reverse so that we can obtain the largest denomination at index 0. Now, starting from index *0* of the sorted list of denominations, sorted_denominations, we iterate and apply the greedy technique:

```
for i in sorted_denominations:
    div = total_amount // i
    total_amount = total_amount % i
    if div > 0:
        number_of_denoms.append((i, div))
```

The loop will run through the list of denominations. Each time the loop runs, it obtains the quotient, div, by dividing the total_amount by the current denomination, *i*. The total_amount variable is updated to store the remainder for further processing. If the quotient is greater than 0, we store it in number_of_denoms.

However, there are some possible instances where this algorithm may fail. For instance, when passed 12 GHC, our algorithm returned one 8 GHC and four 1 GHC coins. This output is, however, not the optimal solution. The best solution is to use two 5 GHC and two 1 GHC coins.

A better greedy algorithm is presented here. This time, the function returns a list of tuples that allow us to investigate the best results:

```
def optimal_small_change(denom, total_amount):

    sorted_denominations = sorted(denom, reverse=True)

    series = []
    for j in range(len(sorted_denominations)):
        term = sorted_denominations[j:]

        number_of_denoms = []
        local_total = total_amount
        for i in term:
            div = local_total // i
            local_total = local_total % i
            if div > 0:
                number_of_denoms.append((i, div))

        series.append(number_of_denoms)

    return series
```

The outer `for` loop enables us to limit the denominations from which we find our solution:

```
for j in range(len(sorted_denominations)):
    term = sorted_denominations[j:]
    ...
```

Assuming that we have the list [5, 4, 3] in `sorted_denominations`, slicing it with `[j:]` helps us obtain the sublists [5, 4, 3], [4, 3], and [3], from which we try to find the right combination.

Shortest path algorithm

The shortest path problem requires us to find out the shortest possible route between nodes in a graph. It has important applications for mapping and route planning, when plotting the most efficient way to get from point **A** to point **B**.

Dijkstra's algorithm is a very popular method of solving this problem. This algorithm is used to find the shortest distance from a source to all other nodes or vertices in a graph. Here we explain how we can use the greedy approach to solve this problem.

Dijkstra's algorithm works for weighted directed and undirected graphs. The algorithm produces the output of a list of the shortest path from a given source node A in a weighted graph. The algorithm works as follows:

1. Initially, mark all the nodes as unvisited, and set their distance from the given source node to infinity (the source node is set to zero).
2. Set the source node as current.
3. For the current node, look for all the unvisited adjacent nodes; compute the distance to that node from the source node through the current node. Compare the newly computed distance to the currently assigned distance, and if it is smaller, set this as the new value.
4. Once we have considered all the unvisited adjacent nodes of the current node, we mark it as visited.
5. We next consider the next unvisited node which has the shortest distance from the source node. Repeat steps 2 to 4.
6. We stop when the list of unvisited nodes is empty, meaning we have considered all the unvisited nodes.

Consider the following example of a weighted graph with six nodes [A, B, C, D, E, F] to understand how Dijkstra's algorithm works:

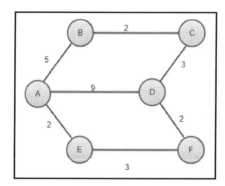

By manual inspection, the shortest path between node **A** and node **D** at first glance seems to be the direct line with a distance of 9. However, the shortest route means the lowest total distance, even if this comprises several parts. By comparison, traveling from node **A** to node **E** to node **F** and finally to node **D** will incur a total distance of 7, making it a shorter route.

We would implement the shortest path algorithm with a single source. It would determine the shortest path from the origin, which in this case is **A**, to any other node in the graph.

In Chapter 8, *Graphs and Other Algorithms*, we discussed how to represent a graph with an adjacency list. We use an adjacency list along with the weight/cost/distance on every edge to represent the graph, as shown in the following Python code. A table is used to keep track of the shortest distance from the source in the graph to any other node. A Python dictionary will be used to implement this table.

Here is the starting table:

Node	Shortest distance from source	Previous node
A	0	None
B	∞	None
C	∞	None
D	∞	None
E	∞	None
F	∞	None

The adjacency list for the diagram and table is as follows:

```
graph = dict()
graph['A'] = {'B': 5, 'D': 9, 'E': 2}
graph['B'] = {'A': 5, 'C': 2}
graph['C'] = {'B': 2, 'D': 3}
graph['D'] = {'A': 9, 'F': 2, 'C': 3}
graph['E'] = {'A': 2, 'F': 3}
graph['F'] = {'E': 3, 'D': 2}
```

The nested dictionary holds the distance and adjacent nodes.

When the algorithm starts, the shortest distance from the given source node (**A**) to any of the nodes is unknown. Thus, we initially set the distance to all other nodes to infinity, with the exception of node **A**, as the distance from node **A** to node **A** is 0.

No prior nodes have been visited when the algorithm begins. Therefore, we mark the previous node column of the node **A** as None.

In step 1 of the algorithm, we start by examining the adjacent nodes to node **A**. To find the shortest distance from node **A** to node **B**, we need to find the distance from the start node to the previous node of node B, which happens to be node **A**, and add it to the distance from node **A** to node **B**. We do this for other adjacent nodes of **A**, which are **B**, **E**, and **D**. This is shown in the following diagram:

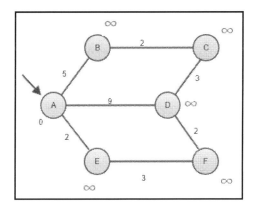

We take the adjacent node **B** as its distance from node **A** is minimum; the distance from the start node (**A**) to the previous node (None) is 0, and the distance from the previous node to the current node (**B**) is **5**. This sum is compared with the data in the shortest distance column of node **B**. Since **5** is less than infinity(∞), we replace ∞ with the smaller of the two, which is **5**.

Any time the shortest distance of a node is replaced by a smaller value, we need to update the previous node column too for all the adjacent nodes of the current node. After this, we mark node **A** as visited:

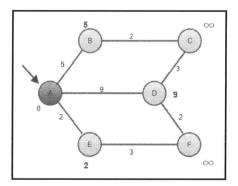

At the end of the first step, our table looks as follows:

Node	Shortest distance from source	Previous node
A*	0	None
B	5	A
C	∞	None
D	9	A
E	2	A
F	∞	None

At this point, node **A** is considered visited. As such, we add node **A** to the list of visited nodes. In the table, we show that node **A** has been visited by making the text bold and appending an asterisk sign to it.

In the second step, we find the node with the shortest distance using our table as a guide. Node **E**, with its value of 2, has the shortest distance. This is what we can infer from the table about node **E**. To get to node **E**, we must visit node **A** and cover a distance of **2**. From node A, we cover a distance of 0 to get to the starting node, which is node **A** itself.

The adjacent nodes to node **E** are **A** and **F**. But node **A** has already been visited, so we will only consider node **F**. To find the shortest route or distance to node **F**, we must find the distance from the starting node to node **E** and add it to the distance between node **E** and **F**. We can find the distance from the starting node to node **E** by looking at the shortest distance column of node **E**, which has the value **2**. The distance from node **E** to **F** can be obtained from the adjacency list we developed in Python earlier in this section.

This distance is **3**. These two sum up to 5, which is less than infinity. Remember we are examining the adjacent node **F**. Since there are no more adjacent nodes to node **E**, we mark node **E** as visited. Our updated table and the figure will have the following values:

Node	Shortest distance from source	Previous node
A*	0	None
B	5	A
C	∞	None
D	9	A
E*	2	A
F	5	E

After visiting node **E**, we find the smallest value in the shortest distance column of the table, which is 5 for nodes **B** and **F**. Let us choose **B** instead of **F** purely on an alphabetical basis (we could equally have chosen **F**).

The adjacent nodes to **B** are **A** and **C**, but node **A** has already been visited. Using the rule we established earlier, the shortest distance from **A** to **C** is 7. We arrive at this number because the distance from the starting node to node **B** is 5, while the distance from node **B** to **C** is 2.

Since 7 is less than infinity, we update the shortest distance to 7 and update the previous node column with node **B**:

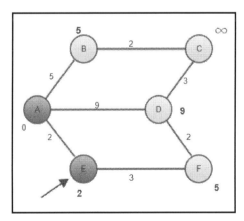

Now, **B** is also marked as visited. The new state of the table and the figure is as follows:

Node	Shortest distance from source	Previous node
A*	0	None
B*	5	A
C	7	B
D	9	A
E*	2	A
F	5	E

The node with the shortest distance yet unvisited is node **F**. The adjacent nodes to **F** are nodes **D** and **E**. But node **E** has already been visited. As such, we focus on finding the shortest distance from the starting node to node **D**.

We calculate this distance by adding the distance from node **A** to **F** to the distance from node **F** to **D**. This sums up to 7, which is less than **9**. Thus, we update the **9** with **7** and replace **A** with **F** in node **D**'s previous node column:

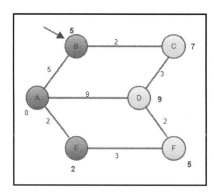

Node **F** is now marked as visited. Here is the updated table and the figure up to this point:

Node	Shortest distance from source	Previous node
A*	0	None
B*	5	A
C	7	B
D	7	F
E*	2	A
F*	5	E

Now, only two unvisited nodes are left, **C** and **D**, both with a distance cost of **7**. In alphabetical order, we choose to examine **C** because both nodes have the same shortest distance from the starting node **A**:

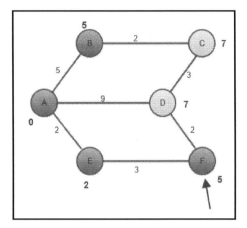

However, all the adjacent nodes to **C** have been visited. Thus, we have nothing to do but mark node **C** as visited. The table remains unchanged at this point:

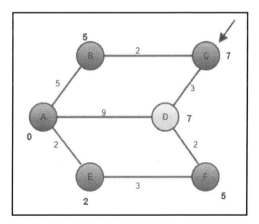

Lastly, we take node **D**, and find out that all its adjacent nodes have been visited too. We only mark it as visited. The table remains unchanged:

Node	Shortest distance from source	Previous node
A*	0	None
B*	5	A
C*	7	B
D*	7	F
E*	2	A
F*	5	E

Let's verify this table with our initial graph. From the graph, we know that the shortest distance from **A** to **F** is **5**. We will need to go through **E** to get to node **F**:

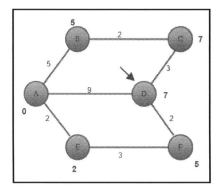

According to the table, the shortest distance from the source column for node **F** is 5. This is true. It also tells us that to get to node **F**, we need to visit node **E**, and from **E** to node **A**, which is our starting node. This is actually the shortest path.

To implement Dijkstra's algorithm to find the shortest path, we begin the program for finding the shortest distance by representing the table that enables us to track the changes in our graph. For the diagram we used, here is a dictionary representation of the table:

```python
table = dict()
table = {
    'A': [0, None],
    'B': [float("inf"), None],
    'C': [float("inf"), None],
    'D': [float("inf"), None],
    'E': [float("inf"), None],
    'F': [float("inf"), None],
}
```

The initial state of the table uses `float("inf")` to represent infinity. Each key in the dictionary maps to a list. At the first index of the list, the shortest distance from the source A is stored. At the second index, the previous node is stored:

```
DISTANCE = 0
PREVIOUS_NODE = 1
INFINITY = float('inf')
```

To avoid the use of magic numbers, we use the preceding constants. The shortest path column's index is referenced by `DISTANCE`. The previous node column's index is referenced by `PREVIOUS_NODE`.

Now all is set for the main function of the algorithm. It will take the graph, represented by the adjacency list, the table, and the starting node as parameters:

```
def find_shortest_path(graph, table, origin):
    visited_nodes = []
    current_node = origin
    starting_node = origin
```

We keep the list of visited nodes in the `visited_nodes` list. The `current_node` and `starting_node` variables will both point to the node in the graph we choose to make our starting node. The `origin` value is the reference point for all other nodes with respect to finding the shortest path.

The heavy lifting of the whole process is accomplished by the use of a `while` loop:

```
while True:
    adjacent_nodes = graph[current_node]
    if set(adjacent_nodes).issubset(set(visited_nodes)):
        # Nothing here to do. All adjacent nodes have been visited.
        pass
    else:
        unvisited_nodes =
            set(adjacent_nodes).difference(set(visited_nodes))
        for vertex in unvisited_nodes:
            distance_from_starting_node =
                get_shortest_distance(table, vertex)
            if distance_from_starting_node == INFINITY and
                current_node == starting_node:
                total_distance = get_distance(graph, vertex,
                                                  current_node)
            else:
                total_distance = get_shortest_distance (table,
                    current_node) + get_distance(graph, current_node,
                                                  vertex)
```

```
                if total_distance < distance_from_starting_node:
                    set_shortest_distance(table, vertex,
                                             total_distance)
                    set_previous_node(table, vertex, current_node)

        visited_nodes.append(current_node)

        if len(visited_nodes) == len(table.keys()):
            break

        current_node = get_next_node(table,visited_nodes)
```

Let's break down what the `while` loop is doing. In the body of the `while` loop, we obtain the current node in the graph we want to investigate with `adjacent_nodes = graph[current_node]`. Now, `current_node` should have been set prior. The `if` statement is used to find out whether all the adjacent nodes of `current_node` have been visited.

When the `while` loop is executed for the first time, `current_node` will contain A and `adjacent_nodes` will contain nodes B, D, and E. Furthermore, `visited_nodes` will be empty too. If all nodes have been visited, we only move on to the statements further down the program. Otherwise, we begin a whole new step.

The `set(adjacent_nodes).difference(set(visited_nodes))` statement returns the nodes that have not been visited. The loop iterates over this list of unvisited nodes:

```
        distance_from_starting_node = get_shortest_distance(table, vertex)
```

The `get_shortest_distance(table, vertex)` helper method will return the value stored in the shortest distance column of our table, using one of the unvisited nodes referenced by `vertex`:

```
        if distance_from_starting_node == INFINITY and current_node ==
    starting_node:
            total_distance = get_distance(graph, vertex, current_node)
```

When we are examining the adjacent nodes of the starting node, `distance_from_starting_node == INFINITY and current_node == starting_node` will evaluate to `True`, in which case we only have to find the distance between the starting node and vertex by referencing the graph:

```
        total_distance = get_distance(graph, vertex, current_node)
```

The `get_distance` method is another helper method we use to obtain the value (distance) of the edge between `vertex` and `current_node`.

If the condition fails, then we assign to `total_distance` the sum of the distance from the starting node to `current_node`, and the distance between `current_node` and `vertex`.

Once we have our total distance, we need to check whether `total_distance` is less than the existing data in the shortest distance column of our table. If it is less, then we use the two helper methods to update that row:

```
if total_distance < distance_from_starting_node:
    set_shortest_distance(table, vertex, total_distance)
set_previous_node(table, vertex, current_node)
```

At this point, we add `current_node` to the list of visited nodes:

```
visited_nodes.append(current_node)
```

If all nodes have been visited, then we must exit the `while` loop. To check whether all the nodes have been visited, we compare the length of the `visited_nodes` list to the number of keys in our table. If they have become equal, we simply exit the `while` loop.

The `get_next_node` helper method is used to fetch the next node to visit. It is this method that helps us find the minimum value in the shortest distance column from the starting nodes using our table.

The whole method ends by returning the updated table. To print the table, we use the following statements:

```
shortest_distance_table = find_shortest_path(graph, table, 'A')
for k in sorted(shortest_distance_table):
    print("{} - {}".format(k, shortest_distance_table[k]))
```

This is the output for the preceding statement:

```
>>>
A - [0, None]
B - [5, 'A']
C - [7, 'B']
D - [7, 'F']
E - [2, 'A']
F - [5, 'E']
```

For the sake of completeness, let's find out what the helper methods are doing:

```
def get_shortest_distance(table, vertex):
    shortest_distance = table[vertex][DISTANCE]
    return shortest_distance
```

The `get_shortest_distance` function returns the value stored in index 0 of our table. At that index, we always store the shortest distance from the starting node up to `vertex`. The `set_shortest_distance` function only sets this value as follows:

```
def set_shortest_distance(table, vertex, new_distance):
    table[vertex][DISTANCE] = new_distance
```

When we update the shortest distance of a node, we update its previous node using the following method:

```
def set_previous_node(table, vertex, previous_node):
    table[vertex][PREVIOUS_NODE] = previous_node
```

Remember that the, `PREVIOUS_NODE` constant equals 1. In the table, we store the value of `previous_node` at `table[vertex][PREVIOUS_NODE]`.

To find the distance between any two nodes, we use the `get_distance` function:

```
def get_distance(graph, first_vertex, second_vertex):
    return graph[first_vertex][second_vertex]
```

The last helper method is the `get_next_node` function:

```
def get_next_node(table, visited_nodes):
    unvisited_nodes =
        list(set(table.keys()).difference(set(visited_nodes)))
    assumed_min = table[unvisited_nodes[0]][DISTANCE]
    min_vertex = unvisited_nodes[0]
    for node in unvisited_nodes:
        if table[node][DISTANCE] < assumed_min:
            assumed_min = table[node][DISTANCE]
            min_vertex = node

    return min_vertex
```

The `get_next_node` function resembles a function to find the smallest item in a list.

The function starts off by finding the unvisited nodes in our table by using `visited_nodes` to obtain the difference between the two sets of lists. The very first item in the list of `unvisited_nodes` is assumed to be the smallest in the shortest distance column of `table`.

If a lesser value is found while the `for` loop runs, the `min_vertex` will be updated. The function then returns `min_vertex` as the unvisited vertex or node with the smallest shortest distance from the source.

The worst-case running time of Dijkstra's algorithm is $O(|E| + |V| \log |V|)$, where $|V|$ is the number of vertices and $|E|$ is the number of edges.

Complexity classes

Complexity classes group problems on the basis of their difficulty level, and the resources required in terms of time and space to solve them. In this section, we discuss the N, NP, NP-Complete, and NP-Hard complexity classes.

P versus NP

The advent of computers has sped up the rate at which certain tasks can be performed. In general, computers are good at perfecting the art of calculation and solving problems that can be reduced to a set of mathematical computations.

However, this assertion is not entirely true. There are some classes of problems that take an enormous amount of time for the computer to make a sound guess, let alone find the right solution.

In computer science, the class of problems that computers can solve within polynomial time using a step-wise process of logical steps is known as P-type, where P stands for polynomial. These are relatively easy to solve.

Then there is another class of problems that are considered very hard to solve. The word *hard problem* is used to refer to the way in which problems increase in difficulty when trying to find a solution. However, despite the fact that these problems have a high growth rate of difficulty, it is possible to determine whether a proposed solution solves the problem in polynomial time. These are known as NP-type problems. NP here stands for nondeterministic polynomial time.

Now the million dollar question is, does $P = NP$?

The proof for P = *NP* is one of the Millennium Prize Problems from the Clay Mathematics Institute, offering a million dollar prize for a correct solution.

The Traveling Salesman problem is an example of an NP-type problem. The problem statement says: given n number of cities in a country, find the shortest route between them all, thus making the trip a cost-effective one.

When the number of cities is small, this problem can be solved in a reasonable amount of time. However, when the number of cities is above any two-digit number, the time taken by the computer is remarkably long.

A lot of computer and cybersecurity systems are based on the RSA encryption algorithm. The strength of the algorithm is based on the fact that it uses the integer factoring problem, which is an NP-type problem.

Finding the prime factors of a prime number composed of many digits is very difficult. When two large prime numbers are multiplied, a large non-prime number is obtained. Factorization of this number is where many cryptographic algorithms borrow their strength.

All P-type problems are subsets of **NP** problems. This means that any problem that can be solved in polynomial time can also be verified in polynomial time:

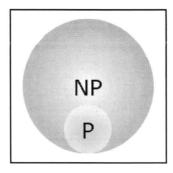

But P = **NP** investigates whether problems that can be verified in polynomial time can also be solved in polynomial time. In particular, if they are equal, it means that problems that are solved by trying a number of possible solutions can be solved without the need to actually try all the possible solutions, invariably creating some sort of shortcut proof.

The proof, when finally discovered, will certainly have serious consequences for the fields of cryptography, game theory, mathematics, and many other fields.

NP-Hard

A problem is NP-Hard if all other problems in NP can be polynomial-time-reducible, or mapped to it. It is at least as hard as the hardest problem in NP.

NP-Complete

NP-Complete problems are the most difficult problems. A problem is considered an **NP-Complete** problem if it is an **NP-Hard** problem that is also found in the **NP** class.

Here, we show the Venn diagram for various complexity groups:

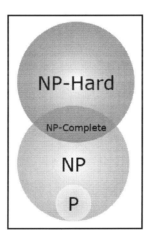

Summary

In this chapter, we discussed in detail algorithm design techniques, which are very important in the computer science field. Without too much mathematical rigor, we also discussed some of the main categories into which algorithms are classified.

Other design techniques in the field, such as the divide and conquer, dynamic programming, and greedy algorithms, were also covered, along with implementations of important sample algorithms. Lastly, we presented a brief discussion on complexity classes. We saw how proof for P = NP will definitely be a game-changer in a number of fields, if such a proof is ever discovered.

In the next chapter, we will be discussing some real-world applications, tools, and the basics of machine learning applications.

14
Implementations, Applications, and Tools

Learning about algorithms without any real-life application remains a purely academic pursuit. In this chapter, we will explore the data structures and algorithms that are shaping our world.

One of the golden nuggets of this age is the abundance of data. Emails, phone numbers, text documents, and images contain large amounts of data. In this data, there is valuable information that makes the data more important. But to extract this information from the raw data, we have to use data structures, processes, and algorithms that specialize in this task.

Machine learning employs a significant number of algorithms to analyze and predict the occurrence of certain variables. Analyzing data on a purely numerical basis still leaves much of the latent information buried in the raw data. Presenting data visually thus enables one to understand and gain valuable insights too.

By the end of this chapter, you should be able to do the following:

- Prune and present data accurately
- Use both supervised and unsupervised learning algorithms for the purposes of prediction
- Visually represent data in order to gain more insight

Technical requirements

In order to proceed with this chapter, you will need to install the following packages. These packages will be used to pre-process and visually represent the data being processed. Some of the packages also contain a well-written implementation of the algorithms that will operate on our data.

Preferably, these modules should be installed using `pip`. So, firstly, we need to install pip for Python 3 using the following commands:

- `sudo apt-get update`
- `sudo apt-get install python3-pip`

Furthermore, the following commands are to be run to install the `numpy`, `scikit-learn`, `matplotlib`, `pandas`, and `textblob` packages:

```
# pip3 install numpy
# pip3 install scikit-learn
# pip3 install matplotlib
# pip3 install pandas
# pip3 install textblob
```

If you are using the old version of Python (that is, Python 2), the packages can be installed using the same commands by replacing `pip3` with `pip`.

You are also required to install the `nltk` and `punkt` packages, which provide inbuilt text processing functions. To install them, open the Python Terminal and run the following commands:

```
>>import nltk
>>nltk.download('punkt')
```

These packages may require other platform-specific modules to be installed first. Take note and install all dependencies:

- **NumPy**: A library with functions to operate on n-dimensional arrays and matrices.
- **Scikit-learn**: A highly advanced module for machine learning. It contains an implementation of many algorithms for classification, regression, and clustering, among others.
- **Matplotlib**: This is a plotting library that makes use of NumPy to graph a good variety of charts, including line plots, histograms, scatter plots, and even 3D graphs.
- **Pandas**: This library deals with data manipulation and analysis.

The GitHub link is as follows: `https://github.com/PacktPublishing/Hands-On-Data-Structures-and-Algorithms-with-Python-3.x-Second-Edition/tree/master/Chapter14`.

Knowledge discovery in data

To extract useful information from the given data, we initially collect the raw data that is to be used to learn the patterns. Next, we apply the data preprocessing techniques to remove the noise from the data. Further more, we extract the important features from the data, which are representative of the data, to develop the model. Feature extraction is the most crucial step for machine learning algorithms to work effectively. A good feature must be informative and discriminating for the machine learning algorithms. Feature selection techniques are used to remove the irrelevant, redundant, and noisy features. Further more, the prominent features are fed to the machine learning algorithms to learn the patterns in the data. Finally, we apply the evaluation measure to judge the performance of the developed model and use visualization techniques to visualize the results and data. Here are the steps:

1. Data collection
2. Data preprocessing
3. Feature extraction
4. Feature selection
5. Machine learning
6. Evaluation and visualization

Data preprocessing

To analyze the data, first of all, we have to preprocess the data to remove the noise and convert it in to an appropriate format so that it can be further analyzed. A collection of data from the real world is mostly full of noise, which makes it difficult to apply any algorithm directly. The raw data collected is plagued by a lot of issues so we need to adopt ways to sanitize the data to make it suitable for use in further studies.

Processing raw data

The data collected may also be inconsistent with other records collected over time. The existence of duplicate entries and incomplete records warrant that we treat the data in such a way as to bring out hidden and useful information.

To clean the data, we totally discard irrelevant and noisy data. Data with missing parts or attributes can be replaced with sensible estimates. Also, where the raw data suffers from inconsistency, detecting and correcting that becomes necessary.

Let's explore how we can use NumPy and pandas for data preprocessing techniques.

Missing data

The performance of the machine learning algorithm deteriorates if the data has missing values. Just because a dataset has missing fields or attributes does not mean it is not useful. Several methods can be used to fill in the missing values. Some of these methods are as follows:

- Using a global constant to fill in the missing values.
- Using the mean or median value in the dataset.
- Supplying the data manually.
- Using the attribute mean or median to fill in the missing values. The choice is based on the context and sensitivity of what the data is going to be used for.

Take, for instance, the following data:

```
import numpy as np
data = pandas.DataFrame([
    [4., 45., 984.],
    [np.NAN, np.NAN, 5.],
    [94., 23., 55.],
])
```

As we can see, the data elements data[1][0] and data[1][1] have values of np.NAN, representing the fact that they have no value. If the np.NAN values are not desired in a given dataset, they can be set to a constant figure.

Let's set data elements with the value np.NAN to 0.1:

```
print(data.fillna(0.1))
```

The new state of the data becomes the following:

```
    0     1      2
0   4.0  45.0  984.0
1   0.1   0.1    5.0
2  94.0  23.0   55.0
```

To apply the mean values instead, we do the following:

```
print(data.fillna(data.mean()))
```

The mean value for each column is calculated and inserted into those data areas with the `np.NAN` value:

```
   0     1      2
0   4.0  45.0  984.0
1  49.0  34.0    5.0
2  94.0  23.0   55.0
```

For the first column, column 0, the mean value was obtained by `(4 + 94)/2`. The resulting `49.0` is then stored at `data[1][0]`. A similar operation is carried out for columns `1` and `2`.

Feature scaling

The columns in a data frame are known as its features. The rows are known as records or observations. The performance of the machine learning algorithm decreases if one attribute has values in a higher range compared to other attributes' values. Thus, it is often required to scale or normalize the attribute values in a common range.

Consider an example, the following data matrix. This data will be referenced in subsections so please do take note:

```
data1= ([[ 58.,     1.,    43.],
  [  10.,  200.,    65.],
  [  20.,   75.,     7.]]
```

Feature one, with data of `58`, `10`, and `20`, has its values lying between `10` and `58`. For feature two, the data lies between `1` and `200`. Inconsistent results will be produced if we supply this data to any machine learning algorithm. Ideally, we will need to scale the data to a certain range in order to get consistent results.

Once again, closer inspection reveals that each feature (or column) lies around different mean values. Therefore, what we want to do is to align the features around similar means.

One benefit of feature scaling is that it boosts the learning parts of machine learning. The `scikit` module has a considerable number of scaling algorithms that we shall apply to our data.

Min-max scalar form of normalization

The min-max scalar form of normalization uses the mean and standard deviation to box all the data into a range lying between certain min and max values. Generally, the range is set between 0 and 1; although other ranges may be applied, the 0 to 1 range remains the default:

```
from sklearn.preprocessing import MinMaxScaler

scaled_values = MinMaxScaler(feature_range=(0,1))
results = scaled_values.fit(data1).transform(data1)
print(results)
```

An instance of the `MinMaxScaler` class is created with the range `(0,1)` and passed to the `scaled_values` variables. The `fit` function is called to make the necessary calculations that are used internally to change the dataset. The `transform` function affects the actual operation on the dataset, returning the value to `results`:

```
[[ 1.          0.          0.62068966]
 [ 0.          1.          1.        ]
 [ 0.20833333  0.3718593   0.        ]]
```

We can see from the preceding output that all the data is normalized and lies between 0 and 1. This kind of output can now be supplied to a machine learning algorithm.

Standard scalar

The mean values for the respective features in our initial dataset or table are 29.3, 92, and 38. To make all the data have a similar mean, that is, a zero mean and a unit variance across the data, we can apply the standard scalar algorithm, shown as follows:

```
stand_scalar = preprocessing.StandardScaler().fit(data)
results = stand_scalar.transform(data)
print(results)
```

data is passed to the `fit` method of the object returned from instantiating the `StandardScaler` class. The `transform` method acts on the data elements in the data and returns the output to the results:

```
[[ 1.38637564 -1.10805456  0.19519899]
 [-0.93499753  1.31505377  1.11542277]
 [-0.45137812 -0.2069992  -1.31062176]]
```

Examining the results, we observe that all our features are now evenly distributed.

Binarizing data

To binarize a given feature set, we can make use of a threshold. If any value within a given dataset is greater than the threshold, the value is replaced by 1, and if the value is less than the threshold, it is replaced with 0. Consider the following code snippet, where we take 50 as the threshold to binarize the original data:

```
results = preprocessing.Binarizer(50.0).fit(data).transform(data)
print(results)
```

An instance of `Binarizer` is created with the argument `50.0`. `50.0` is the threshold that will be used in the binarizing algorithm:

```
[[ 1.  0.  0.]
 [ 0.  1.  1.]
 [ 0.  1.  0.]]
```

All values in the data that are less than 50 will have a value of 0, and hold a value of 1 otherwise.

Learning about machine learning

Machine learning is a subfield of artificial intelligence. Machine learning is basically an algorithm that can learn from the example data and can provide predictions based on that. Machine learning models learn the patterns from the data examples and use those learned patterns to make predictions for unseen data. For example, we feed many examples of spam and ham email messages to develop a machine learning model that can learn the patterns in emails and can classify new emails as spam or ham.

Types of machine learning

There are three broad categories of machine learning, as follows:

- **Supervised learning**: Here, an algorithm is fed a set of inputs and their corresponding outputs. The algorithm then has to figure out what the output will be for an unseen input. Supervised learning algorithms try to learn the patterns in the input features and target output in such a way that the learned model can predict the output for the new unseen data. Classification and regression are two kinds of problem that are solved using a supervised learning approach, in which the machine learning algorithm learns from the given data and labels. Classification is a process that classifies the given unseen data into one of the predefined sets of classes, given a set of input features and labels associated with them. Regression is very similar to classification, with one exception—in this, we have continuous target values instead of a fixed pre-defined set of classes (nominal or categorical attribute), and we predict the value in a continuous response for new unseen data. Examples of such algorithms include naive bayes, support vector machines, k-nearest neighbors, linear regression, neural networks, and decision tree algorithms.
- **Unsupervised learning**: Without using the relationship that exists between a set of input and output variables, the unsupervised learning algorithm uses only the input to learn the patterns and clusters within the data. Unsupervised algorithms are used to learn the patterns in the given input data without labels associated with them. Clustering problems are one of the most popular types of problems that are solved using an unsupervised learning approach. In this, the data points are grouped together to form groups or clusters on the basis of the similarities among the features. Examples of such algorithms include k-means clustering, agglomerative clustering, and hierarchical clustering.
- **Reinforcement learning**: The computer in this kind of learning method dynamically interacts with its environment in such a way as to improve its performance.

The hello classifier

Let's take a simple example to understand how machine learning works; we begin with a `hello world` example of a text classifier. This is meant to be a gentle introduction to machine learning.

This example will predict whether the given text carries a negative or positive connotation. Before this can be done, we need to train our algorithm (model) with some data.

The naive bayes model is suited for text classification purposes. Algorithms based on the naive bayes models are generally fast and produce accurate results. It is based on the assumption that features are independent of each other. To accurately predict the occurrence of rainfall, three conditions need to be considered. These are wind speed, temperature, and the amount of humidity in the air. In reality, these factors do have an influence on each other to determine the likelihood of rainfall. But the abstraction in naive bayes is to assume that these features are unrelated in any way and thus independently contribute to the chances of rainfall. Naive bayes is useful in predicting the class of an unknown dataset, as we will see soon.

Now, back to our hello classifier. After we have trained our model, its prediction will fall into either the positive or negative categories:

```
from textblob.classifiers import NaiveBayesClassifier
train = [
    ('I love this sandwich.', 'pos'),
    ('This is an amazing shop!', 'pos'),
    ('We feel very good about these beers.', 'pos'),
    ('That is my best sword.', 'pos'),
    ('This is an awesome post', 'pos'),
    ('I do not like this cafe', 'neg'),
    ('I am tired of this bed.', 'neg'),
    ("I can't deal with this", 'neg'),
    ('She is my sworn enemy!', 'neg'),
    ('I never had a caring mom.', 'neg')
]
```

First, we will import the `NaiveBayesClassifier` class from the `textblob` package. This classifier is very easy to work with and is based on the bayes theorem.

The `train` variable consists of tuples that each hold the actual training data. Each tuple contains the sentence and the group it is associated with.

Now, to train our model, we will instantiate a `NaiveBayesClassifier` object by passing train to it:

```
cl = NaiveBayesClassifier(train)
```

The updated naive bayesian model `cl` will predict the category that an unknown sentence belongs to. Up to this point, our model has known of only two categories that a phrase can belong to, `neg` and `pos`.

The following code runs tests using our model:

```
print(cl.classify("I just love breakfast"))
print(cl.classify("Yesterday was Sunday"))
print(cl.classify("Why can't he pay my bills"))
print(cl.classify("They want to kill the president of Bantu"))
```

The output of our tests is as follows:

```
pos
pos
neg
neg
```

We can see that the algorithm has had some degree of success in classifying the input phrases into their categories correctly.

This contrived example is overly simplistic, but it does show the promise that if given the right amount of data and a suitable algorithm or model, it is possible for a machine to carry out tasks without any human help.

In our next example, we will use the `scikit` module to predict the category that a phrase may belong to.

A supervised learning example

Let's consider an example of the text classification problem, which can be solved using a supervised learning approach. The text classification problem is to classify a new document into one of the pre-defined sets of categories of documents when we have a set of documents related to a fixed number of categories. As with supervised learning, we need to first train the model in order to accurately predict the category of an unknown document.

Gathering data

The `scikit` module comes with sample data that we can use for training the machine learning model. In this example, we will use the newsgroups documents, which have 20 categories of documents. To load those documents, we will use the following lines of code:

```
from sklearn.datasets import fetch_20newsgroups
training_data = fetch_20newsgroups(subset='train', categories=categories,
                                    shuffle=True, random_state=42)
```

Let's take only four categories of documents for training the model. After we have trained our model, the results of the prediction will belong to one of the following categories:

```
categories = ['alt.atheism',
              'soc.religion.christian','comp.graphics', 'sci.med']
```

The total number of records we are going to use as training data is obtained by the following:

```
print(len(training_data))
```

Machine learning algorithms do not work on textual attributes directly, so the names of the categories that each document belongs to are denoted as numbers (for example, alt.atheism is denoted as 0) using the following code line:

```
print(set(training_data.target))
```

The categories have integer values that we can map back to the categories themselves with print(training_data.target_names[0]).

Here, 0 is a numerical random index picked from set(training_data.target).

Now that the training data has been obtained, we must feed the data to a machine learning algorithm. The bag of words model is an approach to convert the text document into a feature vector in order to turn the text into a form on which the learning algorithm or model can be applied. Furthermore, those feature vectors will be used for training the machine learning model.

Bag of words

Bag of words is a model that is used for representing text data in such a way that it does not take into consideration the order of words but rather uses word counts. Let's consider an example to understand how the bag of words method is used to represent text. Look at the following two sentences:

```
sentence_1 = "as fit as a fiddle"
sentence_2 = "as you like it"
```

Bag of words enables us to split the text into numerical feature vectors represented by a matrix.

To reduce our two sentences using the bag of words model, we need to obtain a unique list of all the words:

```
set((sentence_1 + sentence_2).split(" "))
```

This set will become our columns in the matrix, called the features in machine learning terminology. The rows in the matrix will represent the documents that are being used for training. The intersection of a row and column will store the number of times that word occurs in the document. Using our two sentences as examples, we obtain the following matrix:

	as	fit	a	fiddle	you	like	it
Sentence 1	2	1	1	1	0	0	0
Sentence 2	1	0	0	0	1	1	1

The preceding data has many features that are generally not important for text classification. The stop words can be removed to make sure only relevant data is analyzed. Stop words include is, am, are, was, and so on. Since the bag of words model does not include grammar in its analysis, the stop words can safely be dropped.

To generate the values that go into the columns of our matrix, we have to tokenize our training data:

```
from sklearn.feature_extraction.text import CountVectorizer
from sklearn.feature_extraction.text import TfidfTransformer
from sklearn.naive_bayes import MultinomialNB
count_vect = CountVectorizer()
training_matrix = count_vect.fit_transform(training_data.data)
```

`training_matrix` has a dimension of (2,257 x 35,788) for the four categories of data we used in this example. This means that 2,257 corresponds to the total number of documents while 35,788 corresponds to the number of columns, which is the total number of features that make up the unique set of words in all documents.

We instantiate the `CountVectorizer` class and pass `training_data.data` to the `fit_transform` method of the `count_vect` object. The result is stored in `training_matrix`. `training_matrix` holds all the unique words and their respective frequencies.

Sometimes, frequency counts do not perform well for a text-classification problem; instead of using frequency count, we may use the **term frequency-inverse document frequency (TF-IDF)** weighting method for representing the features.

Here, will import `TfidfTransformer`, which helps to assign the weights of each feature in our data:

```
matrix_transformer = TfidfTransformer()
tfidf_data = matrix_transformer.fit_transform(training_matrix)

print(tfidf_data[1:4].todense())
```

`tfidf_data[1:4].todense()` only shows a truncated list of a three rows by 35,788 columns matrix. The values seen are the TF-IDF; it is a better representation method compared to using a frequency count.

Once we have extracted features and represented them in a tabular format, we can apply a machine learning algorithm for training. There are many supervising learning algorithms; let's look at an example of the naive bayes algorithm to train a text classifier model.

The naive bayes algorithm is a simple classification algorithm that is based on the bayes theorem. It is a probability-based learning algorithm that constructs a model by using the term frequency of a feature/word/term to compute the probability of belonging. The naive bayes algorithm classifies a given document into one of the predefined categories where there is the maximum probability of observing the words of the new document in that category. The naive bayes algorithm works as follows—initially, all training documents are processed to extract the vocabulary of all the words that appear in the text, then it counts their frequencies among the different target classes to obtain their probabilities. Next, a new document is classified in the category, which has the maximum probability of belonging to that particular class. The naive bayes classifier is based on the assumption that the probability of word occurrence is independent of position within the text. Multinomial naive bayes can be implemented using the `MultinomialNB` function of the `scikit` library, shown as follows:

```
model = MultinomialNB().fit(tfidf_data, training_data.target)
```

`MultinomialNB` is a variant of the naive bayes model. We pass the rationalized data matrix, `tfidf_data`, and categories, `training_data.target`, to its `fit` method.

Prediction

To test how the trained model works to predict the category of an unknown document, let's consider some example test data to evaluate the model:

```
test_data = ["My God is good", "Arm chip set will rival intel"]
test_counts = count_vect.transform(test_data)
new_tfidf = matrix_transformer.transform(test_counts)
```

The `test_data` list is passed to the `count_vect.transform` function to obtain the vectorized form of the test data. To obtain the TF-IDF representation of the test dataset, we call the `transform` method of the `matrix_transformer` object. When we pass new test data to the machine learning model, we have to process the data in the same way as we did in preparing the training data.

To predict which category the docs may belong to, we use the `predict` function as follows:

```
prediction = model.predict(new_tfidf)
```

The loop can be used to iterate over the prediction, showing the categories they are predicted to belong to:

```
for doc, category in zip(test_data, prediction):
    print('%r => %s' % (doc, training_data.target_names[category]))
```

When the loop has run to completion, the phrase, together with the category that it may belong to, is displayed. A sample output is as follows:

```
'My God is good' => soc.religion.christian
'Arm chip set will rival intel' => comp.graphics
```

All that we have seen up to this point is a prime example of supervised learning. We started by loading documents whose categories were already known. These documents were then fed into the machine learning algorithm most suited for text processing, based on the naive bayes theorem. A set of test documents was supplied to the model and the category was predicted.

To explore an example of an unsupervised learning algorithm, we will discuss the k-means algorithm for clustering some data.

An unsupervised learning example

Unsupervised learning algorithms are able to discover inherent patterns in the data that may exist and can cluster them in groups in such a way that the data points in one cluster are very similar and data points from two different clusters are highly dissimilar in nature. An example of these algorithms is the k-means algorithm.

K-means algorithm

The k-means algorithm uses the mean points in a given dataset to cluster and discover groups within the dataset. The K is the number of clusters that we want and are hoping to discover. After the k-means algorithm has generated the groupings/clusters, we can pass unknown data to this model to predict which cluster the new data should belong to.

Note that in this kind of algorithm, only the raw uncategorized data is fed to the algorithm without any labels associated with the data. It is up to the algorithm to find out if the data has inherent groups within it.

The k-means algorithm iteratively assigns the data points to the clusters based on the similarities among the features provided. K-means clustering groups the data points in k clusters/groups using the mean point. It works as follows. Firstly, we create k non-empty sets, and we compute the distance between the data point and the cluster center. Next, we assign the data point to the cluster that has the minimum distance and is closest. Next, we recalculate the cluster point and we iteratively follow the same process until all the data is clustered.

To understand how this algorithm works, let's examine `100` data points consisting of x and y values (assuming two attributes). We will feed these values to the learning algorithm and expect that the algorithm will cluster the data into two sets. We will color the two sets so that the clusters are visible.

Let's create a sample data of 100 records of *x* and *y* pairs:

```
import numpy as np
import matplotlib.pyplot as plt
original_set = -2 * np.random.rand(100, 2)
second_set = 1 + 2 * np.random.rand(50, 2)
original_set[50: 100, :] = second_set
```

First, we create 100 records with `-2 * np.random.rand(100, 2)`. In each of the records, we will use the data in it to represent *x* and *y* values that will eventually be plotted.

The last 50 numbers in `original_set` will be replaced by `1+2*np.random.rand(50, 2)`. In effect, what we have done is to create two subsets of data, where one set has numbers in the negative while the other set has numbers in the positive. It is now the responsibility of the algorithm to discover these segments appropriately.

We instantiate the KMeans algorithm class and pass it n_clusters=2. That makes the algorithm cluster all its data into two groups. In the k-means algorithm, the number of clusters has to be known in advance. The implementation of the k-means algorithm using the scikit library is as shown:

```
from sklearn.cluster import KMeans
kmean = KMeans(n_clusters=2)

kmean.fit(original_set)

print(kmean.cluster_centers_)

print(kmean.labels_)
```

The dataset is passed to the fit function of kmean, kmean.fit(original_set). The clusters generated by the algorithm will revolve around a certain mean point. The points that define these two mean points are obtained by kmean.cluster_centers_.

The mean points when printed appear as follows:

```
[[ 2.03838197 2.06567568]
 [-0.89358725 -0.84121101]]
```

Each data point in original_set will belong to a cluster after our k-means algorithm has finished its training. The k-mean algorithm represents the two clusters it discovers as ones and zeros. If we had asked the algorithm to cluster the data into four, the internal representation of these clusters would have been 0, 1, 2, and 3. To print out the various clusters that each dataset belongs to, we do the following:

```
print(kmean.labels_)
```

This gives the following output:

```
[1 1 1 1 1 1 1 1 1 1 1 1 1 1 1 1 1 1 1 1 1 1 1 1 1 1 1 1 1 1 1 1 1 1 1 1 1
 1 1 1 1 1 1 1 1 1 1 1 1 1 0 0 0 0 0 0 0 0 0 0 0 0 0 0 0 0 0 0 0 0 0 0 0 0
 0 0 0 0 0 0 0 0 0 0 0 0 0 0 0 0 0 0 0 0 0 0 0 0 0 0]
```

There are 100 ones and zeros. Each shows the cluster that each data point falls under. By using matplotlib.pyplot, we can chart the points of each group and color it appropriately to show the clusters:

```
import matplotlib.pyplot as plt
for i in set(kmean.labels_):
    index = kmean.labels_ == i
    plt.plot(original_set[index,0], original_set[index,1], 'o')
```

`index = kmean.labels_ == i` is a nifty way by which we select all points that correspond to group `i`. When `i=0`, all points belonging to group zero are returned to the variable index. It's the same for `index =1, 2`, and so on.

`plt.plot(original_set[index,0], original_set[index,1], 'o')` then plots these data points using o as the character for drawing each point.

Next, we will plot the centroids or mean values around which the clusters have formed:

```
plt.plot(kmean.cluster_centers_[0][0],kmean.cluster_centers_[0][1],
        '*', c='r', ms=10)
plt.plot(kmean.cluster_centers_[1][0],kmean.cluster_centers_[1][1],
        '*', c='r', ms=10)
```

Lastly, we show the whole graph with the two means illustrated by red star using the code snippet `plt.show()` as follows:

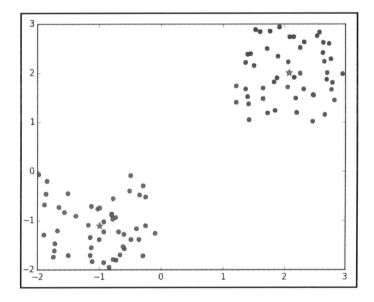

The algorithm discovers two distinct clusters in our sample data.

Prediction

With the two clusters that we have obtained, we can predict the group that a new set of data might belong to.

Let's predict which group the points `[[-1.4, -1.4]]` and `[[2.5, 2.5]]` will belong to:

```
sample = np.array([[-1.4, -1.4]])
print(kmean.predict(sample))

another_sample = np.array([[2.5, 2.5]])
print(kmean.predict(another_sample))
```

The output is as follows:

```
[1]
[0]
```

Here, two test samples are assigned to two different clusters.

Data visualization

The numerical analysis is sometimes not that easy to understand. In this section, we show you some methods to visualize the data and results. Images present a quick way to analyze data. Differences in size and length are quick markers in an image, upon which conclusions can be drawn. In this section, we will take a tour of the different ways to represent data. Besides the graphs listed here, there is more that can be achieved when dealing with data.

Bar chart

To chart the values 25, 5, 150, and 100 into a bar graph, we will store the values in an array and pass it to the `bar` function. The bars in the graph represent the magnitude along the *y*-axis:

```
import matplotlib.pyplot as plt

data = [25., 5., 150., 100.]
x_values = range(len(data))
plt.bar(x_values, data)

plt.show()
```

`x_values` stores an array of values generated by `range(len(data))`. Also, `x_values` will determine the points on the *x*-axis where the bars will be drawn. The first bar will be drawn on the *x*-axis where *x* is zero. The second bar with data 5 will be drawn on the *x*-axis where *x* is 1:

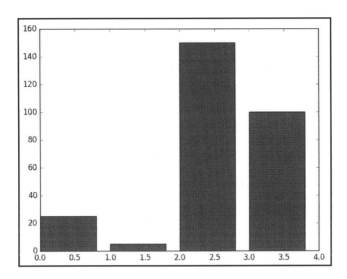

The width of each bar can be changed by modifying the following line:

```
plt.bar(x_values, data, width=1.)
```

This should produce the following graph:

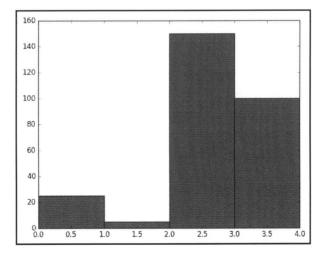

However, this is not visually appealing because there is no space between the bars anymore, which makes it look clumsy. Each bar now occupies one unit on the *x*-axis.

Multiple bar charts

In trying to visualize data, stacking a number of bars enables one to further understand how one piece of data or variable varies compared to another:

```
data = [
        [8., 57., 22., 10.],
        [16., 7., 32., 40.],
        ]

import numpy as np
x_values = np.arange(4)
plt.bar(x_values + 0.00, data[0], color='r', width=0.30)
plt.bar(x_values + 0.30, data[1], color='y', width=0.30)

plt.show()
```

The y values for the first batch of data are `[8., 57., 22., 10.]`. The second batch is `[16., 7., 32., 40.]`. When the bars are plotted, 8 and 16 will occupy the same x position, side by side.

`x_values = np.arange(4)` generates the array with values `[0, 1, 2, 3]`. The first set of bars are drawn first at position x_values + 0.30. Thus, the first x values will be plotted at `0.00, 1.00, 2.00 and 3.00`.

The second batch of x_values will be plotted at `0.30, 1.30, 2.30 and 3.30`:

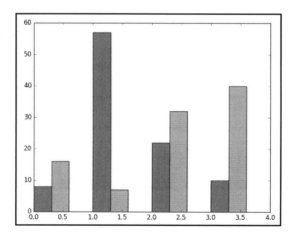

Box plot

The box plot is used to visualize the median value and low and high ranges of a distribution. It is also referred to as a box and whisker plot.

Let's chart a simple box plot.

We begin by generating 50 numbers from a normal distribution. These are then passed to `plt.boxplot(data)` to be charted:

```
import numpy as np
import matplotlib.pyplot as plt

data = np.random.randn(50)

plt.boxplot(data)
plt.show()
```

The following diagram is what is produced:

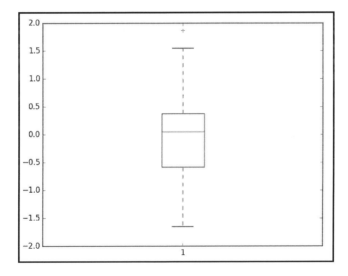

A few comments on the preceding diagram—the features of the box plot include a box spanning the interquartile range, which measures the dispersion; the outer fringes of the data are denoted by the whiskers attached to the central box; the red line represents the median.

The box plot is useful to easily identify the outliers in a dataset, as well as determining in which direction a dataset may be skewed.

Pie chart

The pie chart interprets and visually represents the data as if to fit into a circle. The individual data points are expressed as sectors of a circle that add up to 360 degrees. This chart is good for displaying categorical data and summaries too:

```
import matplotlib.pyplot as plt
data = [500, 200, 250]

labels = ["Agriculture", "Aide", "News"]

plt.pie(data, labels=labels,autopct='%1.1f%%')
plt.show()
```

The sectors in the graph are labeled with the strings in the labels array:

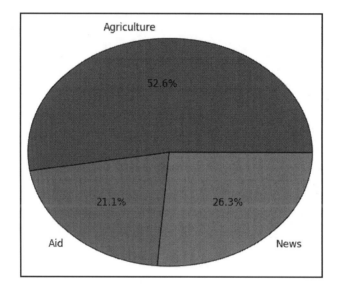

Bubble chart

Another variant of the scatter plot is the bubble chart. In a scatter plot, we only plot the x and y points of the data. Bubble charts add another dimension by illustrating the size of the points. This third dimension may represent sizes of markets or even profits:

```
import numpy as np
import matplotlib.pyplot as plt
```

```
n = 10
x = np.random.rand(n)
y = np.random.rand(n)
colors = np.random.rand(n)
area = np.pi * (60 * np.random.rand(n))**2

plt.scatter(x, y, s=area, c=colors, alpha=0.5)
plt.show()
```

With the n variable, we specify the number of randomly generated x and y values. This same number is used to determine the random colors for our x and y coordinates. Random bubble sizes are determined by `area = np.pi * (60 * np.random.rand(n))**2`.

The following diagram shows this bubble chart:

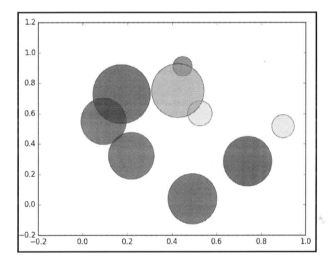

Summary

In this chapter, we have explored how data and algorithms come together to aid machine learning. Making sense of huge amounts of data is made possible by first pruning our data through data cleaning techniques and scaling and normalization processes. Feeding this data to specialized learning algorithms, we are able to predict the categories of unseen data based on the patterns learned by the algorithm from the data. We also discussed the basics of machine learning algorithms.

We explained supervised and unsupervised machine learning algorithms in detail with the naive bayes and k-means clustering algorithms. We also provided the implementation of these algorithms using the `scikit-learn` Python-based machine learning library. Finally, some important visualization techniques were discussed, as charting and plotting the condensed data helps you to better understand and make insightful discoveries.

I hope you had a good experience with this book and that it helps in your future endeavors with data structures and Python 3.7!

Other Books You May Enjoy

If you enjoyed this book, you may be interested in these other books by Packt:

Learn Python Programming - Second Edition
Fabrizio Romano

ISBN: 9781788996662

- Get Python up and running on Windows, Mac, and Linux
- Explore fundamental concepts of coding using data structures and control flow
- Write elegant, reusable, and efficient code in any situation
- Understand when to use the functional or OOP approach
- Cover the basics of security and concurrent/asynchronous programming
- Create bulletproof, reliable software by writing tests
- Build a simple website in Django
- Fetch, clean, and manipulate data

Mastering Python Design Patterns - Second Edition
Kamon Ayeva

ISBN: 9781788837484

- Explore Factory Method and Abstract Factory for object creation
- Clone objects using the Prototype pattern
- Make incompatible interfaces compatible using the Adapter pattern
- Secure an interface using the Proxy pattern
- Choose an algorithm dynamically using the Strategy pattern
- Keep the logic decoupled from the UI using the MVC pattern
- Leverage the Observer pattern to understand reactive programming
- Explore patterns for cloud-native, microservices, and serverless architectures

Leave a review - let other readers know what you think

Please share your thoughts on this book with others by leaving a review on the site that you bought it from. If you purchased the book from Amazon, please leave us an honest review on this book's Amazon page. This is vital so that other potential readers can see and use your unbiased opinion to make purchasing decisions, we can understand what our customers think about our products, and our authors can see your feedback on the title that they have worked with Packt to create. It will only take a few minutes of your time, but is valuable to other potential customers, our authors, and Packt. Thank you!

Index

Made in the
USA
Middletown, DE